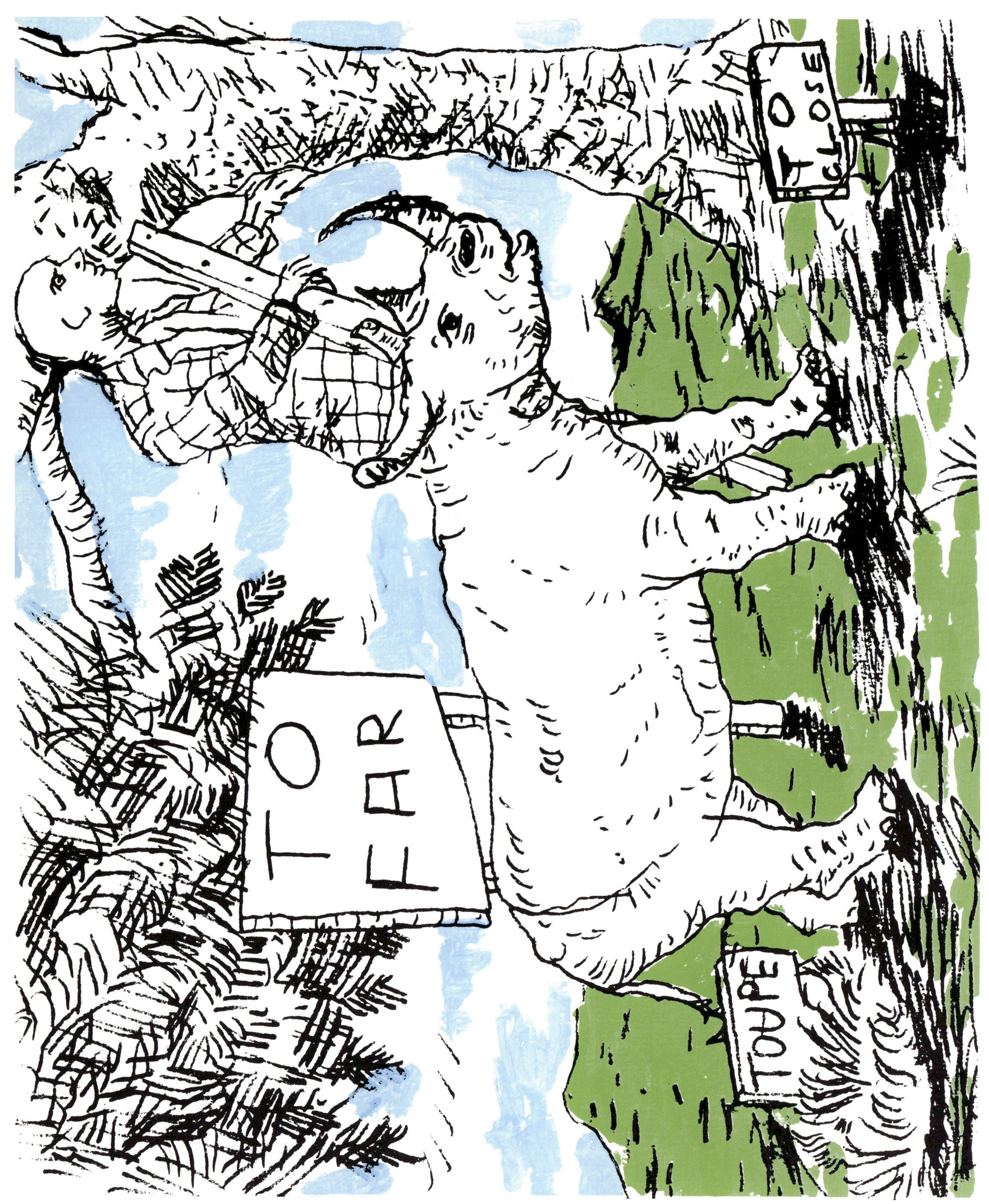

TO CLOSE
TO FAR
TO RIPE

British & American Art
The Uneasy Dialectic

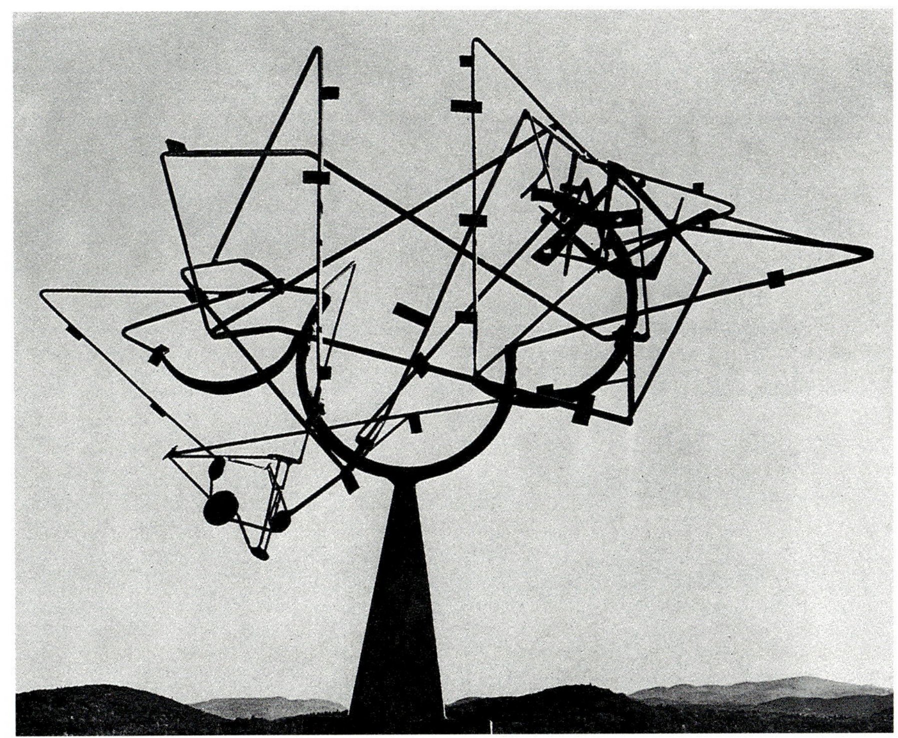

David Smith, *Star Cage*, 1950

STEVEN CAMPBELL
An original colour graphic
specially designed by the artist

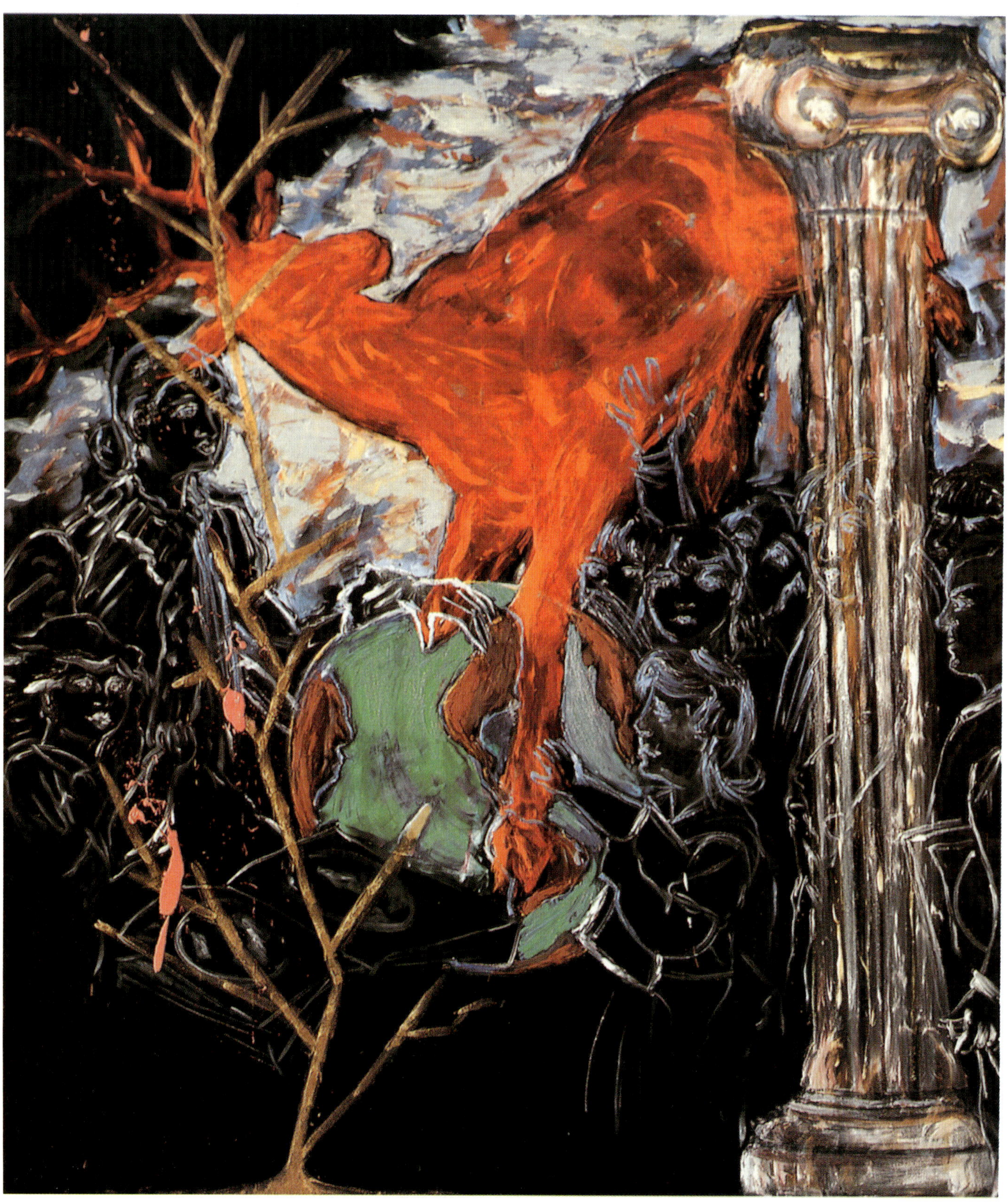

Julian Schnabel, *The Geography Lesson*, 1980, oil on velvet

AD An Art & Design Profile

British & American Art
The Uneasy Dialectic

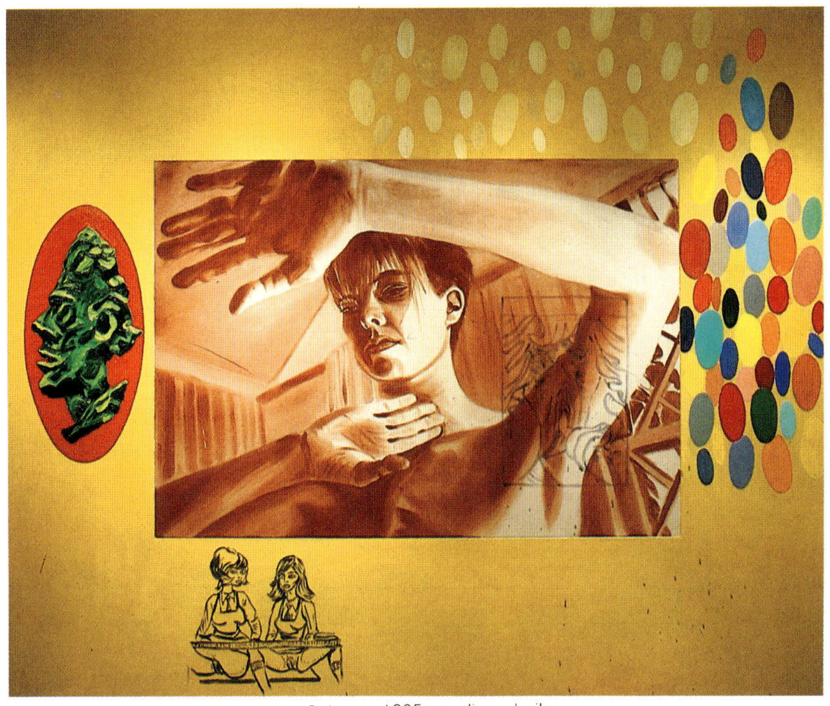

David Salle, *Reliance*, 1985, acrylic and oil on canvas

THIS ISSUE TAKES ITS THEME FROM THE *INTERCHANGES: British and American Painting 1945-87* symposium at the Tate organised by the British American Arts Association. A series of major international exhibitions concurrent with the symposium highlight and extend issues raised by it. *Individuals: A Selected History of Contemporary Art 1945-86* at the Museum of Contemporary Art, Los Angeles, brings together the major figures who have provoked the imaginative advances in American art today. *NY Art Today* at the Saatchi Gallery provides an opportunity to see the very latest American art which has built on the legacy of Minimalism and Pop, while the essential formal component of Pop expression, the contemporary icon, is the subject of a major analytical exhibition at the ICA, *Comic Iconoclasm*.

In a major interview, Robert Rosenblum discerns the main trends and artists in British and American art since 1945. Emphasising the formal influence and innovations of Abstract Expressionism, Rosenblum goes on to chart the increasing cultural role of art and assess the effects of the Post-Modern revaluation of neglected traditions. Peter Fuller provides a strong and provoking analysis of the vital years of aesthetic innovation following the war, when both British and American art had distinct yet shared themes and concerns. Mary Rose Beaumont compares the main movements in both countries up to the present day, and describes the figures and groups that have contributed to indigenous traditions.

The current trends in New York art are the subject of Dan Cameron's survey of the work in the forthcoming exhibition at the Saatchi Gallery. John Griffiths brings together the major figures in American art since 1945, whether in Abstract Expressionism, Pop art, Minimalism, realism, or Post-Modernism.

Charles Jencks examines the nature of Narrative Classicism in the work of contemporary British and American artists, highlighting a clear and mutual engagement with both innovation and tradition. The importance of the popular cultural icon during the heyday of Pop and its abiding attraction to contemporary artists is looked at by Sheena Wagstaff. An essential record of seminal statements by Grace Hartigan, Patrick Heron, Bryan Robertson and Robert Rosenblum from the *Interchanges* symposium brings together the major concerns that have intrigued and influenced British and American artists over the past 40 years.

THE EXHIBITIONS AND EVENTS FEATURED IN THIS ISSUE INCLUDE THE FOLLOWING:

Interchanges: British and American Painting at the Tate Gallery (organised by British American Arts Association), June 27, 1987.

Mark Rothko 1903-70, 17 June - 1 September 1987, Tate Gallery, 23 September - 2 January, 1988, Fundacion March, Madrid, 28 January -25 March, 1988, Museum Ludwig, Cologne.

Comic Iconoclasm, ICA London, October-November 1987, Douglas Hyde Galllery Dublin, January-February 1988, Cornerhouse Gallery, Manchester.

NY Art Today, from 11 September 1987, Saatchi Collection, London.

Individuals: A Selected History of Contemporary Art 1945-1986: (organised by Julia Brown Turrel) December 1986 - January 1988. The Museum of Contemporary Art, Los Angeles.

Eduardo Paolozzi; Sculptures from a Garden 6 August - 25 October, Serpentine Gallery, London, a Glynn Vivian Art Gallery and Museum, Swansea, 8 November 1987 - 10 January 1988 11 March-2 May, The Whitworth Art Gallery May - September 1988, Glasgow Garden Festival.

The works illustrated on pages 19, 24 and 25 have been reproduced by kind permission of the Henry Moore Foundation.

We would especially like to thank Jennifer Williams and Dani Salvadori of the British American Arts Association for their permission to reproduce extracts from the Interchange symposium and for providing related material.

We would also like to thank Janice Blackburn of the Saatchi Collection for providing illustrations related to the *NY Art Today* exhibition and other illustrative material related to the theme of this issue.

We would like to thank the ICA for providing illustrations relating to the *Comic Iconoclasm* exhibition.

We would also like to thank the following for providing illustrations for this issue: Waddington Gallery, The Henry Moore Foundation, Gimpel Fils, Serpentine Gallery, Whitechapel Art Gallery, Tate Gallery, Barbican Art Gallery, Anthony D'Offay Gallery, The Fruitmarket Gallery, Lisson Gallery.

The following works were of assistance in the preparation of this issue: *Mark Rothko 1903-1970*, The Tate Gallery, *Comic Iconoclasm*, ICA, *British Art in the 20th Century*, Royal Academy of Arts/Prestel, Frank H. Goodyear Jr, *Contemporary American Realism since 1960*, NYGS, Marina Vaizey, Peter Blake Weidenfeld & Nicolson, Gail Levin, *Edward Hopper; the Complete Prints*, Norton/Whitney, Ed. Jorn Merkert, *David Smith: Sculpture and Drawings*, Prestel, Barbara Rose, *American Twentieth Century Painting*, Skira/Rizzoli, Elizabeth Frank, *Jackson Pollock*, Abbeville, Ed. Wim Beeren and Talitha Schoon, *David Salle*, Museum Boymans-van Beunigen, James Thrall Soby/*Ben Shahn*, Penguin, Nikos Stangos, *Pictures by David Hockney*, Thames and Hudson, Terry Fenton, Anthony Caro, Thames & Hudson, *Individuals: A Selected History of Contemporary Art 1945-86* MOCA/Abbeville, Henry Moore, and John Hedgecoe. *Henry Moore* Ebury Press, Ed. Dr David Mellor, *Paradise Lost*, Lund Humphries/Barbican Art Gallery, St Ives, Tate Gallery.

Editor: Dr Andreas C Papadakis

First published in Great Britain in 1987 by Art & Design
an imprint of the
ACADEMY GROUP LTD, 7 HOLLAND STREET, LONDON W8 4NA

Art & Design Profile 5 is published as part of Art & Design Volume 3 9/10-1987
Distributed in the United States of America by
St Martin's Press, 175 Fifth Avenue, New York 10010

ISBN: 0-85670-930-1 (UK)

Printed in Great Britain by E G Bond Ltd

THE ASCENDANCY OF ART
An Interview with Robert Rosenblum

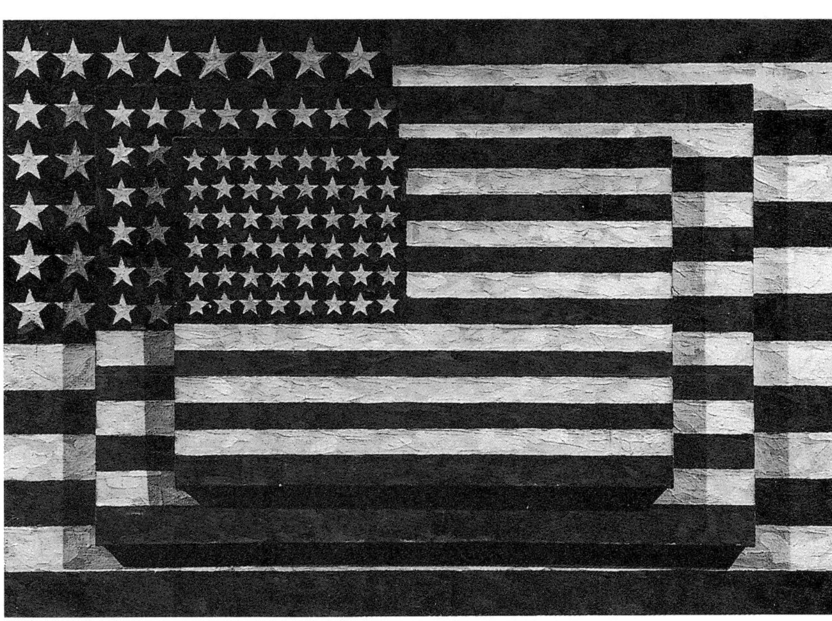

Jasper Johns, *Three Flags*, 1958

ROBERT ROSENBLUM

Abstraction, Pop art, Minimalism, Conceptualism, and now Post-Modernism, have dominated British and American art since 1945. In a major interview Robert Rosenblum discusses with Hugh Cumming the shared concerns, the differences and the imaginative interchange between the two cultures, as well as the emergent re-evaluation of respective visual traditions.

HC   Do you think there actually has been, especially when Abstract Expressionism and then Pop art were the significant movements of the moment, an interchange between Britain and America? Were artists inspiring one another, and then improving on anything they might have seen, or is that a superficial judgment, and were the major movements, such as Pop and Abstract Expressionism, really created by one country, and was the other country just copying them?

RR   Yes, I would think you could say that there has been one dominant centre of high creative activity. In the early 20th century, as well as in the later 19th century, this was Paris, then it seems to have moved to New York during the war years. This is a familiar myth, and maybe it will be challenged. Yet it still seems to me that in terms of not only chronological priority, but also the thrust, the impact, the innovation of the work, New York had the lead in the late 40s, 50s and early 60s. The question of abstract art in England in the late 50s and early 60s, as well as Pop art, is one that is maybe a little vexed vis-à-vis the American story. But it still seems very clear to me that abstract painters like Robyn Denny, or Hoyland, or Turnbull, could not have done what they did without the precedent of the likes of Rothko or Newman. And artists like Johns and Rauschenberg in the late 50s certainly left their impact on the likes of Richard Smith, or Allen Jones, or Peter Blake. Despite the fact that there really was a kind of early phase

of Pop art in England in the 50s, and even in the late 40s with Paolozzi, there was also this in America too. I doubt really that there were any artists in England who had the grandeur, the thrust, the centrality of artists like Warhol or Lichtenstein on the Pop side, or Stella, or some of the early Minimalist sculptors like André, Judd and Morris on the side of abstract art. It should be said too that England was very precocious in terms of giving the American artists sometimes their first major one man shows on this side of the Atlantic, rather than in New York, so that the material was visually accessible throughout the late 50s and early 60s.

The Abstract Vision

HC   If we just concentrate on Abstract Expressionism for a moment, who would you say was the major artist of that particular group?

RR   I think, in terms of the impact on England, it would be Rothko and Newman. A lot of the huge British abstract paintings that were done in the early 60s, especially under the aegis of the Situation Group, seem to be direct reflections, almost clones of Rothko and Newman. Nobody really took on Pollock, or de Kooning, or Kline. They seemed to be much too savage and chaotic for the traditional British temperament. But the very lean abstractions of the likes of Stella, these had immediate repercus-

Mark Rothko, *Horizontals White over Dark*, 1961, oil on canvas, 56½×93¼"

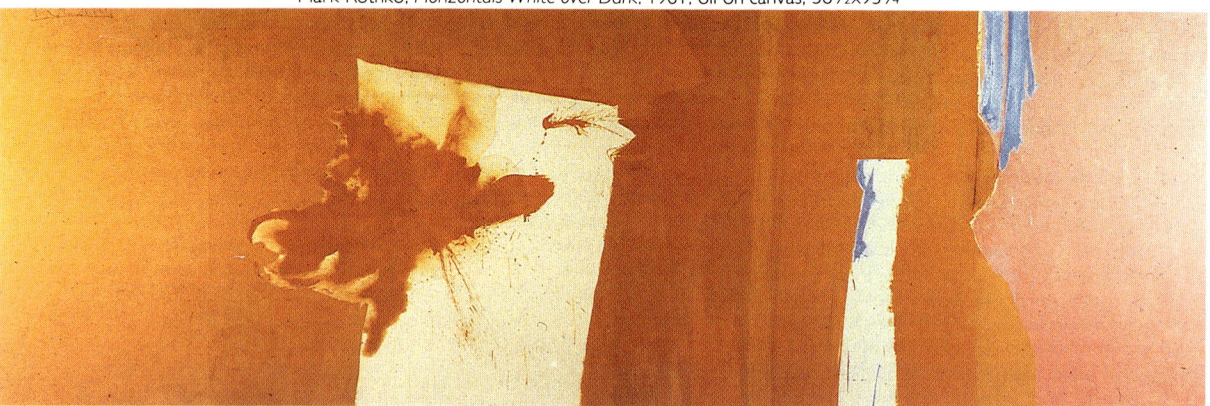

Robert Motherwell, *The Golden Fleece*, 1961, oil on canvas, 82×180"

sions in London. They seemed to be more congenial.

HC Did those artists share something between them? Did Rothko, Pollock, Stella, have something in common, or were they in actual fact distinct?

RR Like any group – you can say the same thing about the Cubists or Impressionists – they shared something, but they were also, if they were masters, distinct individuals. So that Rothko and Pollock couldn't look less alike: one seems to be all action, the other seems to be all inaction. But at the same time, the feeling of something primordial, something that is a basic ABC language, something that gets to the absolute roots of the sensation – these are experiences that are shared by many of those American artists of the late 40s and 50s, the so-called heroic generation. This is true as well of the Minimalist artists of the early 60s. Nobody would mistake a Carl André for a Donald Judd or a Frank Stella, but they all share this feeling of getting down to elementary basics of geometry, plotting, measurement in the early 60s. They are distinctive, and alike, in the way that

Picasso and Braque often look alike in the 1910s and their Cubist years, but are nevertheless quite different artists.

HC Do you think it's significant that they were, as you say, looking for a primordial basic language?

RR I think there are many ways to approach it. It's always been a recurrent theme in the history of modern art to chuck the past, to overthrow tradition, and to start as if you were the first artist and the first human being on earth. This seems to be the way that modern art regenerates itself, to shut out the past, and start from scratch with a clean slate. All of this is part of a long heritage. You can find earlier examples in the 20th century in the work of abstractionists like Malevich or Mondrian. Even the idea of Impressionism is of a kind of naive child's eye, looked at in a simplified way. But I would say also that in the particular time and space situation of America after 1945, there was the extra thrust of the devastating conclusion of the Second World War, the atom bomb, Hiroshima. This made Americans, as it certainly did Europeans, feel as though the world had come to an end. There

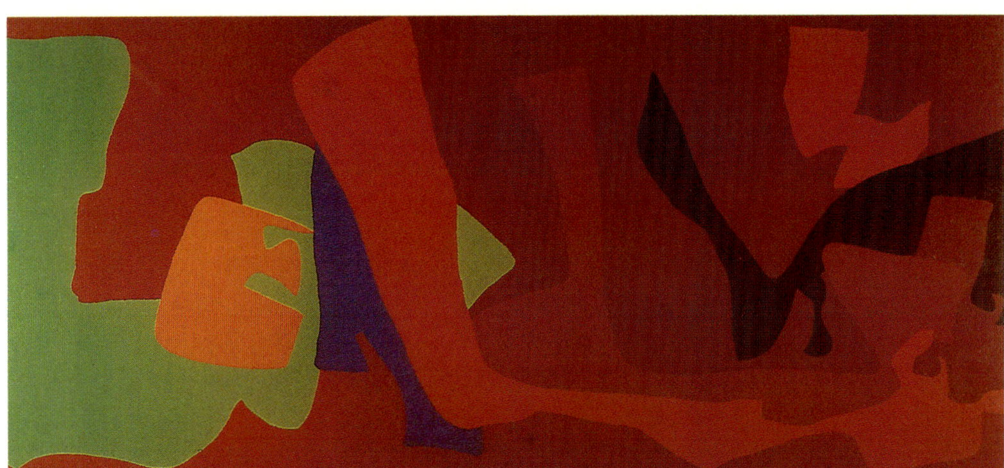

Patrick Heron, *March, April*, 1975, oil on canvas, 69x204"

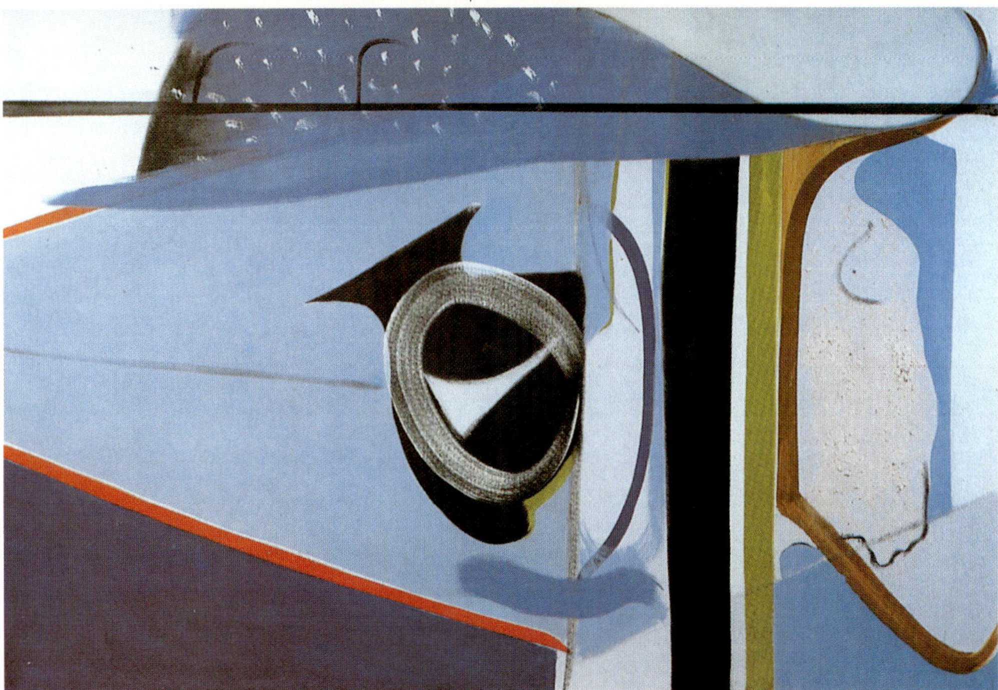

Peter Lanyon, *Clevedon Bandstand*, 1964, oil on canvas, 48x72"

was a sense of total annihilation, not only metaphorically, but literally in many cases. It was a kind of back-to-the-beginning-of-everything experience; first light, first chaos, first shape. So I think that this mythology of total devastation, a kind of post-apocalyptic feeling, was in part responsible for this search for origins, even though this is also a long tradition in the modern experience.

HC So, would you say this distinguished the work of Rothko from that of someone like Kandinsky or Malevich? What makes their abstract work different? Is it an advance on it?

RR Well, it's not about advance. In some ways there are works by Kandinsky, not to mention Malevich or Mondrian, which are also a response to world crisis situations. It's often been pointed out that Kandinsky's abstractions emerged on the eve of the First World War, and they have an end-of-the-world feeling, as if there were going to be a total immolation, which in fact there almost was. Similarly Malevich and Mondrian are post-war ex-pressions of starting from scratch. They have the image of

reconstruction, of a kind of simple, pure language of primary shapes and colours that might presumably present ethical and visually unpolluted ground plans for the future. These conditions, in general terms, help to explain a lot of the character of abstract art in the early part of this century. What is very different about the Americans, just in visual terms, is the sense of scale. I think that is something that had really no precedent in early 20th-century abstract art. These were pictures that everybody commented on, in the late 40s and 50s, as looking huge. This sense of an overwhelming cosmic scale was often attributed – and I think this is in good part true – to the different sense of actual scale in the American continent vis-à-vis Europe. There is a sense of vastness, of infinite spaces, of openness. In fact many of the artists came from the West, as is the case with Pollock or Still. Even so, the sense of a big picture that couldn't really be walked past, the way you could walk past a smaller easel picture, this was very conspicuous then. It was certainly an image that many British artists tried to live up to in the 60s. This is something else that I think is very clearly a question of a British response to American priority.

HC A lot of people, for instance, that are used to more complicated figurative or symbolic work, prior to those particular paintings, would say that the work of Pollock or Rothko had an initial superficial attraction, because of its immediacy, and as time has gone on, that's worn off, and the actual formal innovations are in fact all there is to it, and that is just it. What would you say to a comment like that?

RR It goes completely counter to my own experience, which is the first place I would look. It also seems to go counter to the consensus of younger audiences, and the most conspicuous example of this seems to be the current Tate show of Rothko's work. I do remember people who didn't like Rothko in the late 40s and 50s tended to think he was utterly vacuous. I remember a quip that he looked like a Buddhist television set. There was a sense that he was a con artist and painting, as they said about Turner, pictures of nothing. But the fact is that then, and more

artists who have spiritual visions who don't have the language to convey it. If he didn't have the feeling, and the force, and the conviction, it's true it wouldn't be there, but he also had the language which seemed to fuse perfectly with what he apparently felt about the human situation in general, or his in particular. But the fact is that there are any number of other artists, not even followers, but actually predecessors, like Josef Albers, who worked within a similar context of floating abstract colour planes. Their pictures, now I'm thinking of Albers, don't yield any particularly dramatic emotions. They look to me like didactic and beautiful exercises in the arrangement of planes, and colours, and intervals, whereas Rothko's work really seems to evoke all kinds of last judgements. So that I think in his case it has to be a fusion of this pictorial genius and the fact that, as the phrase goes, he had something to say.

HC Do you see any figures today working on either side of the Atlantic who have an equivalent formal ability and vision?

RR I don't think that in the language of abstraction there is

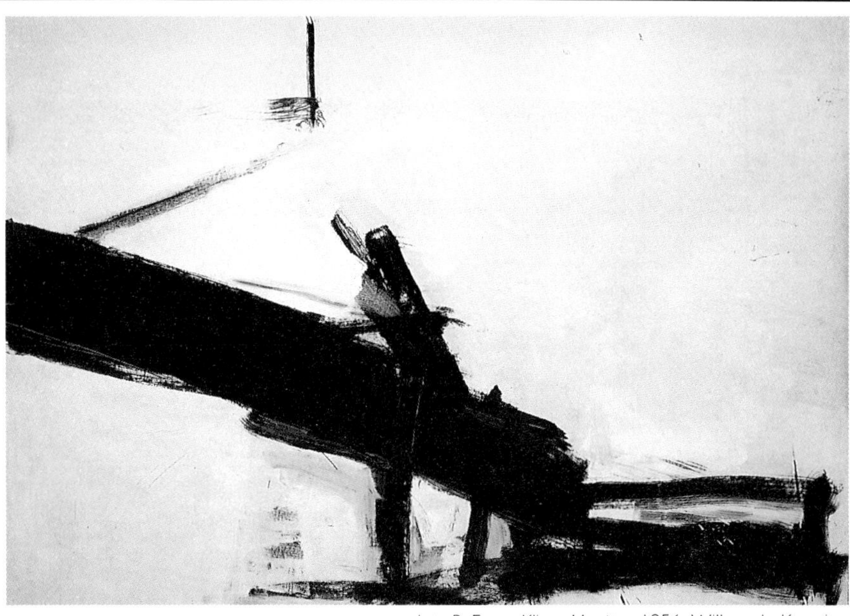 

L to R: Franz Kline, *Monitor*, 1956, Willem de Kooning, *Untitled*, 1963

and more now, people seem to find something emotionally compelling, haunting about his work. It seems to be very gloomy, it seems to be very serious, and even to have a rather religious, sanctified aura to it. These are experiences extracted from his work that seem particularly prominent in the Tate show today and that most viewers seem to have responded to. Rather than diminishing in terms of their emotional power, the works of Rothko have expanded and I would certainly say the same was true for the works of Pollock or Newman. I think when they were first seen the language was so strong that people tended not to get much of an emotional response to it because they were put off by the sheer newness of the surface. But once you got used to that, the sense of energy, the sense of heroic drama in the work began to percolate through. It seems very conspicuous to me now, and I think it does to most audiences in the 1980s.

HC Does that particular quality that you mention, Rothko's spiritual vision, make him a great painter for you?

RR It has to be a combination of the two. There are many

anybody who comes up to that. Because I think in general in the late 20th century the feeling is, not only about abstraction, but art in general, that its force for change, moral good, drama, seems to be a thing of the past. We're in what might be called, in the phrase of the day, a Post-Modernist situation, and the feeling that modern art can be heroic, that it makes a difference to the world, all this seems sort of quaint and nostalgic rather than a part of living reality. So I certainly think that on the level of abstract artists, I've never seen anybody who can come up to those ambitions. That's all right, things have changed, and people don't believe that art has that much power. Most abstract art today seems to be like most Post-Modernist 'things': these are artists who look back to the glories of the abstract past and repeat it, paraphrasing it, but it's always with a sense of being an historical repetition of a long ago era. There are even some artists now, Phillip Taaffe is one, who re-do Barnett Newman. There's an extraordinary painting which is a visual paraphrase, to mix metaphors, of Barnett Newman's *Vir Heroicus Sublimis* which repeats the picture, but instead of those zips, there is a kind of coiled rope band which tends to de-existentialise it and make it look as though it's coming off a computer.

Post-Modernism: Innovation as Tradition

HC   Would you say that some of the contemporary American artists you mentioned are looking back to American traditions, or are they creating something new?

RR   It's not American traditions. Some of them do respectful repetitions with variations of Bridget Riley, Lissitsky, Moholy Nagy, you name it, or in other cases, Barnett Newman. So it's not a national thing, it's just the international history of abstract art, preferably hardedged. They are very much, as their name 'Neo-Geo' suggests, historicists in the way that Carlo Maria Mariani is an historicist, resurrecting the look of Neo-Classicism. I think of them as two sides of the same coin. It's fascinating that today in the 1980s artists are so aware of history. Instead of trying to obliterate it in the way the Rothko-Pollock generation did, they

of 20th-century artists from Picasso and de Kooning to even Giorgio Morandi. He just does exact replicas of them and that is his way of bowing down to the muse of history and the fact of reproductions of works of art.

HC   What is the difference between that and an artist who just doesn't have any imagination? Do you find that a valid art form?

RR   This is a very curious phenomenon. It means that nowadays, when you look at a work say by Mike Bidlo, you don't say this is a Lichtenstein, you say this is a Mike Bidlo. If there were a one-shot affair of one artist copying *Les Demoiselles d'Avignon* you might pooh-pooh it, but this is an artist who spent years and years passionately copying works of art. When you see his studio it's absolutely mind-boggling because it looks as if the Museum of Modern Art has been closed for the bombing and this is the storeroom. So collecting the anthology of works has a special poignance. It seems like some kind of bomb shelter history of the 20th century . So I have nothing but interest and respect for that.

HC   Would you recognise Post-Modernism as a valid tenden-

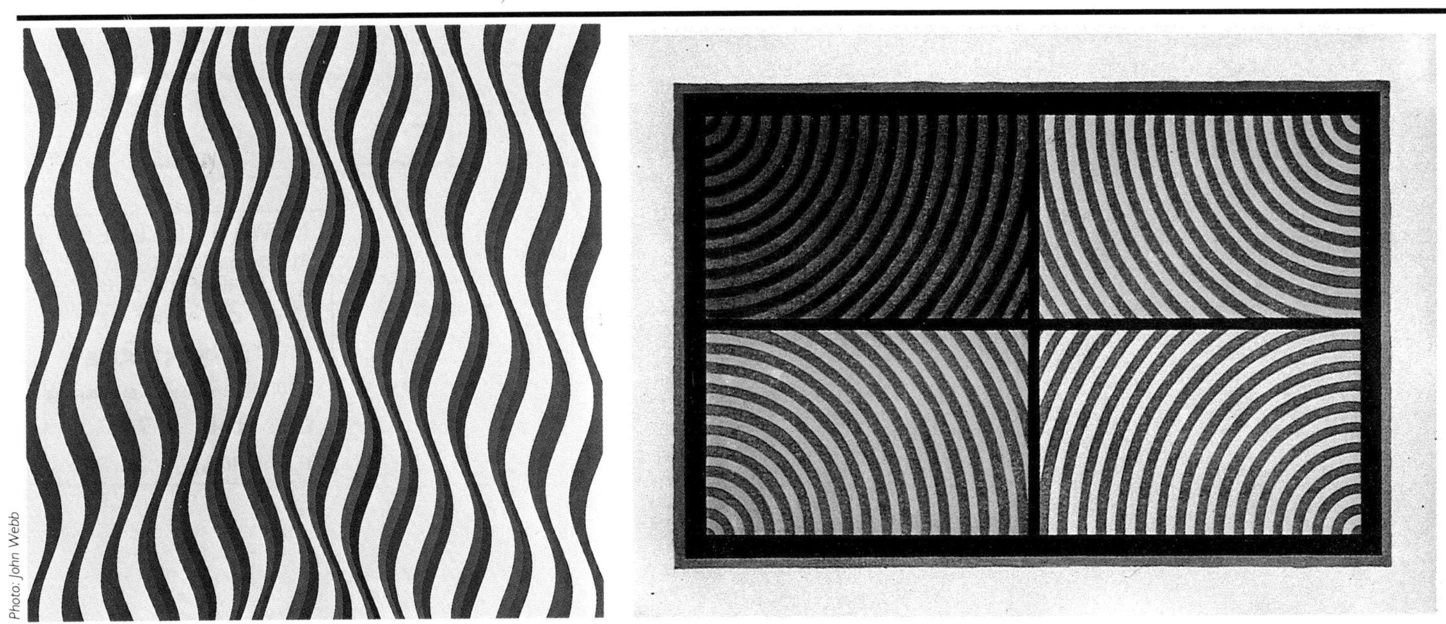

L to R: Bridget Riley, *Cataract 1*, 1967; Sol LeWitt, *Arcs from four corners*, 1986

are using it as a kind of touchstone of nostalgia, sentiment, to look back and to reconstruct the 20th century. It's rather scary in terms of the fact that I think it's a symptom of the way in which younger people, like the older people, cannot bear the thought of what might happen in the future. The future of the world seems to be so blank. Nobody any longer, I think, believes in progress, and I think the 21st century is almost inconceivable.

HC   So do you see this as a lack of cultural inspiration or a form of decadence in a way?

RR   Well, I wouldn't want to moralise about it. It's an expected response to the way people tend to feel at the end of the 20th century. They don't want to face the future. There is also of course the culture of history which is so dense now. I mean the proliferation of knowledge, of reproductions and so on, is all around us, so that history itself has become a kind of present reality. As you know, there are lots of painters in New York in the 1980s who actually just do copies of earlier works of art, like Mike Bidlo, who does as literal copies as possible of any number

cy? For instance someone like Charles Jencks would argue that there's been a reaction against Modernism in art and what you see now is a tendency that combines certain things from Modernism with certain things from tradition to make a new aesthetic. This is an aesthetic that is as valid as Modernism, and is a source of optimism a source of innovation, a new international movement. Obviously he's charted it in architecture but he's saying it exists in art as well. I don't know if that ties in any way with what you were saying about a nostalgic attitude towards the past in art?

RR   It seems to clear to me and I think it does to practically everybody that the heyday of Modernism is long behind us. The whole sense that art is linear or progressive, or that there were groups of artists pointing in the same direction, that myth of an artistic forward march, has been shattered since the 70s, if not earlier. Therefore you have to have a word to describe the new position and the history of the modern movement seems to have closed its last chapter. So we're somewhere else, and the only word that seems to cover it all is Post-Modernism, which is a bit

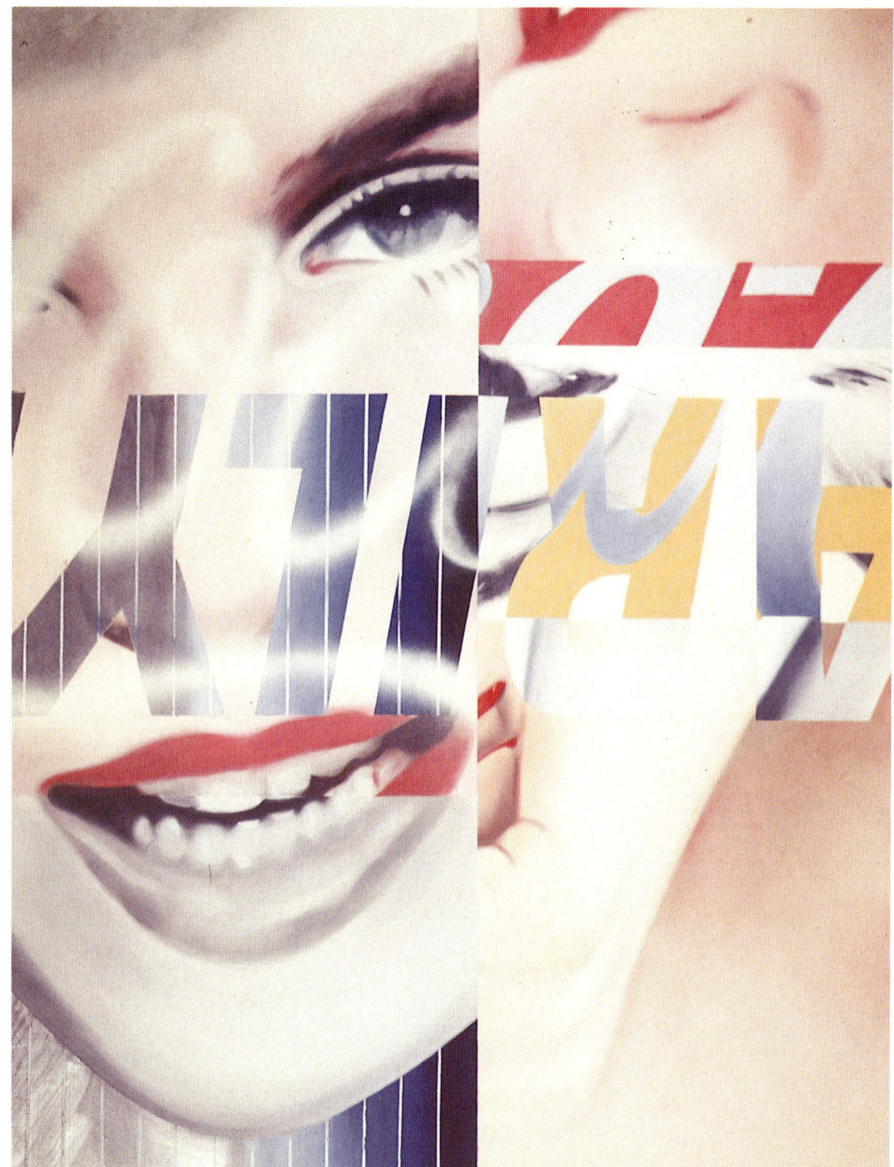

J Rosenquist, *Marilyn Monroe*, 1962

like Post-Impressionism, which is pretty diverse, but it's after some event. Whether this is a coherent movement, or just some sort of death rattle of eclecticism and confusion, I can't say. I don't proselytise or predict, I'm just trying to keep score with what is happening. I hope that whatever we have now will result in works of art that are terrific and keep our attention, not just now but over the decades. I certainly think there are enough candidates for that in the 1980s to make me cheerful.

The Legacy of Pop: Gilbert & George

HC   If we look at contemporary art in Britain for the moment, do you think that there are any artists of international stature creating significant works right now?

RR   I am a great fan of Gilbert and George who seem to be very topical, now having a show at the Hayward Gallery which has been all around the world. One of the things that fascinates me about them is not only their British insularity, which is very wilful, but their Post-Modernist internationalism. It seems to me

that they fit in very comfortably with this sense of revival, nostalgia for the past. They probably wouldn't agree that they're nostalgic, but they really seem to me to be evangelical reformers cast in the mould of some sort of Victorian proselytisers. Their art in so many ways seems retrospective, and at the same time very much here and now, as a comment on British social realities. They strike me as world-class artists. Their images are not only just plain gorgeous, even if you don't care about what's going on inside of them, but they also intersect with so many of the concerns of this historical retrospection which is common in the 1980s, and I assume will still be in the 90s. They are, in the rarest of British traditions, both insular and international in character, because they seem to be accessible to people on both sides of the Atlantic and the Channel.

HC   What are the characteristics of their concerns? You mentioned their Victorian evangelical role, for instance. What particular problems do they deal with?

RR   It looks to me – and I'm viewing it from another planet,

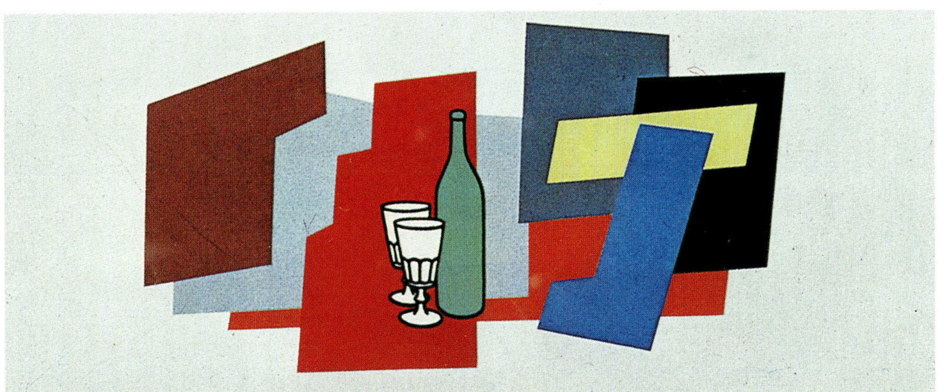

Patrick Caulfield, *Still Life with Green Bottle*, 1964

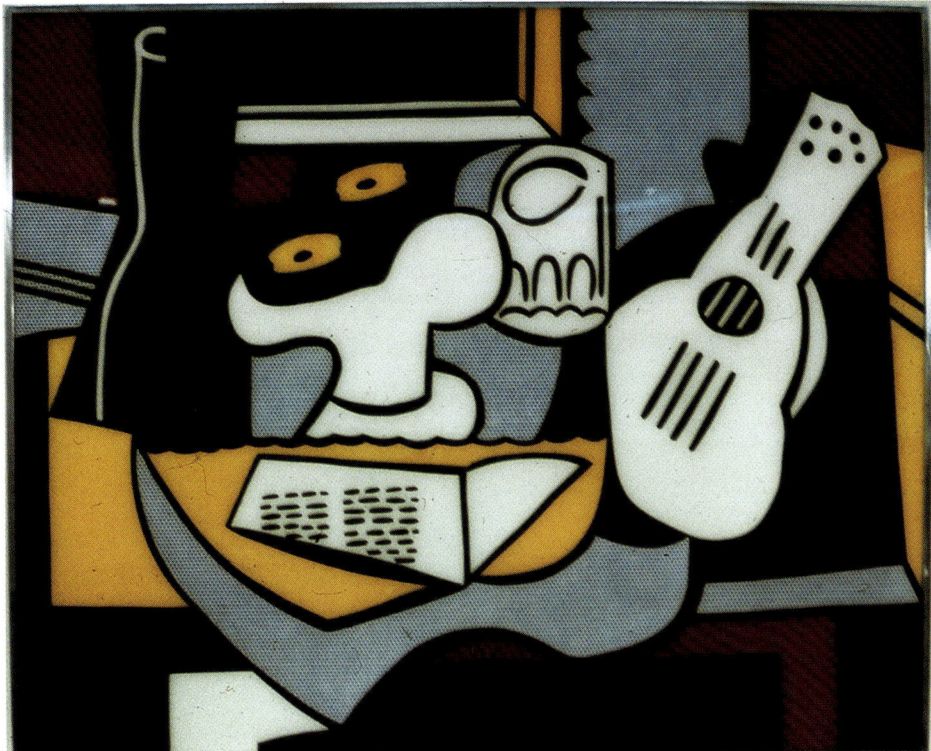

Roy Lichtenstein, *Still Life*, 1964, magna on plexiglass, 48x60"

New York – that they're reportorial in character. They are very interested in photographing, documenting and presenting, in clear and journalistic ways, the facts of life, especially the seamier side, in London and the East End where they live. This looks to me like an extraordinary photo-documentary of a major social, cultural reality of London today. That in itself, even if they were photo-journalists, would be something of an achievement. I don't know of anybody else who's come to grips with those facts in such a potent manner. The other part of their art is a kind of reconstruction of these roots of social reality in that population in terms of a grand Victorian religious vision. It's been said, and I certainly sense it, that their pictures look like Victorian stained glass. They're constructed that way. They have the character of a shrine or altar in terms of the way they're composed. The figures of Gilbert and George, at least for me, have taken on a kind of mythic stature, of people who have an almost extra-terrestrial character, who've come down to observe life on earth, being the East End of London, and to offer some kind of sermons about heaven and hell. All this may seem kind of peculiar and nostalgic in terms of the hard facts of religion and salvation in the late 20th century, and that's part of its historicising or British Post-Modernist flavour. I think it sets up in the most visually and emotionally poignant way what can be felt, or done, or not done. What can't be done is often as potent an image to work on as what can be done regarding the problems of religion, of the supernatural, of the here and now as opposed to the beyond, in terms of a large segment of British society, and by implication, the whole world today. And I find this an extraordinary programme. I find it even more extraordinary that the images resulting from it come off, just as dazzling works of art on the first level, but also as something to chew on, to conjure with, on the second.

HC You could say that in some of their work there is a predominance of authoritarian symbols, of authoritarian figures. Are they treating those particular images with irony, or do you think they approve of them? Does the same attitude apply to their sexual obsessions, or the particular sexual angle they take?

Some people might say, are they interested in women? Where do women come into the work of Gilbert and George? Is it exclusive?

RR Looked at from any point of view, it's a very narrow segment of reality. There are no women. There are tough East End kids who for all I know are out to start a revolution here, Paki-bashers, anti-or-pro Thatcherites, depending on your angle of vision. And it's only a small part of the world. But this is true of practically every artist in Britain as elsewhere. There may not be many women in Gilbert and George, but there aren't too many naked women in Francis Bacon either, or in David Hockney's work. And, after all, Allen Jones isn't interested in nude men, and he shows a particular segment of society, so there's nothing so peculiar about that. The spectator can deduce from the work of Renoir and Picasso, for example, implications about those artists' sexual preferences, too. I don't see anything distinctive about Gilbert and George here as opposed to any other artists who deal with their particular obsessions.

who seem to be working in the shadow of Gilbert and George. The idea of artists being doubles or working as a pair, a group, is something that is becoming more and more common today. Whether it has to do with the direct impact of Gilbert and George or rather the way things are going, I can't say. There are identical twin photographers, the Starn twins, and there's a marvellous pair of New York painters, McGough and McDermott, who dress in a uniformly foppish way like late 19th-century dandies, and who do pictures that are reconstructions of Victorian and early 20th-century styles. So they have a kind of historical science-fiction character that reminds me somewhat of Gilbert and George. But I can't think of anybody who has their stature except looking back to Warhol. So I think even on that wave-length Warhol is a kind of major figure who can be picked up and varied and explored by countless younger artists doing a million different things. His range and his visual innovation are like nothing else I know. He's also the first artist, it seems to me, who was aware that art would just be a commodity. He knew very

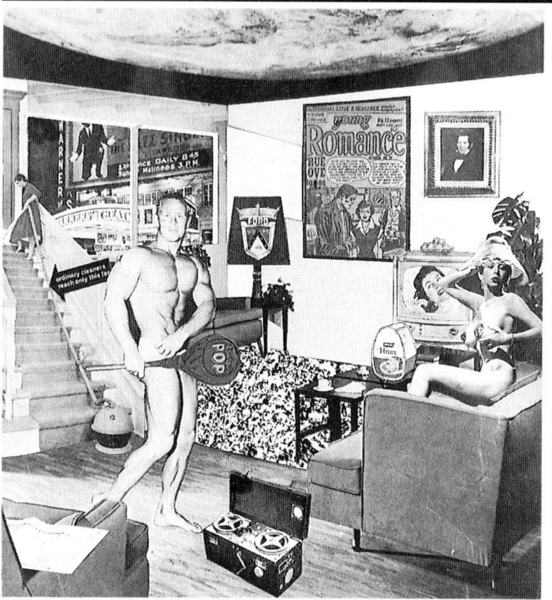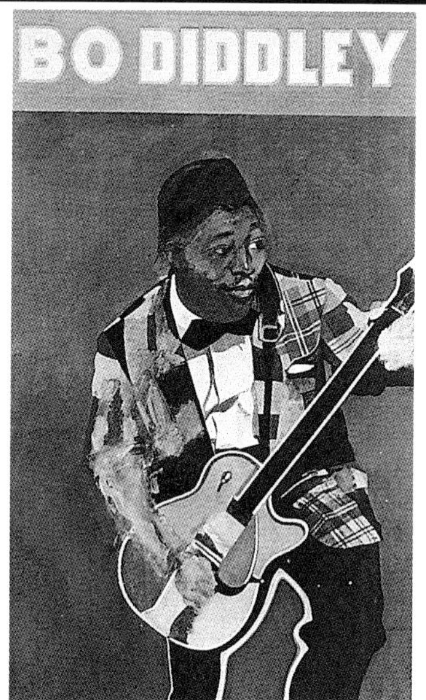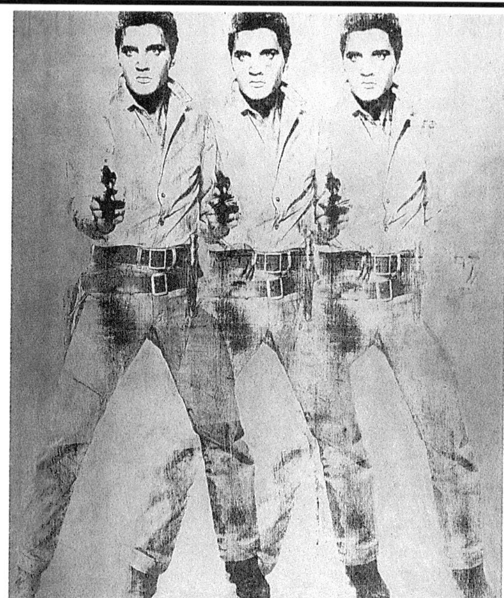

L to R: Richard Hamilton, Just What is it that Makes Today's Homes, so Different, so Appealing?, 1956; Peter Blake, Bo Diddley, 1963; Andy Warhol, Triple Elvis, 1962

HC Does their work relate to any particular American or British movement within recent years? Do they relate to Pop? You also mentioned photography.

RR Well, I think that their great predecessor, and he seems to be everybody's great predecessor now that he's dead, is Andy Warhol. Because I can think of very few artists who had such a scope, in terms of reporting as a photographic journalist, the realities of, in his case, American life, and letting the spectator draw his own conclusions.

Warhol is important not only in terms of transforming photo-documentation, but also in terms of a kind of irony about what he presents, a kind of detachment that puts him in the centre of his universe. This seems to me to have interesting repercussions in the Gilbert and George direction. I would think that no artist could tell us as much as Andy Warhol did about the facts of American society in the 60s and 70s. And probably the same is true about Gilbert and George. So on many counts they seem to be related to him. There are younger artists in New York now

quickly that it could be a factory, it could be a business, that it was money. Just by his ironic awareness of this, his use of it for his own purposes, he set into motion a whole point of view that's very current today amongst younger artists; the idea that art does not have to have a great aesthetic or social message in that it's only business. That sounds perhaps very jaded, but I think it's a perfectly ok point of view as long as the art that's being produced is something that I want to look at.

HC Is this a good thing or a bad thing? Is this just a means of covering up the fact that they're ripping people off, or not?

RR No, I think they are responding to the facts of modern life and they're not ripping people off anymore than the thousands of 19th-century artists who painted pictures that could be bought. I think it's just a change of mythology that is there. The whole myth of an artist starving in order to produce serious or authentic works of art is something that went out with the Abstract Expressionists. It doesn't do anybody any good and there have been always very wealthy artists who have also been great artists such as Rubens, Delacroix, Degas. It's not been a hindrance.

HC Do you think art is as vital, or has as much urgency, as far as most people are concerned, as it did when Abstract Expressionism was the dominant movement in contemporary art? Or is it that there just happen to be one or two figures like Gilbert and George, and that, for instance, people culturally look to another art form for something more pertinent or visionary about their lives?

RR I don't think very many people look to art for anything visionary or religious, except for the fact that it seems in a very curious way to have replaced religion in most people's lives. The only thing I can think of that's comparable is the way people queue up for any great exhibition such as a Picasso, Renoir, or van Gogh show. Well they stand in line for hours and hours, and they file by with great piety. This seems to me an extraordinary transformation of religious pilgrimages or processions, in earlier, more pious days. They've got to see this show, they don't care how much effort it takes to get there, the way they had to go to

York with the heyday of Abstract Expressionism, that art, especially contemporary art, was perceived by an audience that you could count on the fingers of a couple of hands. It seems that today there is a huge audience out there just waiting to pounce on the next new artist, not to mention to go again and again to see retrospectives of middle-aged artists, or venerable artists, or what have you. Just in statistical terms, in New York in particular, the sheer quantity of people out there who are involved with art, who rush around from one gallery to another, and will go to every museum exhibition on the books, is absolutely staggering. I think the main effect of it hasn't anything to do with purifying people's lives, or saving their souls, or anything of that sort. Probably the main effect is to fill in time because there's much more leisure time now for 'cultural activities' which seem to be good for you and high-minded. The effect is also to make money because the whole international art market scene now is pretty spectacular in terms of a network of finances and the number of people who buy and sell and exchange things all over the world,

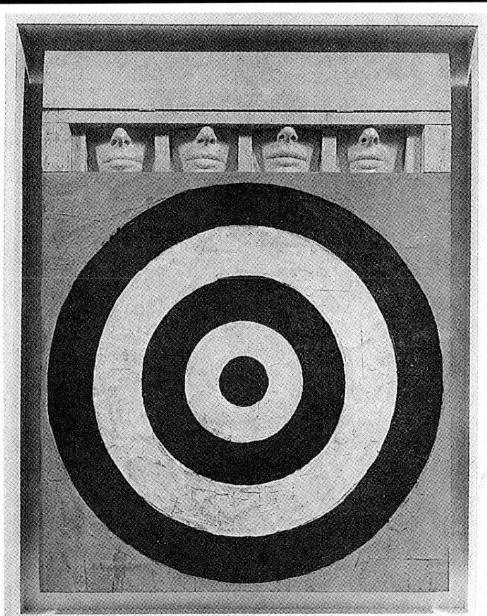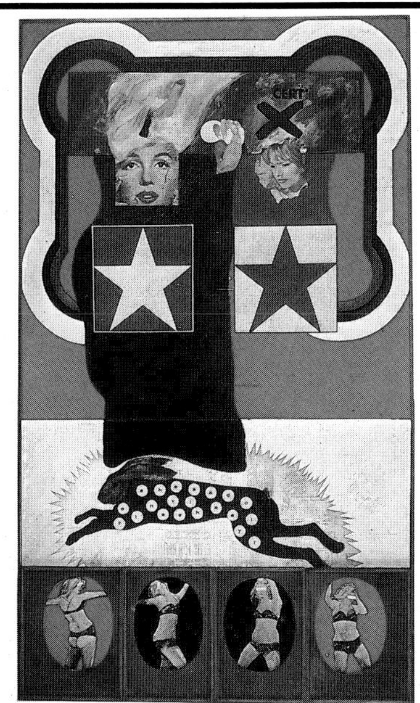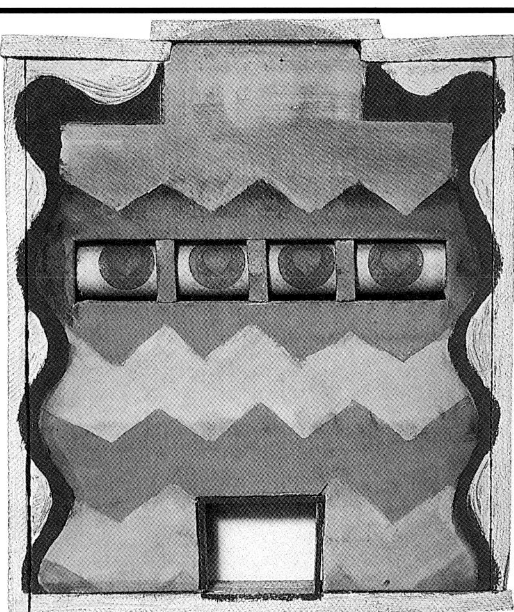

L to R: Jasper Johns, *Target with Four Faces*, 1955; Peter Philips, *For Men Only, Starring MM and BB*, 1961; Richard Smith, *Slot Machine*, 1960

this or that religious shrine in another century. But I think that the world is much too jaded now, except in the case of teenage idealists, to think that art's going to change anybody's life. It may change artists' lives in so far as they may believe passionately in what they do, but I don't think it's going to make too much difference in terms of the actual moral, or political, or social behaviour of anybody who absorbs a picture by Gilbert and George, or Andy Warhol, or anybody else.

The Ascendancy of Art

HC Do you think other art forms have a similar role in people's lives, like architecture, or the movies, or literature? It seems to me you could say that certain art forms become more dominant in a particular era, and then fade into the background, and then come back into the foreground in another.

RR One thing that is very clear now is that I can't imagine when there was ever as much popular interest in art as there is now. I mean it used to be, and I'm thinking back to the situation in New

and must infinitely surpass anything that's ever been in the history of art as commerce.

HC Do you see this as a good thing or a bad thing? Or is it just the sign of the times?

RR I think it's a good thing. Although it was very nice to say that van Gogh or Picasso, Kline or Pollock, were starving to death at a certain point in their lives, I don't see why this is good. I don't see any reason why artists shouldn't make money the way other people do. The whole myth of the artist being pure and poverty-stricken and not having the goods and comfort of ordinary people is ridiculous. There've been a lot of rich artists throughout history who were just as great as the poor ones. If artists realise that art is a commodity and that they can make money on it, I don't see any reason why this is bad or why it should in some way pollute their art. I mean artists ideally have patrons, and they always did. It was the 19th and early 20th century that tended to upset that balance. Now things have caught up. Artists always used to complain that they were

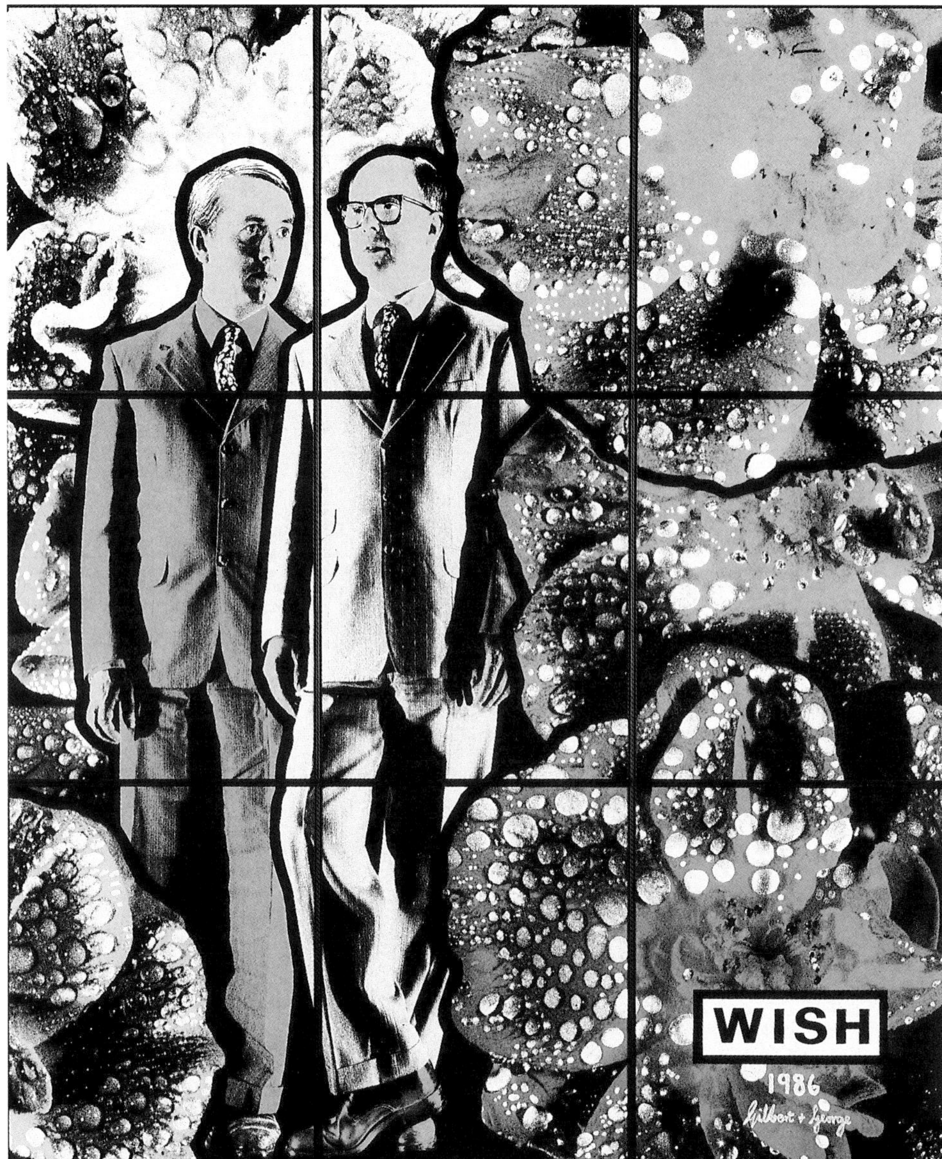

Gilbert and George, *Wish*, 1986, photo-piece 71½x59½″, from the recent exhibition at the Anthony d'Offay gallery

alienated, but they aren't any more. We should all be happy that art is thriving and selling at least on my side of the Atlantic.

HC Would you say it was symptomatic of a trend toward a more predominantly visual culture as opposed to a literary culture?

RR I think so absolutely. One of the reasons art is so successful in the late 20th century is because of, among other things, TV. The fact is that most people have stopped reading, or stopped being involved with any high-minded cultural activity that takes too long a time. I mean people's attention span in the late 20th century is very very short. Most people can't wait for the commercial to come on because the news itself is too lengthy. Whatever, art seems to be perfectly tuned to the minimal attention span for culture. If you listen to music or read a book, it takes imposed minutes, or hours, or days, whereas you can look at a work of art at your own tempo. The number of seconds that people devote to each work of art is probably pitiful, but then there's so much art to see. But I think it is an activity that can be

reduced to practically nothing more than blinking and people register things very quickly. It's a kind of instant gratification that suits the unbelievably rapid tempo of information we receive in the late 20th century. Now I think that's really one of the reasons it's been such a huge success.

HC Do you think this has an effect on the kind of paintings people produce? Are they tending to produce paintings that will have more of an initial sensory impact that doesn't stand up to continual re-examination and exploration of detail?

RR I think that a lot of art is geared to make a big show in a fast way. Most artists have to deal with the attention span of gallery-goers or museum-goers and they have to make them look fast. They have to shout their identity, and be recognised. It's certainly clear in Gilbert and George. The identity thing is really the important issue. I think that obviously television and the big bang image is important today, but I don't think that it necessarily dominates many artists who are now, in a kind of 'neo' way, going back to old-fashioned oil paint techniques and looking like

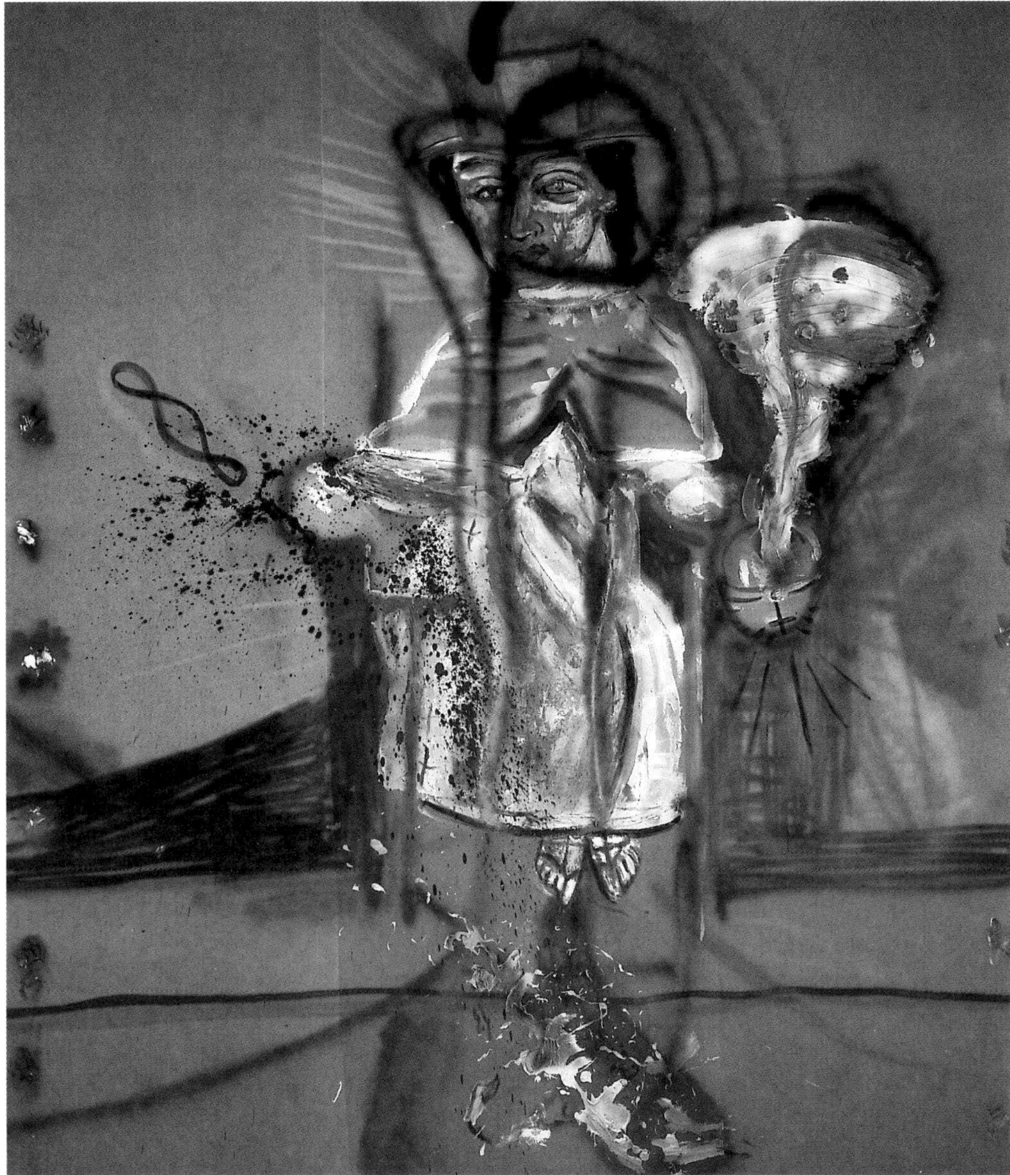

Julian Schnabel, *Resurrection: Albert Finney meets Malcolm Lowry*, 1984, oil and modelling paste on velvet, 10×9", from the recent exhibition at the Whitechapel

Tintoretto, El Greco, Rubens, you name it.

HC   Would you say that the expansion of visual culture and the widening of the audience has produced an inquisitive attitude towards the past?

RR   Oh yes. The thirst for information and new things to see seems to be unquenchable. The sheer expansion of knowledge about 19th- and 20th-century art, not to mention pre 19th-century art, in the last 10 to 20 years has been mind-boggling. I remember seeing in London last year an exhibition of Scandinavian late 19th- and early 20th-century art which would have been really unthinkable 20 to 30 years ago. Now there's a whole new repertory of lesser artists whose names are mainly unpronounceable to us, but this has been happening all over. It has to do with museums, and it has to do with dealers who have to sell new things, and it has to do with a kind of sating of a large part of the informed art audience with familiar things, and the need to see unfamiliar things, to dig them up, excavate them, dust them off and start from scratch. Otherwise people would get bored.

The sheer quantity of things to look at from the past these days surpasses anything that we've known in the mid or early 20th century and I don't know when it will stop. I mean the data banks are flooded, and it keeps coming.

HC   Do you think people are just consuming then? Or do you think that the constant exposure to rediscovered artists as well as recognised ones will have an effect on their creative capacity? Will we see more new works of art?

RR   I don't know what the influence is going to be in terms of artists, how they're going to deal with the constant expansion of history. Although I think that part of the sense of quotation, a feeling that history, that data from the past are what the stuff of reality is, is something that is reflected in that whole Post-Modernist situation of pinching and choosing among the fossils of the Western past. But it's anybody's guess what the future holds in terms of this flood of new art. My own sense is that there might even be some kind of backlash, and that in the future people are only going to deal with masterpieces.

ART & DESIGN 15

The Rediscovery of Tradition

HC   You mentioned Rothko earlier as an important American artist. You also talked about Gilbert and George. Are there any other figures you see on either side of the Atlantic since the war, who you think have made an important contribution either as individuals or as groups apart from the ones we've discussed? We were talking earlier about Hockney and Bacon. Do you see them as important and in what sense?

RR   Hockney and Bacon. Well they're very different. I saw the Bacon retrospective at the Tate last summer. Although I went to it simply out of duty, I was far more impressed than I expected to be, first of all by how simply gorgeous and seductive the paintings were. I had never expected to experience Bacon as such a terrific colourist. He almost looked as though he was Britain's one major and original response to Matisse, and that was not the usual approach to Bacon. But that's what really bowled me over first, and all the *Grand Guignol* subject matter seemed rather secondary. So I really think he's something. But he strikes me as being in

country, or not?

RR   Well, my own vision of British art, coming from abroad, is to look at what is most peculiar, what is most native about it. Therefore what attracts me most in looking at the history of 20th-century British art generally is what seems to have to do with landscape, rural traditions, mystical traditions. In other words exactly that aspect of British art that is not under the shadow of, first, Paris, in the earlier 20th century, and then New York, after the 1940s. The perfect capsule version of what happens to attract me is in a show I just saw at the Barbican Gallery about Neo-Romantic British art from the mid 30s until after the war, which is the other side of the British abstract coin that we usually learn about in the 30s. What is not Barbara Hepworth and Ben Nicholson, what is not in the Circle Group, but what has to do with a kind of Romantic retrogression to ruins, to nationalist history, to British landscape.

This is something which has a particularly strong and special flavour for me, whereas general, British abstract art tends, again

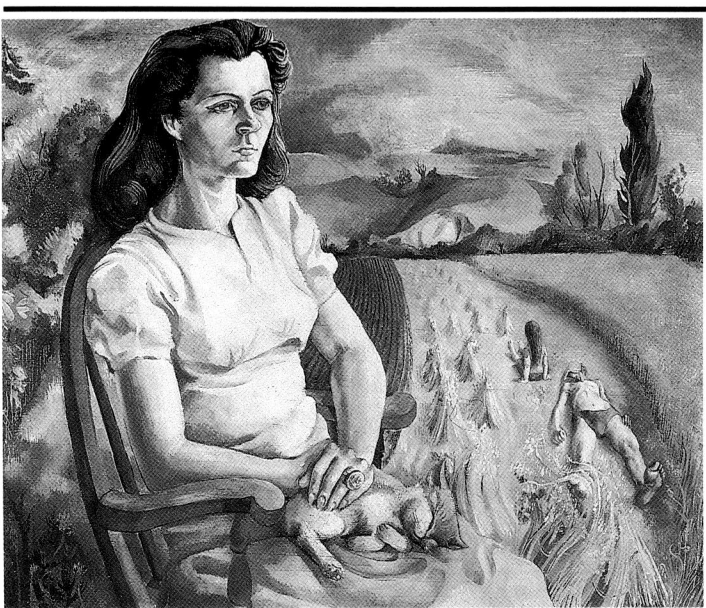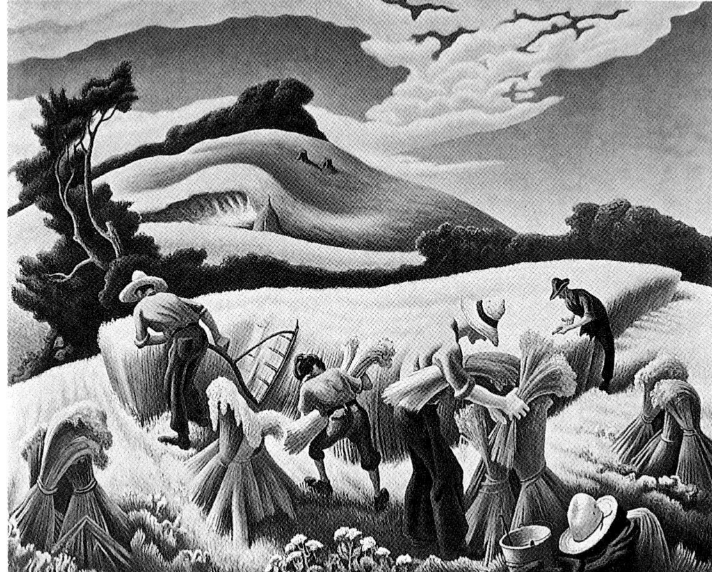

L to R: Michael Ayrton, *Joan in the Fields*, 1943; Thomas Hart Benton, *Cradling Wheat*, 1938

some way like Henri Fuseli, a kind of very mannered and grand style practitioner of bizarre and fantastic subject matter. But he is there, and he's in the best tradition of being a grand private British eccentric who can hold his own in any company.

David Hockney's work I enjoy immensely. I particularly like his non paintings, that is, I find him much more cheerful, ebullient, original and so on, when he's being something like a swimming pool decorator, or a stage designer. I like that jack-of-all-trades aspect of him right down to the photography. In many ways he reminds me of Jennifer Bartlet. He's that kind of prodigious and productive sort of artist. If I say that I find his work decorative, I mean it in the best sense, the way that I would say that a lot of Matisse's work is decorative. So he's very much there.

HC   Do you think there are any figures or movements in English art that have been ignored so far? Some people would say that there's a strong romantic tendency, say, in landscape and symbolic work that has been ignored so far, and that was still there. Would you say that something like that existed in this

I'm speaking in personal terms, to have a kind of diluted look vis-à-vis the sources. But the landscapes of Sutherland or Piper, and the visionary fantasies of the like of Cecil Collins, all this has a tremendous appeal to me. I assume that it's an underground tradition that will have a long life. I don't know too much about current artists who are working within it. In general I would prefer to look at something like this when I'm here because it seems to be something I can only find in England, as opposed to something that is just international coinage.

HC   Is there an equivalent in America? Or is the art that is internationally recognised as American the equivalent of what you were describing in England?

RR   One of the things that's curious and I suppose parallel to it, is that in recent years, say the last decade, younger generation audiences and scholars have been digging up the American regionalist art of 30s and 40s. The situation is in some ways parallel to Britain in so far as the Abstract Expressionists felt they were not really American so much as they were universal. They

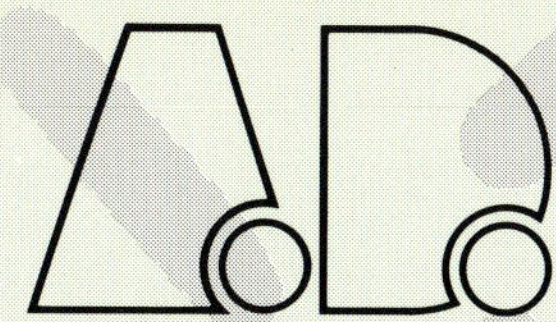

Art & Design
Architectural Design

NEW FOR 1987

From January 1987 *Art & Design* and *Architectural Design* will be published six times a year in alternate months. Each issue will be fatter, and devoted to a specific theme, although the outer pages will still be packed with news and views of all that is going on in the worlds of art and architecture.

Art & Design will cover the whole spectrum of the arts, and each issue will deal in depth with a particular theme. Individual issues will be £7.95/US$14.95.

Architectural Design will continue to provide you with up-to-date information on the architecture of the present and the past, and each issue will contain an analysis of a theme of relevance to present-day architectural practice. Individual issues will be on sale at £7.95/US$14.95.

You may subscribe to either magazine alone – or to both at a special rate. If you are already a subscriber, you will continue to receive both magazines until your subscription expires.

Please complete the order form opposite and send it with your payment NOW.

Subscriptions Department
ACADEMY GROUP LTD
7/8 Holland Street
London W8
Tel: 01-402 2141

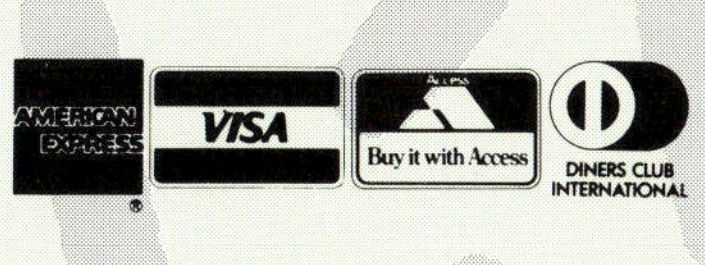

All major credit cards accepted

ART & DESIGN MAGAZINE SUBSCRIPTION

Please send me one year's subscription to Art & Design

Full rate UK £29.50 Europe £34.00 Overseas US$49.50 Students UK £25.00 Europe £29.50 Overseas US$45.00

☐ **Payment enclosed by cheque/postal order/draft**

☐ **Please charge £ . . . . . to my credit card account no:**

Expiry date . . . .

Signature ....
Name ....
Address..
....
....

Subscriptions Department
ACADEMY GROUP LTD
7/8 Holland Street
LONDON W8 4NA

ARCHITECTURAL DESIGN + ART & DESIGN

Please send me one year's subscription to both magazines

Full rate: UK £59.50 Europe £69.50 Overseas US$105.00
Student rate: UK £55.00 Europe £65.00 Overseas US$95.00

☐ **Payment enclosed by cheque/postal order/draft**

☐ **Please charge £ . . . . . to my credit card account no:**

Expiry date . . . .

Signature ....
Name ....
Address..
....
....

felt they had finally joined the united nations of artists and painted pictures that could be exported and that were not regionalist. They were in particular battling against the authority of American art for American people about American subjects in the 1930s. All that had about it a sort of right-wing political flavour, and people felt that American art should be internationalised and not look to its own past. Now enough time has passed so that these works no longer have the polemical character they used to. I mean, it was assumed that if you like an artist like John Steuart Curry or Thomas Hart Benton, who happens to have been Pollock's teacher, it meant that you hated what the Museum of Modern Art and what the Modern Movement represented. But that battle is ancient now and younger people have been fascinated, in a kind of retrospective and nostalgic way, with the wilfully American grassroots art of the 30s and 40s. They're looking at it, not only sympathetically, because it has its own distinctive flavour, but also as a mirror of American cultural history – a kind of isolationism, regionalism, unwillingness to join

occasions when respectable museums like the Metropolitan Museum and now the National Gallery in Washington have a Wyeth show presumably to appease the public. And that is considered giving in to Satan. My own feelings about him are that he is not the devil and he's not Christ either. He's a perfectly memorable American illustrator who paints very nostalgic images of rural Arcadian America, in some ways the counterpart to those British Neo-Romantic artists I've been looking at in the Barbican Gallery in London. That is, he is a kind of retrogressive image painter who tells about a pre-industrial world of escapism, in his case the backwoods of Pennsylvania or Maine. This has enormous popular appeal as getting away from the horrible modern social problems, modern industrial scenes, modern cities, you name it. So he has his role and I neither love him nor hate him; I just think he's there, he's pretty good. If that many people like him that's fine. They have their right to see him.

Ben Shahn is a more curious case because, in the 40s especially, he was a major figure in American art. It would be impossible to

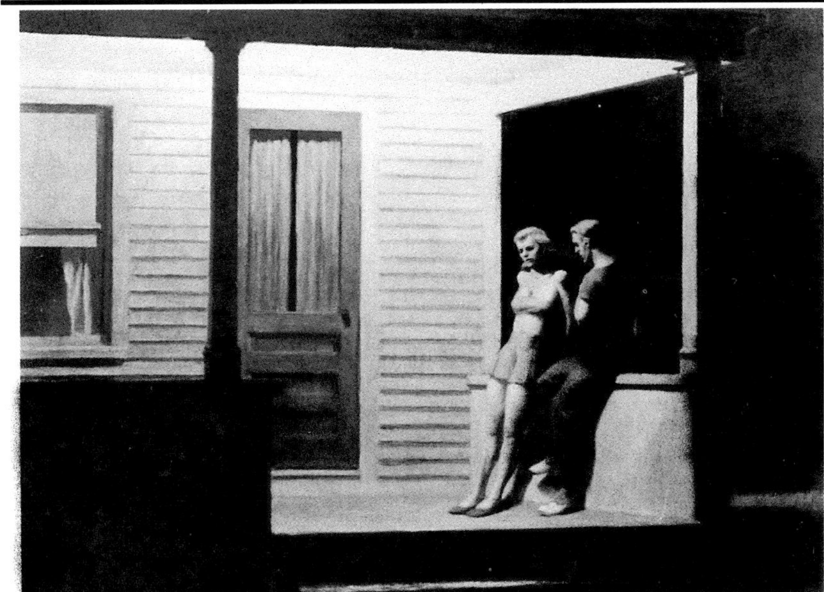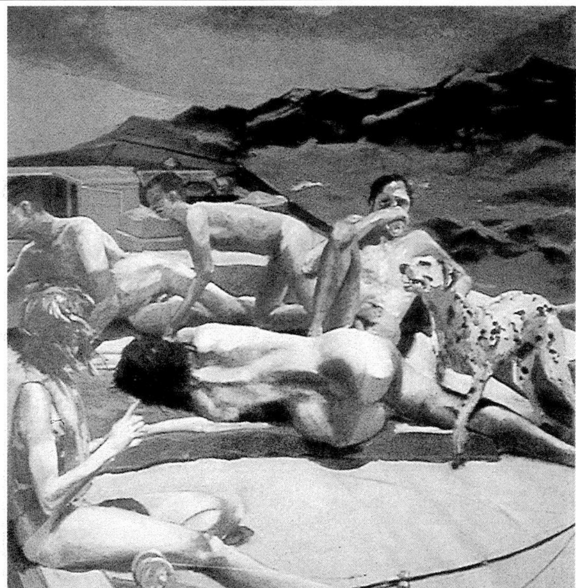

L to R: Edward Hopper, *Summer Evening*, 1947; Eric Fischl, *The Old Man's Boat and the Old Man's Dog*, 1982

forces with Europe. The situation is very parallel on a grander scale to the insular character of a lot of British thought and feeling in the 30s and 40s which was cultivating retrospectively its own garden and its own national tradition .

HC   An interesting thing mentioned at the Tate symposium was that artists – who were recognised as being American – before Abstract Expressionism became well publicised and really took off – were Andrew Wyeth and Ben Shahn. What do you think of their work in relation to say Abstract Expressionism? Are they just as valid?

RR   Andrew Wyeth of course is a hot potato in terms of the current American art scene. I have really little idea of his fame or lack of it across the Atlantic, in England, or on the Continent. He is a kind of grassroots American popular artist. People queue up to see his work the way they do to see Renoir and Picasso. But he's always been the devil in terms of the tradition of rightthinking Modernists or Post-Modernists. He's always seemed to be evil because he's so loved by absolutely everybody. There are always

have a survey of American art without his figuring prominently. He got eclipsed by the Abstract Expressionists, but so did many other American figurative artists. He was really so totally eclipsed that I can now only predict there's going to be a Ben Shahn revival not from a popular front, but from a more ironic campy late 20th-century vision of the political commitment, and the social realism in the 30s and 40s. His work really has great nostalgic flavour, and it's just waiting there to be discovered again.

HC   How important is an artist like Edward Hopper for American artists?

RR   Well he, oddly enough, managed to survive all of this. I myself love Edward Hopper, and I sometimes wonder whether he's exportable. The sensations that I get from Hopper's work, of a kind of openness and barrenness and loneliness, these seem to ring so true in terms of an American experience that most Americans know, whether in the city or country. But I constantly wonder whether – like the work of de Chirico, which is very often melancholy, and lonely, and barren – this registers all over the world, in England and on the Continent, or whether it's a uniquely American experience that is understood only on our side of the Atlantic. He somehow had the authority to last the attack on other social scene American artists of the 30s and 40s. He was always respected if I remember correctly, even through the heyday of Abstract Expressionism and Pop art. Everybody somehow had a hallowed place for him as the lone survivor of that generation.

The Contemporary Interchange

HC   What figures do you see, in contemporary American art, as being the artists of the moment, and the artists that will stand up over the next 10 years?

RR   Well it's hard to say, because one of the frightening things is the swift change of fashions. Artists' lifespans these days seem to be two or three seasons. Nevertheless, with the fear and trembling which always go into such statements as to who is terrific, I would say that Eric Fischl happens to be one of my favourites. Interestingly enough he is one of those artists who tend to look back to the American scene painting that was wiped out by the abstract movement. His pictures very often specifically recall works by Winslow Homer or Edward Hopper. They have a very American look in terms of the people, the costume, the settings. They usually revive some kind of narrative situation which is implied as well in many late 19th-century American pictures, Homer and Eakins in particular. So I find him a fascinating artist and completely unexpected, totally against the abstract grain. So much so that a lot of people in the States have found it very difficult to appreciate him. But he currently is quite exportable in terms of his reputation in England and on the Continent.

I'm also a fan of David Salle's. Well, we're now talking about artists like Fischl and Salle who've had a relatively long reputation. Salle seems to have resurrected the likes of Rosenquist and Johns and Magritte, and then more than repaid his debts to them. He also tells us a lot about what it's like to live in New York today in the 1980s. So those are two artists who've now been around a while compared to the lifespan of a lot of artists these days, and I would put my hand in the fire for them.

HC   Are they having an influence on a younger generation do you think, or are they just themselves?

RR   I think they're just themselves. Obviously any artist is going to have imitators, but I can't imagine anybody who looks like a disciple of either Salle or Fischl who's doing anything you'd want to look at.

HC   Do you think there is anyone in the younger generation in Britain who's either doing something similar, or something different, that's just as vital?

RR   I've seen some pictures by Michael Andrews which have a very Eric Fischl look. They seem to be prosaic situations that have a narrative tension, presenting a psychodrama scenario that viewers can make up themselves. He's somebody who functions on that wavelength. There are many British artists who are maybe not of the 'young' young generation, but respectable artists of longstanding like Richard Long or Lucian Freud, whom I love. I think they're both terrific. Lucian Freud is particularly

interesting. I'm glad that he'll finally be shown in the United States, because he's had almost zero visibility there. But he's particularly interesting for American viewers because so many of his nudes look like Philip Pearlstein's nudes which are very well known in the States, though I don't know that they're so well known here.

HC   What do you think of artists like Steven Campbell in Scotland?

RR   Oh I enjoy him. He seems very much to be in an international rough and tumble style of no-holds-barred fantasy images. I mean there are many artists on both sides of the Atlantic who release a free-flow of their id, or imagination, and just let it all tumble out onto their canvases. I like his work for that reason. It also seems to be at once special and private, and public, and intelligible, in the same way that Chia and Clemente are.

HC   Do you think that when people look back at this era, the figures that will be recognised as being important will be the Abstract Expressionists, the Pop artists such as Andy Warhol, the Minimalists and Conceptualists, or will they also be artists like Wyeth and Ben Shahn?

RR   Well, it's always hard to predict, but I would say, judging from the winds going through younger generation attitudes, that whole period in American art is going to be excavated. Younger scholars, museum people, and so on, will be eager to see what was swept under the carpet in terms of our idea of what happened in American art of the 40s, 50s and 60s. I personally — this is an act of faith — doubt that anybody is going to look as good as the greatest of the Abstract Expressionists, or Pop artists, or Minimalists, the usual canon of what was best at the time. I also think that the new all-embracing eclectic attitude is going to permit people to look at all kinds of American painters of the period, with a great deal of pleasure and historical nostalgia, just as in the case of the British Neo-Romantics, all sorts of reputations were dusted off and put on view again, or have been totally newly discovered, like Gerald Wilde. This includes artists who, as I understand it, were virtually unknown here. That will, I'm positive, happen in terms of a revision of American art, but I doubt that the 'great' greats are going to be toppled by this.

HC   So you think this revival of interest is significant for contemporary artists rather than the artists of the past 20 or 30 years?

RR   Yes, I think so. It's a little bit like the current reconstructions of Impressionism. Just recently in the United States there was a terrific historical exhibition of the actual works that were displayed in the Impressionist exhibitions from 1874 to 86. So the point of it was not only archaeological reconstruction but to indicate that there were all kinds of art and painters you'd never heard of who were exhibiting at the same time and the same place as Degas, Renoir, etc. This was a kind of liberation. It was new visual information, new historical information. There were new reputations perhaps to be made. That is clearly what is happening all over the 19th and 20th century. It's certainly happening in terms of the American art that coexisted with Abstract Expressionism.

Robert Rosenblum is Professor of Fine Arts at New York State University. His many books include the influential Modern Painting and the Northern Romantic Tradition

THE EASTWARD MARCH OF CIVILISATION?

Peter Fuller

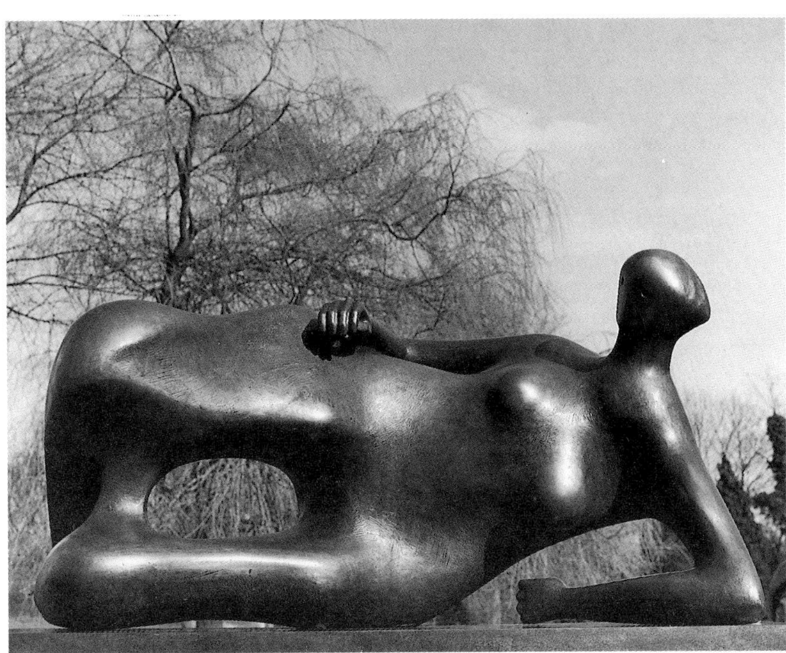

Henry Moore, *Reclining Woman: Elbow*, 1981

The 'official' account of the impact of American art on Europe, and especially on Britain, in recent times is now well-enough known. Indeed, it is reproduced in almost every history of modern art. America is assumed to have taken unto itself many of the most talented figures of the European avant-garde, at the time of the Second World War. This influx is held to have provided the catalyst for a great flowering of America's indigenous tradition; New York is assumed to have usurped the traditional role of Paris as the first city of art, and the crucible of Modernist 'progress'. (Needless to say, London is commonly not even mentioned in all this.) After the war, New York painters and sculptors are presumed to have radiated an enlivening influence throughout the Western world.

As one American scholar has put it, 'beginning immediately after the end of World War II, the vigorous New York school emerged as the dominant one, creating influences which gradually flowed back to Europe, thus reversing the traditional westward march of civilization.' But, in his interview with Hugh Cumming, Robert Rosenblum, an American art historian, is brave enough to hint at the idea that the time may come when this version of events will be questioned: that time is now.

One of the most exciting developments in recent art history is the rediscovery of the richness, stature and variety of the British tradition in the 20th century. This has been reflected in exhibitions such as the Royal Academy's *British Art in the 20th Century* and the Barbican's *A Paradise Lost*. After the latter, the *Sunday Times* critic, herself an American, wrote 'We will never be able to think of this century's British art and literature in quite the same way.' This changing perception can also be seen in increasing international respect for the once-neglected

achievements of British art; Lucian Freud is currently to be seen in Washington, even though the Museum of Modern Art in New York apparently turned down the Freud retrospective on the grounds that he is 'not a modern artist'. It is no secret that prices of British art of all kinds have suddenly begun to soar in the sale-room. This revaluation, and the historical excavation which goes with it, seem destined to transform, and indeed in some ways to reverse, our understanding of the influence of American over British art which has been the received wisdom for the last 30 years.

American art history notwithstanding, Britain emerged from the Second World War supremely confident concerning the stature of her artists, and determined to exert cultural leadership throughout the Western world. America appeared to present no threat to this ambition for at least a decade after the end of hostilities, by which time, of course, 'the moment of Abstract Expressionism', and with it the highest achievements of American Modernism, had long since passed.

In 1946, an exhibition of *Modern British Pictures from the Tate Gallery* was sent abroad for the benefit of 'friends and allies'. It included important recent pictures by Henry Moore, Paul Nash, Ben Nicholson, Graham Sutherland, and John Piper. Works such as Nash's visionary *Landscape from a Dream* and Moore's 'shelter' drawings, of which eight fine examples were included, exerted a powerful impact on war-torn Europe.

The first large-scale exhibition to be held at the Tate Gallery itself after the restoration in 1946 of six of the galleries damaged by bombing, was a show of *American Painting from the 18th Century to the Present Day*. But this was not favourably received by the critics – and appears to have had a negligible effect on the public and practising artists at this time. That same year, however, a major exhibition, *British Contemporary Painters* – again including, among others, Moore, Piper and Sutherland – toured America under the auspices of the Albright Art Gallery and the British Council.

Andrew C Ritchie, the American director of the Albright, contributed an insightful introduction in which he referred to the way in which the severance of links with France, and the initiative of the British Government in commissioning war paintings 'from advanced artists', had led to a great increase in British artistic vitality. 'The very tensions of war and the heroic stand of the British people,' he wrote, 'must also have played

rediscovery of our native landscape, its architecture, its customs, even its reformed religion – all now seemingly threatened with destruction. Rothenstein stressed that those artists most deeply in tune with the wartime sensibility were not (as is still sometimes claimed) Realists; but nor were they the avant-garde, as it was understood elsewhere, or Modernists, most of whom, in any event, had left Britain at the onset of hostilities to exert their influence on the other side of the Atlantic. 'The most impressive memorials to the great armed clashes', as Rothenstein put it, were raised by those 'who had on the whole been disposed to neglect the ebb and flow of life in favour of the cultivation of the imaginative vision or else of formal aesthetic values'. They were, in effect, those who intuited the relationship between immediate historical events, plastic forms, and the spiritual wasteland modern man was constrained to inhabit.

The war caused the best British contemporary artists to abandon vacuous experimentation 'for its own sake', and

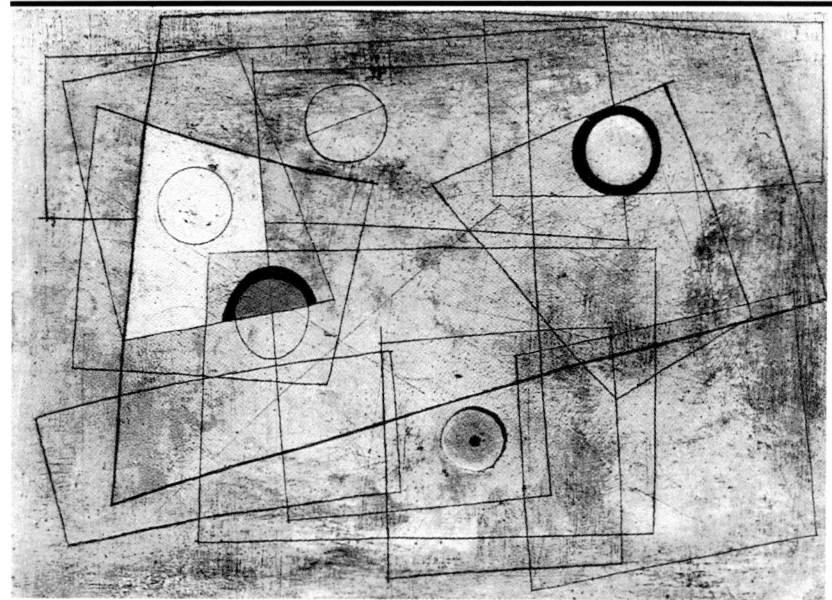
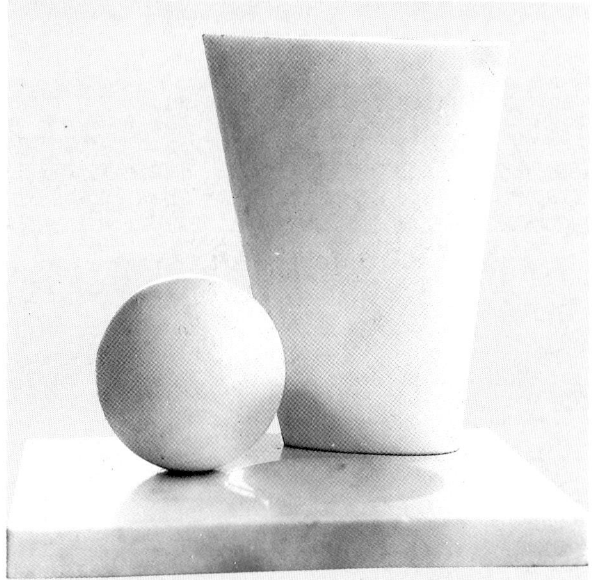

L to R: Ben Nicholson, 1945 (Parrot's Eye), 1945; Barbara Hepworth, Conicoid, Sphere and Hollow 2, 1937

no small part in heightening the perceptions of British artists. A sense of common danger at this time undoubtedly developed a community of feeling between them and the public that has been absent in the Western world for centuries.'

Ritchie, of course, was here referring to the Romantic Revival which swept through British art in the 1930s and 1940s. But it is, I think, important to understand that the social and cultural circumstances which nurtured this revival were antithetical to those which furthered the advance of Abstract Expressionism, and the Modern Movement, in America. In the first place, there was the war itself: this was, so to speak, somewhat closer to home in Europe than in America, and its effects on cultural life in Britain were as profound as they were unexpected.

As John Rothenstein, then Director of the Tate Gallery, has written, 'the public seemed to be quite suddenly transformed'. There was a great surge of interest in the achievements of European, and especially British, culture; this extended to a

replenish their art with what Ruskin would have described as 'theoretic' rather than merely 'aesthetic' content; the imaginative encounter with a scarred and wounded natural world led to vivid and original contributions to, and in some cases profound transformations of, a deeply rooted national tradition. Before Sutherland, nature had rarely been depicted through the creation of fully plastic, rather than scenic, forms. Nature – charred, scorched, blasted, and burned, and yet somehow redeemed through the aesthetic process itself – provided a cogent source of symbols, imagery, and new plastic forms which, though highly original, spoke vividly to a public which was itself experiencing the vicissitudes attendant upon the conflagration.

For Ritchie, Henry Moore was the leading figure in the revival of British art of that time: and, in the same year as the Albright Art Gallery exhibition, Moore held a major retrospective of 58 sculptures and 48 drawings at the Museum of Modern Art in New York. The following year, Moore's work was seen in Chicago and San Francisco, and then throughout Australia. In 1948, Moore's international reputation was further advanced when he was awarded the international prize for sculpture at the Venice Biennale, where his works were exhibited alongside Turner's landscapes. In 1949, he enjoyed a major exhibition in the Musée d'Art Moderne in Paris. Nor was it just Moore: in 1950, Hepworth's sculptures were exhibited in Venice, beside Constable's paintings; and, in 1952 and 1954, Sutherland's and Nicholson's international reputations were confirmed by their respective one-man shows at the Biennale.

Such recognition matched the achievement of these artists; and it must be said that it made what was happening in studios in downtown New York seem a rather provincial and outmoded affair – a matter of precisely those avant-garde 'experiments' and frustration which British artists had outgrown in the late 1940s, as they crossed the brook-of-fire of the Second World War. Indeed, for Modernist American critics like Cle-

means the very opposite – pessimism about man's powers, a fear of facing any reality without precedent.'

This Modernist triumphalism, with its implicit contempt for the element of passivity in man's relationship to nature, helps to explain the hostility felt by the young Greenberg in the face of Moore's achievement. In perhaps the most foolish negative judgment of his career, Greenberg assailed Moore, on the grounds that his work answered 'too perfectly the current notion of how modern sophisticated and inventive sculpture should look, without at the same time disappointing the popular demand for the heroic'. For Greenberg, Moore's 'subservience to taste' condemned him (together with Sutherland) to the category of 'sincere academic modern'; Moore's art became, for him, 'nothing but a fumble and a stammer, a helpless fingering of archaeological reminiscences or a supine surrender to the best taste'.

What sort of sculpture then did Greenberg regard as being free of this 'subservience to taste'? 'More directly and less ambiguously than painting and more nakedly than architecture,'

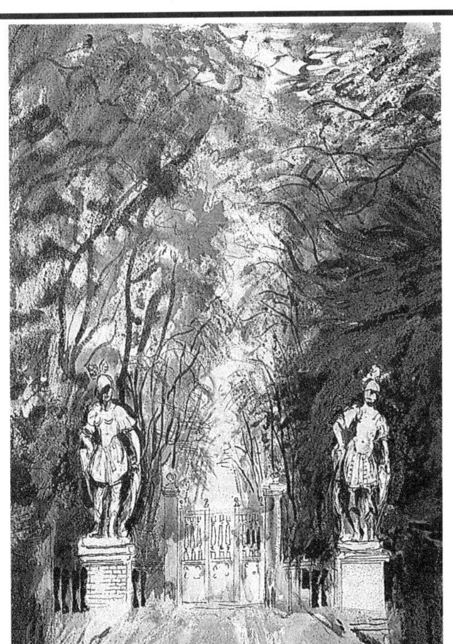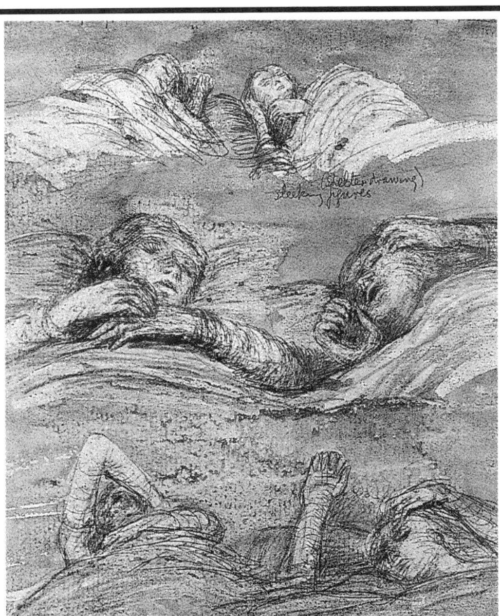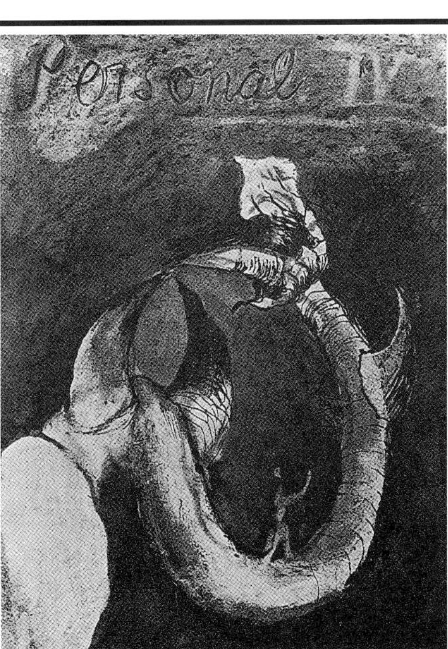

L to R: John Piper, Entrance to the Wilderness, Renishaw, 1942-3; Henry Moore, study for Three Sleeping Shelterers, 1941; Graham Sutherland, Personal, 1942

ment Greenberg, British painting and sculpture, with its affirmation of romantic and humanist values, were principal targets precisely because they seemed to face the world with such splendour and authority. They were an embarrassment to the argument Greenberg had first tried to express in *The Partisan Review* of March 1948, 'that the main premises of Western art have at last migrated to the United States, along with the centre of gravity of industrial production and political power'.

The tastes and the values of Moore and Greenberg were diametrically opposed; and the way in which they were opposed accentuates the distinction between British and American aesthetics at this time. In 1951, Moore himself said, 'I think the most "alive" painting and sculpture from now on will go more "humanist", though at present there are more "abstract" artists than ever (there is a natural time-lag in the work of the majority, who are following past experimental artists).' Clement Greenberg epitomised those who modelled their aesthetics on 'past experimental artists'. 'Today,' Greenberg had written, '"humanism" in art

Greenberg explained elsewhere, 'sculpture realizes the new notion of the work of visual art as an open, more or less transparent object whose effect lies mainly in its total design, its exhibited structure, and which relies relatively little on expressive details.'

Greenberg's wilful incomprehension of just what had been achieved by English artists was again made manifest in his review of the Albright Art Gallery exhibition. He wrote that 'almost all the painters present are emphatically characterized by a lack of conviction that is most marked with respect to color but also affects structure, unity, surface, and everything else required of painting as an art.' And he passed on quickly to celebrate by contrast 'the more or less abstract student paintings of a few young Americans, none over 30, as a demonstration of what begins to seem our superior literacy in the practice, if not consumption, of art.'

But, Greenberg's assumption of a 'superior literacy' notwithstanding, British art undoubtedly exerted a considerable influence over the emerging American school. The fact is that, in

1946, some of those who were to achieve the most in American abstract painting were borrowing freely from precisely those artists whom Greenberg had declared to be lacking in everything 'required of painting as an art'. For example, in the mid 1940s, Rothko briefly produced a number of paintings which referred to conventional Christian imagery; in particular he painted a *Gethsemane* which, as a matter of fact, looks rather more like a Golgotha, with its cruciform shape, and suggestions of bestial and bird-like imagery. In the catalogue of the Guggenheim retrospective, of 1978, this picture was dated 1945; I note that, for the current retrospective at the Tate, the dating of this picture has been revised, I know not by whom, to 1946. This change is significant for two reasons; firstly, it projects *Gethsemane* into the critical year when Rothko adopted 'pure' abstraction for the first time; secondly, it provides strong circumstantial evidence for something suggested by the appearance of the picture itself; namely, that at the time this change was taking place, Rothko was being influenced by, and reacting against, British Neo-Romanti-

natural forms, and that this played some part in his change to a full 'transcendental' abstraction soon after.

Nor was it just Rothko. Has any art historian ever investigated the evolution of Arshile Gorky's forms from 1946 until his death in 1948? We have, of course, heard a great deal about what Gorky took from Cézanne, Picasso, Miró, Kandinsky, Breton, Matta, and even Uccello. But again, that strange prickly sharpening and clarifying of his shapes which took place in his final years — for example in *Agony* of 1947 — certainly suggests to me that Gorky, too, may have started to find something of great potential significance for his development in that exhibition which Greenberg found so unspeakable. (We know from Meyer Schapiro that Gorky was 'a fervent scrutinizer of paintings', and that he 'frequently went to museums'.) Naturally, this is speculation which requires art historical confirmation or denial. Unfortunately, however, it is unlikely to get it; because the question of the influence of British art over American art is not one with which American

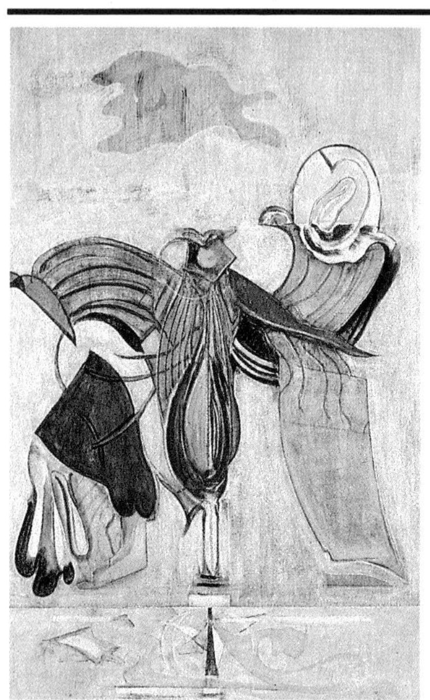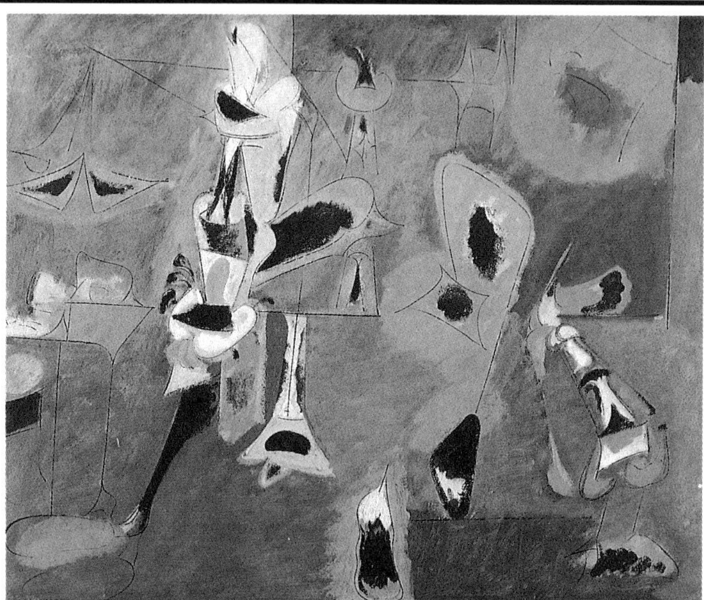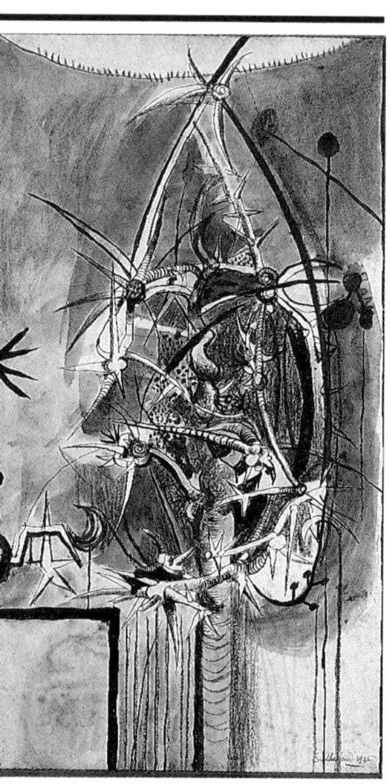

L to R: Mark Rothko, *Gethsemane*, 1946; Arshile Gorky, *Agony*, 1947; Graham Sutherland, *Thorns*, 1945

cism. (Unlike American Abstract Expressionism, English art, at this time, was permeated by references to Christian myths.)

For Rothko's *Gethsemane*, today, looks like nothing so much as a weak Sutherland. In 1944, Graham Hussey, the Vicar of St Matthew's, Northampton, invited Sutherland to paint an Agony in the Garden, or Gethsemane, for his church. Sutherland declined, but offered to paint a crucifixion instead. He was commissioned to do so. While brooding on this theme, he produced his famous *Thorn Tree* pictures, with their mingling bestial and vegetable shapes, and their suggestions of the imagery of Calvary. Two of these — a painting, and an ink and gouache drawing — were in the exhibition which Greenberg purported to find so lacking in everything 'required of painting as an art'. Nonetheless, it is not beyond the bounds of possibility that Rothko studied them rather carefully. It might even be that, after painting his own *Gethsemane*, Rothko realised he was unlikely to excel in this kind of expression of spiritual truths through the metaphoric transformation of

art historians like to trouble themselves.

What are we to deduce from all this? Firstly, that the idea that 'the vigorous New York school' had 'emerged as the dominant one' between 1945 and 1956, was influencing European painting, and causing an eastward march of civilisation, is untenable. The British school in this period was more vigorous, and internationally respected, and its aesthetic achievements more firmly founded. Its influence over New York was greater than New York's influence over it. Of course, this questioning of who was influencing whom is always unilluminating on the issue of *quality*. Nonetheless, the preparedness of Rothko and Gorky, *et alia*, to learn from the British school confirms what has since been established through quite other lines of inquiry; namely that they were not solely interested in those formal and plastic dimensions upon which Greenberg insisted, but rather regarded such devices as means to more numinous ends. In other words, the Abstract Expressionists were not Modernists, in the sense that Greenberg used the term to describe those engaged in a search for the 'ineluctable' essence of their medium. As Robert Rosenblum was later to argue, Rothko's painting, in particular, could more usefully be seen as coming at the very end of a Northern Romantic tradition, rather than as being the beginning of something quite new.

But not even Rosenblum has had the courage to spell out what seems to me to be the implication of this position: namely that if, as I think we must, we look at Abstract Expressionism in this way, we should also recognise that the goals which defeated the classic generation of American Abstract Expressionists were, for a time at least, realised with confidence and authority by the finest artists of the British school. In America, artists did not experience the war in the same way; it was an event on a remote historical stage. There was no impetus for the Romantic resurgence to sever itself from the impingements of a decadent and contradictory Modernism: after all, the emigré avant-garde was right there, in New York, as it had been in London before the war. The British had looked back to Samuel Palmer and then, on that basis, had

communication of ideas between nations'. He expressed the hope that his show would rectify the situation by helping to make 'modern American art better known in Britain'. The exhibition contained works by, among others, Mark Tobey, Arshile Gorky – including *Agony* of 1947 – Willem de Kooning, Robert Motherwell, Mark Rothko, Jackson Pollock, Franz Kline and Clyfford Still.

But within three years, the presentation of American art had changed: from a tentative search for reciprocity, and exchange, the story had become that of the supremacy and dominance of the American school. The tone was set at the Tate in 1959 in a show called *The New American Painting*, which came almost as a signal for the Americanisation of British visual culture: it seemed as if, overnight, the British achievements of the 1940s and early 1950s were simply forgotten. Even the *Times Literary Supplement* announced that 'the flowering of the American imagination has been the chief event in the sphere of living art since the end of the First World War'; while another article in the same issue declared 'that the current style of painting known as Abstract Expression-

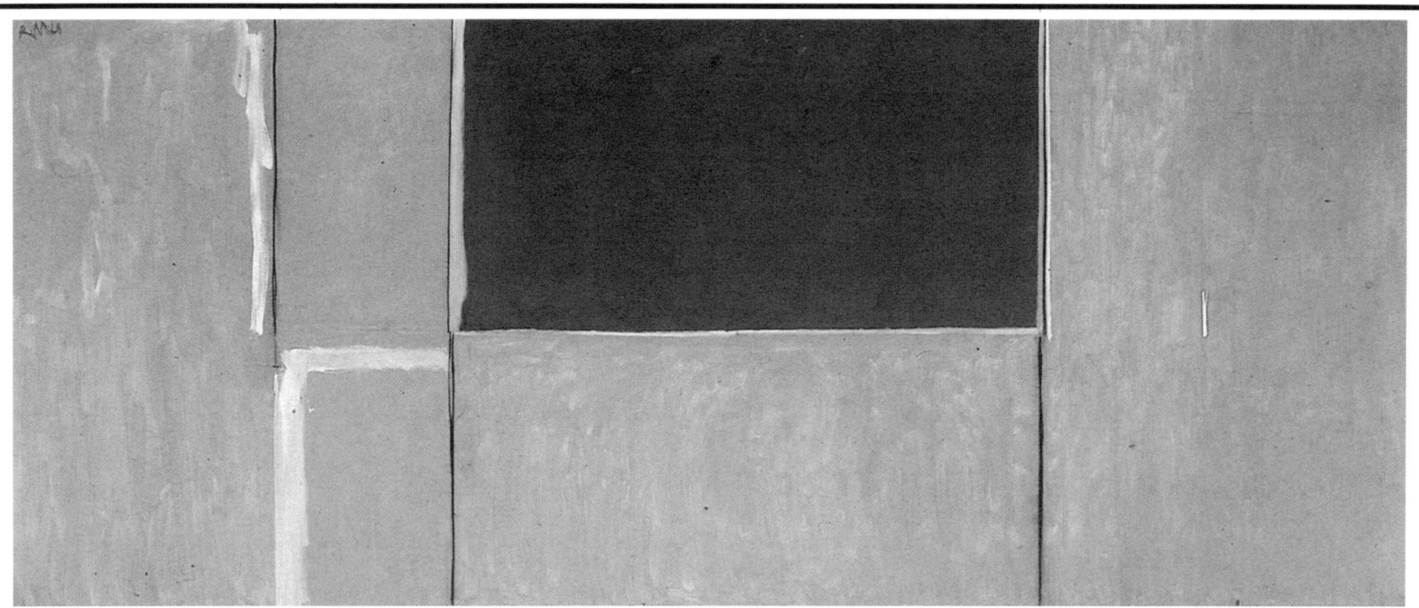

Robert Motherwell, *Open No 11 (in Raw Sienna with Gray)*, 1968, polymer paint and charcoal on canvas

taken what they needed from Picasso, and moved on to find plastic forms appropriate to a new vision of nature in the present. The influence of the great American imaginative painters of nature, such as Albert Pynkham Ryder, Albert Bierstadt or even the Ruskin-inspired Frederick E Church, on the Abstract Expressionist idea of the 'sublime' is now acknowledged; but the Americans' interest in natural form, and in anything other than a 'modern' tradition, remained tenuous – a matter of mood rather than of observation and transformation; of reaction against rather than continuity with. For whatever Gorky may have borrowed from Sutherland, Breton remained of greater importance to him.

As late as 1956, American art was not regarded very seriously in Britain. When the exhibition *Modern Art in the United States*, came to the Tate Gallery in that year, René d'Harnoncourt, then director of the Museum of Modern Art in New York, complained in the catalogue about the lack of active interchange in the visual arts which, he said, 'are among the best media for the

ism radiates the world over from Manhattan Island, more specifically from West Fifty-Third Street, where the Museum of Modern Art stands as the Parthenon on this particular acropolis.' But, for better or for worse, by the late 1950s Abstract Expressionism was in effect an exhausted phenomenon – flickering cinders, rather than a radiant sun; those who had struggled to produce a high and transcendental art, based on abstract forms and colours, had conspicuously failed. Even if, like Pollock, and Rothko, their failure had been on a spectacular scale, it could not be said to constitute *The Triumph of American Painting*. This 'particular acropolis' now supported only the ruins of an aesthetic, and cohorts of imitators who adopted the frayed and mannerist tatters of a style. Meanwhile, however, back in England, Henry Moore was entering a late phase which, in the view of many commentators, was the most original and compelling of his career.

Sadly, however, younger British artists paid very little attention to what he, or others of his generation, were doing. For the tidal wave of Americanisation swept all else before it. An empty and ailing American art rushed through institutions of contemporary art in this country, where it met with no resistance. Many of the best British artists who refused to bow down before the fads of MOMA were simply ignored by the critics and museums.

Take the case of David Bomberg, who died in obscurity at precisely the moment when the American veil descended. There is no doubt, in my mind, that paintings such as *Trendrine, Cornwall*, 1947, rival anything produced by de Kooning at the same date. Bomberg's comparative strength, of course, lay in the fact that although he believed eyes were 'stupid organs', he used them nonetheless. He yearned for the spirit in the mass, and not simply at the base of his own psyche. His paintings from this period have an expressive power comparable to de Kooning's, but they have a richness, specificity, and compactness which the American lacks.

Or consider Leon Kossoff and Frank Auerbach, who learned from Bomberg. Now, in retrospect, these painters might be said to have found a solution to that problem which so dogged Pollock towards the end of his life. In differing ways, they reunited

onwards'. My only qualification to this thesis is, as I have already argued above, that this influence can be traced back a great deal earlier than Heron has suggested.

And yet in the 1960s and 1970s all this was simply forgotten. A new generation of 'Situation' painters sprang up, whose superficial forms, and shallow, jaunty 'professionalism', amounted to little more than a mimicking of American commercialism. And then, of course, there was Pop art . . . In 1964, David Thompson introduced an exhibition of 'New Generation' artists saying, 'They are starting their careers in a boom-period for modern art. British art in particular has suddenly woken up out of a long provincial doze, is seriously entering the international lists and winning prestige for itself.' It was as if all that had been achieved in the 1940s and early 1950s had just been wiped out of history.

Nothing underlines all this more than the case of Sir Anthony Caro, a former assistant to Henry Moore. Caro met Clement Greenberg in 1959, the year of the American invasion of British art. Under Greenberg's influence, and that of the American

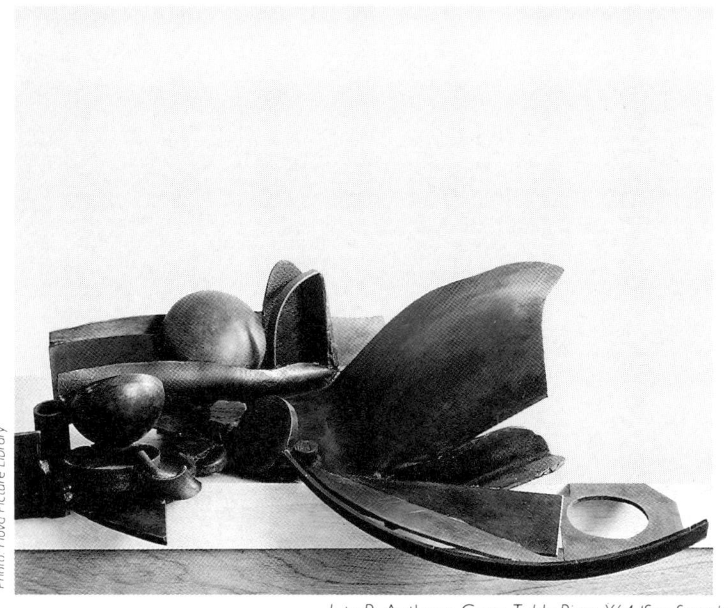
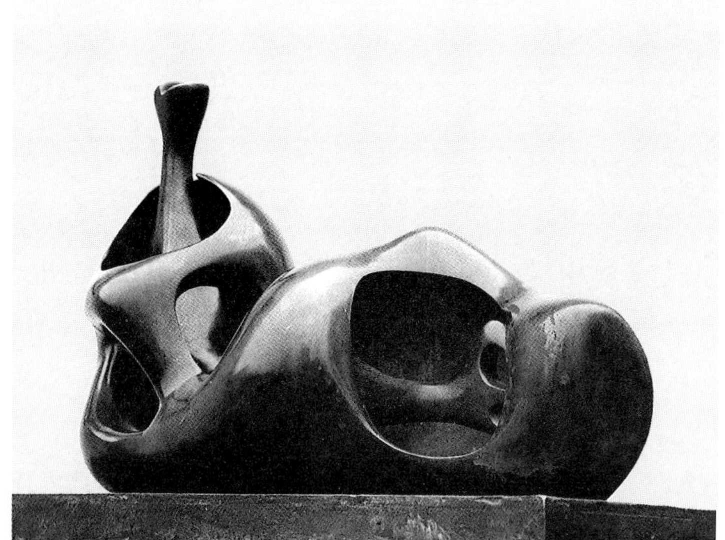

L to R: Anthony Caro, *Table Piece Y64 'Sea Symphony'*, 1985-6; Henry Moore, *Reclining Figure*, 1951

imaginative vision, expressive paint handling and empirical observation. I once asked Greenberg why he had never said anything about their painting. He replied in words to the effect that this was a matter for British criticism. Beneath all the talk about quality, and evaluative judgment, Greenberg's legendary 'eye' was singularly blind to that which could not be harnessed to the American cause. For almost 20 years no attention was paid to Auerbach and Kossoff by critics on either side of the Atlantic, for no better reason than that they were unaffected by, and uninterested in, American culture.

The case made by Patrick Heron concerning 'the Middle Generation' of painters associated with St Ives is well-enough known not to need repeating here. In 1974 Heron pointed out not only that the claims made on behalf of American art had been preposterously extravagant; but that 'far from having always been at the receiving end of influences emanating from New York' several British painters, including himself, had 'exerted crucial influence upon New York painting from the late 1950s

Colour-Field painters Jules Olitski and Kenneth Noland, Caro went 'radically abstract', and produced works which, in the words of his wife, Sheila Girling, called 'in question dependence on the conventions of traditional culture'. Indeed Caro's sculpture began to conform, precisely, to that theoretical 'prototype' which Greenberg had held up against Moore's 'humanism' in the 1940s. Greenberg promptly compared Caro's new structures in painted steel and I-beams to Turner's art, even though he emphasised that Caro's 'breakthrough' was dependent upon the 'radical unlikeness to nature' of his work. And a whole army of American formalist critics arose who made it their business to show how Caro had become great by rejecting everything Moore had stood for, and pursuing 'radical abstraction' beyond bounds so far realised.

For example, in his 1975 book on Caro, William Rubin argued that any sculpture which rises vertically before the spectator, 'retains by that very fact an inference of anthropomorphism even if it is not monolithic in character'. And so, Rubin maintained,

Caro's sculpture attained a more radical degree of abstraction than David Smith's, 'as much by virtue of its horizontality as its morphology'. And yet, of course, anyone who had attended to Henry Moore's great sequence of reclining figures would have recognised immediately not only where the much-vaunted 'horizontality' of works such as *Midday* came from, but also that it no more excluded 'an inference of anthropomorphism' than did verticality. Which is, perhaps, another way of saying that the *qualities* of Caro's work often owed more to Henry Moore than his singularly ignorant American protagonists realised; whereas Caro's weaknesses – ie the triviality and decorativeness of his work, its denial of human or animal forms, and his life-long preference for pictorial planarity, rather than fully cylindrical, *sculptural* roundness – derived from his 'subservience to taste': American taste. For many years, Caro did not so much make sculptures, as illustrations of Greenberg's aesthetic ideas.

Recently, however, there have been signs that Caro, too, is, changing and beginning to acknowledge what he learned from

been greatly exaggerated. Everywhere, we see indications of a desire to rewrite history, to affirm that American art, after Abstract Expressionism, was not simply Modernist, and formalist, as Greenberg and his followers wanted to say it was, but ought also to be esteemed for its 'spiritual' content. But those who argue like this appear, to me, to be setting a trap for themselves. For any one who has the slightest acquaintance with the historic achievements of European civilisation, the spiritual depth of almost all American art must appear cutaneous. American critics, as Greenberg realised, were on safer ground when they staked their claims on modernity and a sensual, materialist aesthetic.

But it would, I think, be a disaster if British artists took too seriously the arguments of those who are now proselytising in favour of 'spiritual' readings of Pop art, Minimalism, and more recent American 'Post-Modern' trends: for the lesson to be learned from the history of the last half century is surely that British art thrives best when it tends its own garden, and draws sustenance from its own indigenous roots, with only half a glance

PETER FULLER

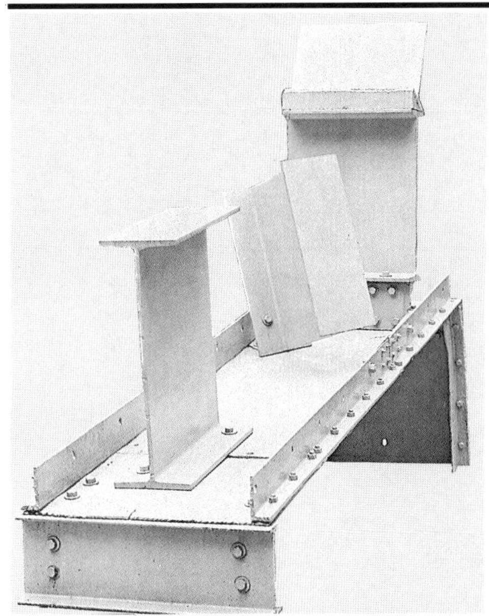
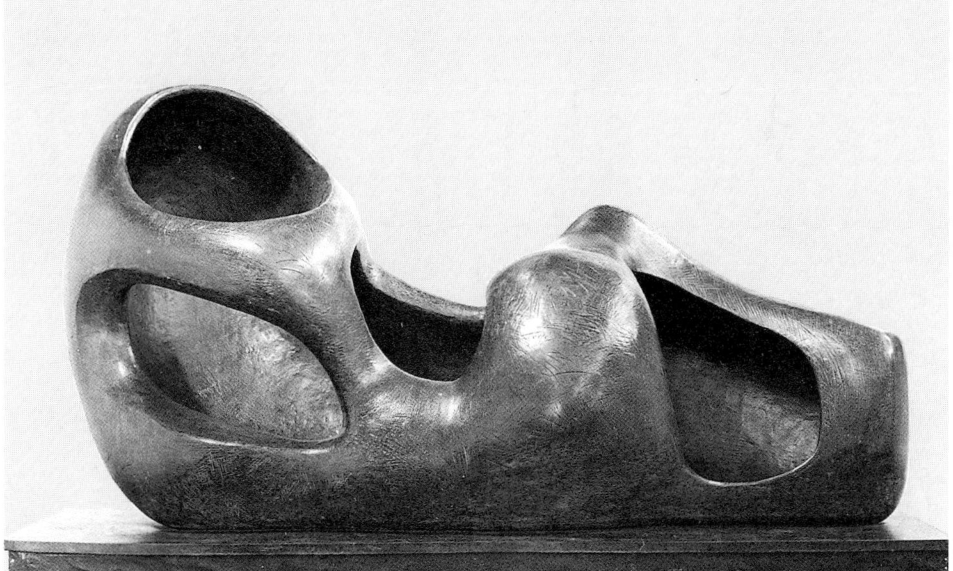

L to R: Anthony Caro, Midday, *1960; Henry Moore,* Reclining Figure Exterior Form, *1953-4*

Moore. The works which Caro showed immediately after Moore's death – such as *Scamander*, made in 1985-86 – demonstrate a desire to recapture a sense of those suggestive, volumetric, expressive, anthropomorphic, reclining forms on which he had worked for Moore when he was his assistant. Indeed, their resemblance to Moore's *Internal and External Forms* of 1953-54, or his *Reclining Figure (External Forms)* of 1953 is striking. This, of course, was exactly the kind of work for which Greenberg had reserved his most undisguised contempt; we do not know what he thinks of his protégé's belated rejection of 'experimental' Modernism and espousal of British, Romantic humanism. But his loss is our gain.

It is not simply that the claims made concerning the stature and originality of American painting have been fraudulent; it is also that the impact of American art on British cultural and aesthetic life, since the Second World War, has been catastrophic. There are signs that even the Americans themselves are coming to realise that the achievement of their artists since the last war has

at what is happening in the rest of the art world.

This is not just because American culture is irredeemably base and spiritually bankrupt. (Those inclined to doubt this should read Allan Bloom's recent book, *The Closing of the American Mind*.) Henry Moore used to stress that the artist must work in contact with society, but that contact must be 'an intimate one'. He went on to say that he believed that the best artists had 'always had their roots in a definite social group or community, or in a particular region'. He pointed out that small and intimate communities produced the great sculpture of Athens, or Chartres, or Florence: the desire for internationalism, and universality, should not blind us to the fact that all great art has been intimately linked to a particular place, and a particular people. It is because he himself grasped this so fully that Henry Moore was able to become among the most international, and universal, of 20th-century artists.

Peter Fuller is a regular contributor to *Art & Design*. He is also author of many publications, including *Art and Psychoanalysis, Images of God, Marches Past* and *The Australian Scapegoat*.

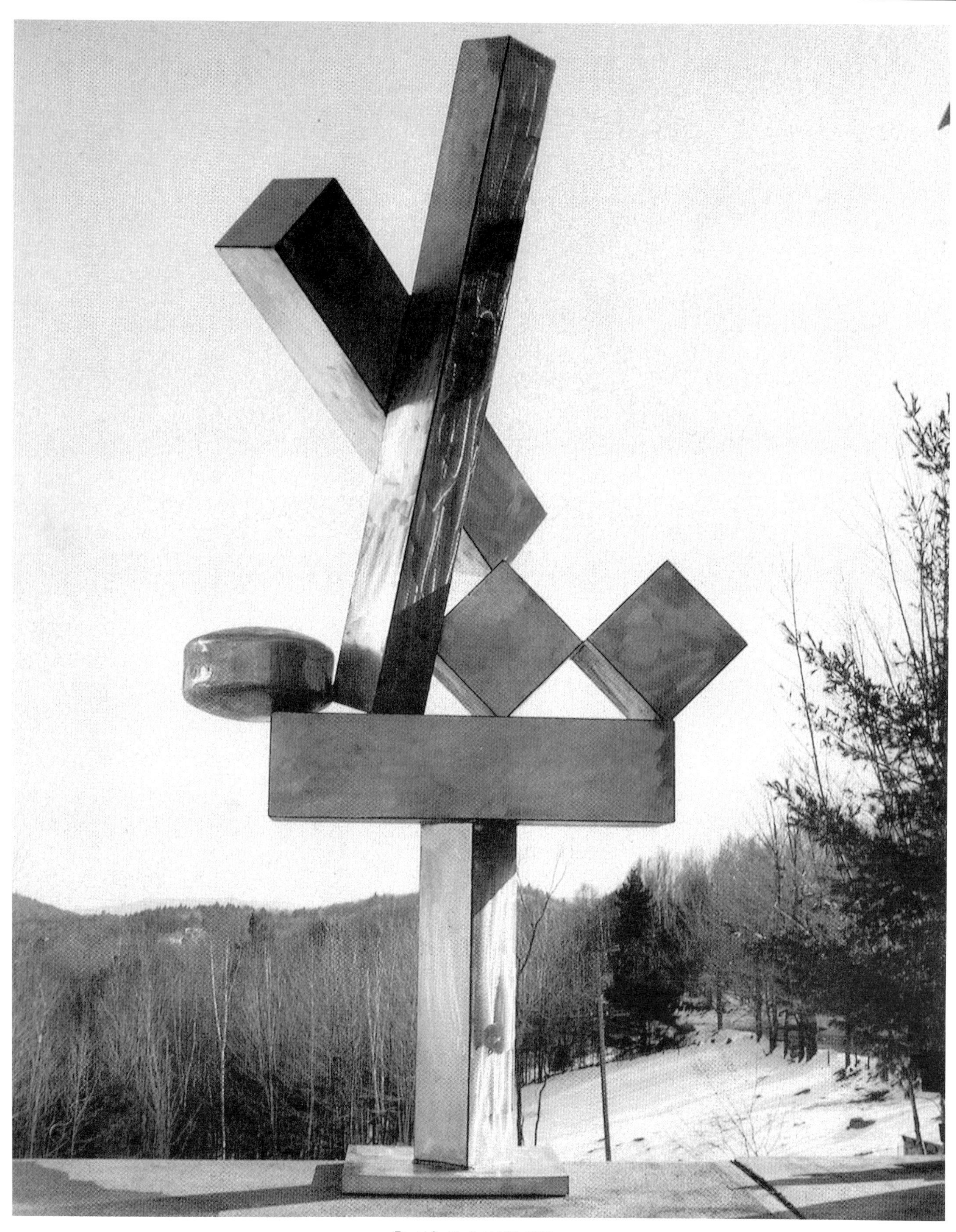

David Smith, *Cubi XIX*, 1964.
Stainless steel 287·5x55x52·5cm

INTERNATIONALISM AND TRADITION:
British and American Art Since 1945
Mary Rose Beaumont

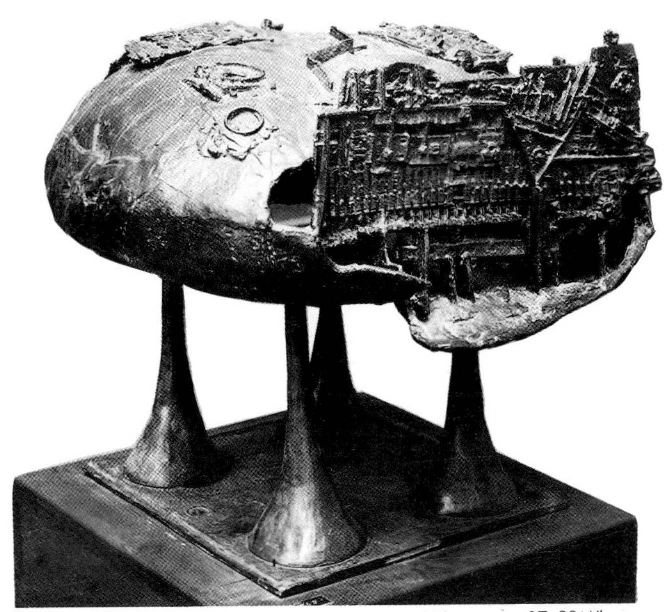

Eduardo Paolozzi, *Large Frog, Version II*, 1958, bronze, 27×32½"

British and American art since 1945 shares a concern with, on the one hand, Modernist innovation, and, on the other, deep-rooted national aesthetic traditions. Mary Rose Beaumont charts both the similarities and unique nature of the most significant movements from Abstract Expressionism and Pop art to Post-Modernism and the new British sculpture.

In the 1940s there was little or no exchange between the visual arts of Britain and America. Literature and music travel more easily and, with the departure of Benjamin Britten and W H Auden for the United States during the war, Americans were certainly aware of British music and British poetry; they were of course even more aware of all the arts of Europe, as so many European, and especially German, artists, writers and musicians had been driven to emigrate following the rise of National Socialism. Some had come to Britain, and some had even stayed, but in general we were a staging post on the way to America. As a result, after the outbreak of war, we were cut off from our artistic contacts with Europe, which at that time meant almost exclusively Paris, and we became, willy-nilly, an island fortress. Connections with Europe having been severed, British painters and draughtsmen turned their eyes towards the Romantic tradition of Samuel Palmer, Edward Calvert and William Blake, artists who had already fed the imagination of Graham Sutherland in the late 1920s.

Neo-Romanticism was essentially a backward-looking and insular art, caused in part by our isolated position. For the same reason it was the last time that there was a specifically 'national' style. John Piper wrote in 1947: 'Romantic art deals with the particular ...[It] is the result of a vision that can see in these things something significant beyond ordinary significance: something that for a moment seems to contain the whole world; and, when the moment is past, carries over some comment on life or experience besides the comment on appearances.' It was intrinsically pastoral in character; Samuel Palmer's shepherds reappeared, scarcely altered, in the paintings of John Craxton or John Minton. And it was parochial, which in part accounts for the fact that Neo-Romantic art has no international reputation. Its wellspring is indigenous and its appeal is indigenous.

After the war, when it was again possible to travel, young British artists rushed to Paris and to the Mediterranean to rediscover broader European roots. For John Piper, nearing 50, it was too late to change. He had experimented with abstraction in the 1930s, in common with Hepworth and Nicholson, and found that he was temperamentally unsuited to it and so has continued to paint wild landscapes and romantic ruins. Graham Sutherland, who had never travelled abroad before the war, finding all that he needed in the folded hills and mysterious valleys of Pembrokeshire, began to visit the south of France in 1947 and settled there permanently in 1956. In 1943 Edward Sackville-West had designated him and Henry Moore as 'two of the most significant artists of our time'. Unfortunately, by deliberately deciding to 'go international' Sutherland cut himself off from the sources of his inspiration and failed to live up to his early promise.

Henry Moore, on the other hand, became the most famous

British artist of the century. Having been reviled and derided in the 1920s and 1930s for his avant-garde and incomprehensible sculptures, he became part of the national consciousness in the 1940s with his *Shelter Drawings* which reflected the actual experience of Londoners during the war. In 1948 he represented Britain at the Venice Biennale and won the International Sculpture Prize. Thereafter honours and prizes were heaped upon him and there is now scarcely a country in the world in which he has not had a major exhibition. Moore was the first 20th-century British artist to transcend the boundaries of nationalism, which may be attributed to his essentially archetypal subject matter: reclining woman as landscape, mother and child, family groups and sculptures which refer to events of world importance such as the atomic bomb. Moore's shapes are organic and telluric; his strength is that his work can be identified as part of the collective unconscious. Moore had a one-man exhibition at the Museum of Modern Art as early as 1946, followed by a tour of the United States.

Heron wrote an enthusiastic article in *Art News*, and his own style of painting was profoundly affected: he abandoned Braque and Matisse for the wide open spaces of Clyfford Still and Mark Rothko. Peter Lanyon who, like Heron, lived in St Ives, was also crucially influenced by de Kooning and Rothko, and made frequent trips to New York to maintain the dialogue. Rothko himself visited St Ives during the late 1950s.

In 1948 a painting by Jackson Pollock, the first to be seen in Britain, was shown at the Southampton City Art Gallery. In 1953 at the ICA an exhibition called '*Opposing Forces*' included Pollock and Sam Francis, but it was not until after the 1956 Tate exhibition, followed by another in 1958 devoted entirely to the Abstract Expressionists, that the momentum really built up for British artists. In 1960 the exhibition '*Situation*' took place at the RBA Galleries. Organised by the artists, one of the conditions of eligibility was that the picture should be wholly abstract and at least 30 feet square. Among the exhibiting artists were John Hoyland, Robyn Denny, Richard Smith and William Turnbull, all

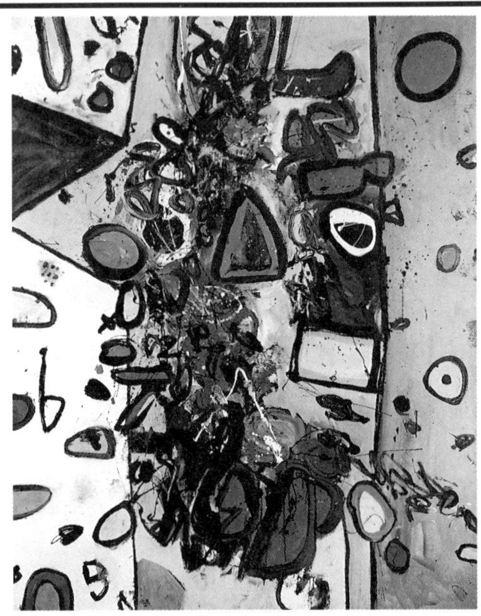 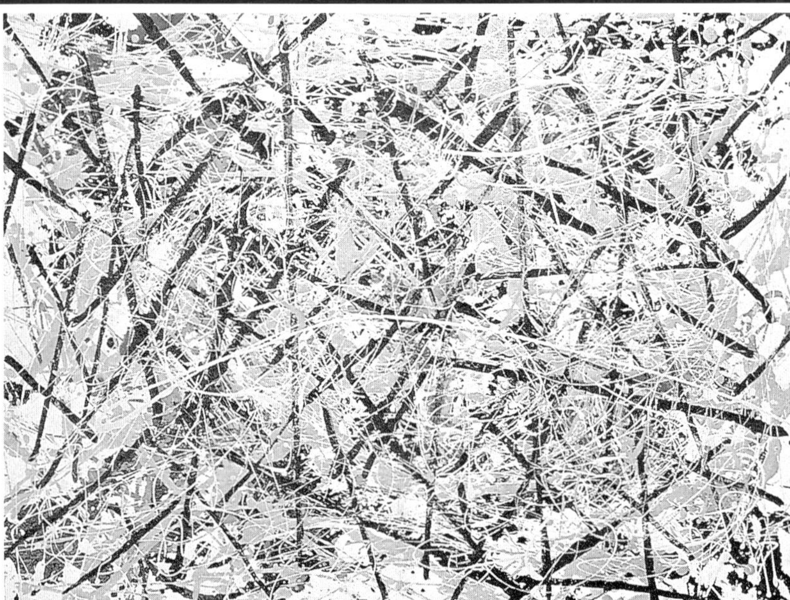

L to R: Alan Davie, *Lush Life No 1*, 1961, oil on canvas; Jackson Pollock, *Number 13*, 1949, enamel on canvas

The only other artists to approach Moore in international repute were Ben Nicholson and Barbara Hepworth, with whom Moore had been in close contact during the 1930s. Nicholson won first prize at the Carnegie International in 1952 and had a retrospective at the Venice Biennale in 1954 whilst Hepworth had represented Britain at Venice in 1950. Thus British art was being widely seen abroad during the late 1940s and early 1950s but British artists were, generally speaking, slow to travel to the United States. Alan Davie was one of the first to realise that something dramatic was germinating in New York, drastically altering his own style after seeing work by Jackson Pollock in Venice in 1948 and then subsequently in New York. Davie had his first one-man exhibition in New York in 1956, a fateful year in more ways than one. In January 1956 '*Modern Art in the United States*' was shown at the Tate Gallery, and in August of that year Jackson Pollock was killed in a car crash. He had never been to Europe. At the Tate Gallery only one room was devoted to the Abstract Expressionists, but the effect was electrifying. Patrick

of them owing allegiance to American Colour-Field painting. The idea, already current in the United States, was to involve the spectator in an 'event' or 'situation' brought about by the largeness of the canvas which occupied the whole field of vision. Arguably the single most important event in the British/American dialogue was the appointment of Bryan Robertson to the Whitechapel Art Gallery in 1952. For the next 16 years he curated a host of international exhibitions, including Moore, Hepworth and Davie for the home team, and Pollock, Rothko and Rauschenberg from across the Atlantic. It was the first time that British and foreign artists had had mid-career exhibitions in this country.

Inevitably the pendulum swung. Reaction against the self-engrossed portentousness of the Abstract Expressionists and their heavy pronouncements about myth and meaning compelled the next generation to present themselves as cheeky and frivolous. In 1957 Richard Hamilton enumerated some of the ingredients of Pop art, which included (obviously) the popular, mass-produced, witty, sexy, gimmicky, glamorous etc... Designed to appeal to a mass audience by using such materials as comics and magazines, it nevertheless turned out to be disappointingly elitist and remote from the man in the street. Peter Blake once remarked sadly that he had thought that by using subject matter such as pop groups, which appeal to a mass audience, his pictures would gain a similarly wide appeal. But alas this is a visually illiterate country and it was not to be. Richard Hamilton and Eduardo Paolozzi, who had been experimenting with collages of pin-ups and incongruously juxtaposed materials as early as 1947, together were the progenitors of British Pop. Indeed Hamilton's collage *Just What is it that Makes Today's Homes so Different, so Appealing?*, 1956, which extols the banal necessities of life as seen through the eyes of an advertisement copywriter, is an icon of English Pop. The same can be said of Peter Blake's *On the Balcony*, 1955-57 loaded with balconic references from Romeo and Juliet, through Manet, to debs and the Royal family. Of the dazzling generation of Blake's contemporaries at the Royal College –

assemblages and installations of, amongst other things, fast food counters and sleazy bars. Oldenburg has said: 'I am for art that is political-erotical-mystical, that does something other than sit on its ass in a museum.' Perhaps the chief attraction of American Pop art is that it is upfront and immediately legible, whereas British Pop art is more complex and·requires greater effort to read. Andy Warhol is certainly the most influential of all American Pop artists. His emphasis on the mechanical aspect of art ('I want to be a machine') and the repetitive nature of his images were crucial for the development of serial art and Minimalism.

Concurrently with the Pop explosion a revolution was taking place in British scuplture. Anthony Caro was assistant to Henry Moore from 1951 to 1953, and was himself at that time making lumpish figurative bronzes. In 1959 he went to the United States and met Kenneth Noland, Clement Greenberg and, most important for his own development, David Smith, America's foremost sculptor who worked exclusively in welded metal. Caro returned to England where his work underwent a sea-change: he

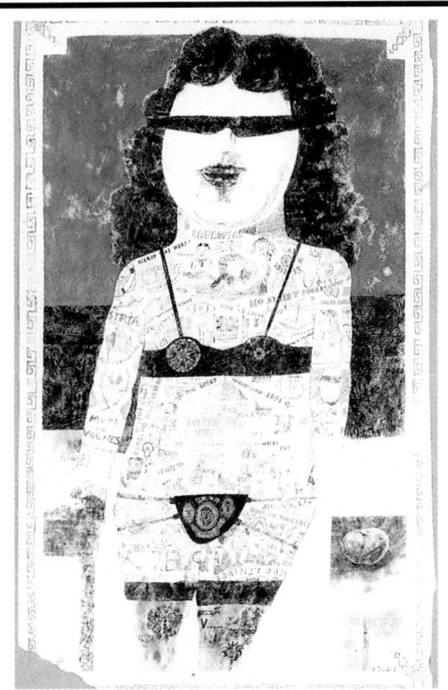
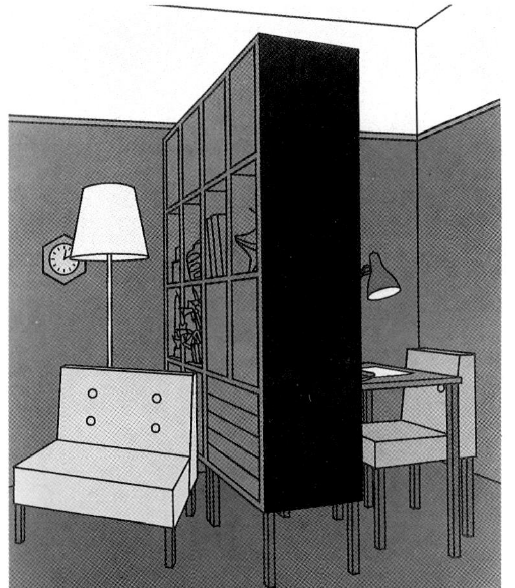
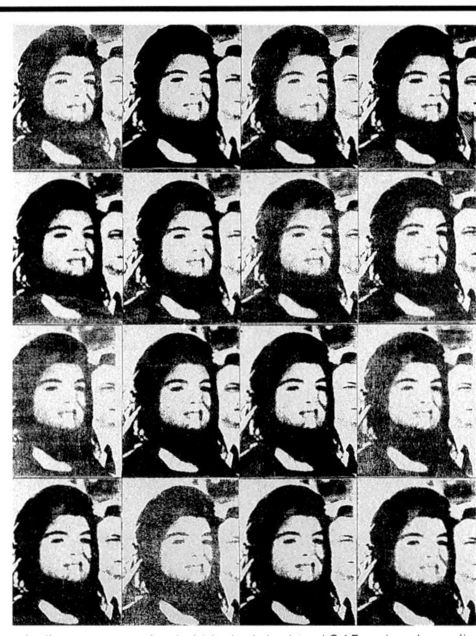

L to R: Peter Blake, Tattooed Lady 1, 1955, mixed media; Patrick Caulfield, Interior with Room Divider, 1971, acrylic and oil on canvas; Andy Warhol, Jackie, 1965, mixed media

David Hockney, Allen Jones, Peter Phillips, Patrick Caulfield – only Allen Jones has remained a Pop artist in the sense of 'witty, sexy, glamorous'. David Hockney was never really a Pop artist, despite attempts to categorise him as such. On his first trip to America while still at the Royal College, which resulted in the series of etchings *The Rake's Progress*, he found his spiritual home, and as soon as he could he settled there.

Compared to British Pop, sometimes regarded as twee, partly because of its small scale, American Pop is large scale, and raunchy. Its forerunners are considered to have been Jasper Johns and Robert Rauschenberg, whose iconoclasm in the mid 1950s was designated as neo-Dada. They both used commonplace imagery and popular kitsch, bound together with a technical brilliance which transcended its subject matter. Subsequently Roy Lichtenstein, Tom Wesselman, James Rosenquist and Andy Warhol began to paint popular images from the world of advertising and comic strips, reproducing commercial techniques. The sculptors Claes Oldenburg and Ed Kienholz made

abandoned bronze figures on a plinth and placed his welded sculptures directly on the floor, sometimes painting them in clear, bright, monocolours so they could be considered as 3-dimensional paintings occupying the same space as the viewer. Caro's new doctrine, which he disseminated at St Martin's School of Art, influenced an entire generation of British sculptors. Caro's younger colleague at St Martin's, Phillip King, is perhaps the most important of all this generation. His work has an ambiguous and enigmatic quality which teases the eye and the mind. His *Genghis Khan*, 1963, has a hieratic presence which is unforgettable. The very solidity of the achievements of Caro and King caused a reaction among their students, who included at that time Gilbert and George, Bruce McLean and Barry Flanagan, all of whom turned to more conceptual forms of art.

Minimal and Conceptual art are peculiarly American phenomena, having comparatively few adherents in Britain. As we have seen, Pop art was a reaction against Abstract Expressionism. Similarly, Minimal and Conceptual art were a reaction against

Pop art, although strands of the preceeding movements are always interwoven into those that succeed them. Minimal art is essentially an art of reduction, and has its roots in Russian Constructivism, Mondrian, Brancusi and Duchamp, as well as, closer to home, the all-white and all-black paintings which Rauschenberg exhibited at the Betty Parsons Gallery, New York, in 1951. It also included certain elements of Pop art, such as Warhol's repetitious imagery. There is very little difference conceptually between Warhol's Brillo boxes and Donald Judd's 'specific objects'. Elements are also derived from Abstract Expressionism, such as the smooth lack of differentiation in the surface of a painting by Barnett Newman. On a philosophical level Minimal and Conceptual artists can be regarded as introducing a cool impersonal note into the hectic and messy world in which we live. As Plato said: 'Only in geometric forms can we find absolute beauty'. This absolute beauty resides in Carl Andre's metal plates as much as in Sol LeWitt's cubic constructions.

In Britain the list of artists who briefly adhered to the tenets of

photographs the landscape through which he is walking and exhibits the results in a gallery. David Nash rearranges the scenery near his studio by pleaching young trees together – the sculpture will not be complete before the year 2000. These works can be seen as a continuation of the Romantic tradition as defined by John Piper. In the United States, on the other hand, if an artist wished to interfere with Nature he used a bulldozer to rearrange the landscape. Michael Heizer and Robert Smithson were of that persuasion.

Gilbert and George, McLean and Flanagan, by using themselves as sculptures or making objects so ephemeral that they had a built-in obsolescence, broke the barriers for the younger generation of sculptors in Britain. On the one hand there are the *bricoleurs* like Bill Woodrow or Tony Cragg, who use discarded objects of urban detritus to make their socially-conscious sculptures. On the other hand, there is Richard Deacon, who can be regarded as a classicist. His shapes are at first sight abstract, but there are nearly always figurative connotations which gradually

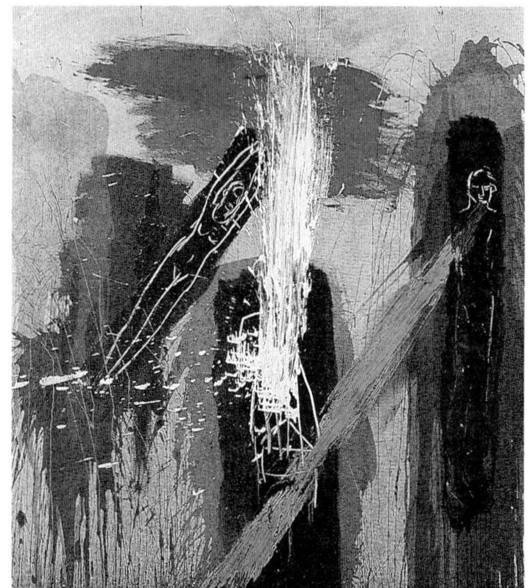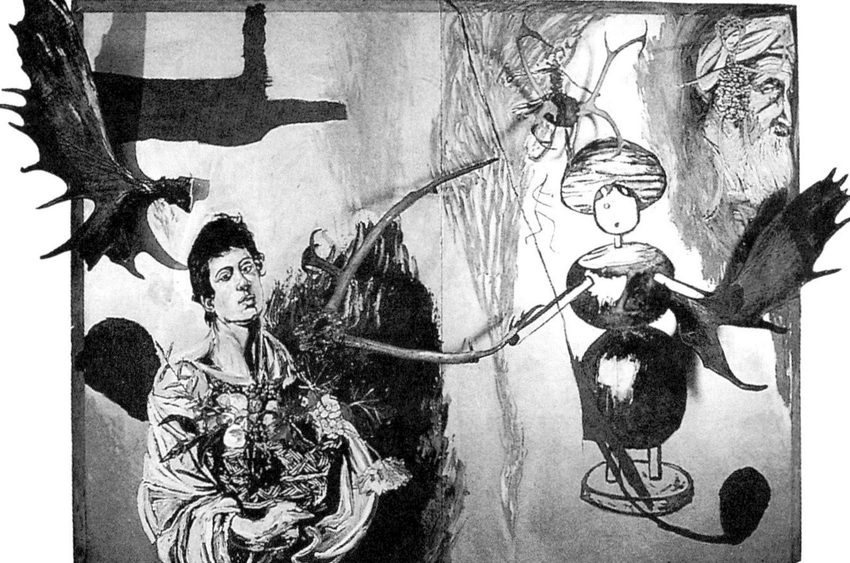

L to R: Bruce McLean, *Untitled*, 1986, acrylic on canvas; Julian Schnabel, *Exile*, 1980, oil and antlers on wood

Conceptualism is not long: Victor Burgin, whose work consists of texts to read which are at odds with the accompanying image; Bruce McLean, who at that time made ephemeral and transitory works; Michael Craig-Martin, whose images were undermined by their titles, to which they bore no relation; and Richard Long, whose walks in remote parts of the world are recorded as photographs and hung in the gallery alongside gnomic texts. Long's more substantial contribution to art in the gallery consists of stone circles or lines which have to be dismantled and stored, or of hand prints with mud as medium, on a wall from which they will perforce have to be washed.

It seems to me that from the mid 1970s Britain and America drew apart in the arena of the visual arts. The dialectic became tenuous indeed. Pluralism was the name of the game, and anyone could join in. One example of the division in attitudes is apparent in the British and American stance with regard to Nature. Richard Long's interference with Nature is minimal: he rearranges a few stones, photographs them and passes on. Hamish Fulton likewise

reveal themselves. His titles, such as *If the Shoe Fits*, are often well-worn clichés to which he gives new meaning, in this case fashioning the sculpture to look like an outsize clog or a Denver boot. Anthony Gormley uses his own body to make sculpture, as the best means of communicating to the world his concern with nothing less than life and death. The only artist in America using his own or other people's bodies to make sculpture who can be compared to Gormley is George Segal. His *Raising the Flag at Iwo Jima* in Cologne and his recently executed memorial in San Francisco to the victims of the holocaust are truly epic.

The weakening of the ties between Britain and America in the mid 1970s was partly due to the fact that Britain had again become more aware of contemporary European art. After the war America was the land of plenty towards which war-weary Europeans looked, but as Europe slowly began to recover from the depredations and horrors of 1939-45, so the artists of Western European countries were able to rejoin the mainstream of avant-garde art from which they had been so long cut off.

Nowhere did the phoenix arise more dramatically from the ashes than in Germany, and it was from West Germany and Italy that the new wave of figurative painting, which came to be known as Neo-Expressionism, first manifested itself. Expressionism is of course anything but new in Northern Europe. It is a tradition which stretches back to Grünewald, Munch, Beckmann and the artist of die Brücke and der Blaue Reiter.

Although I am aware that he repudiates the label of Expressionist, what else is one to call Francis Bacon? He uses expressive distortion to heighten the already highly strung emotions of his powerful paintings. His themes are those of human tragedy, of man's inhumanity to man, and he is existentially aware of the hopelessness of the human condition. He paints in the grand tradition of the Old Masters: Michelangelo, Velásquez and Goya are his mentors; Aeschylus and the letters of van Gogh are his bedside reading. The Eumenides are ever present. Henry Geldzahler said in his introduction to Bacon's exhibition at the Metropolitan Museum of Art in 1975: 'His achievement is to have

tives, with a cast of stock characters who get into impossible situations. Campbell's paintings are light relief from the serious business of life.

American painters have no such tradition to draw on, and the so-called Neo-Expressionist artists in American have been looking hard at German painters. David Salle, for example, could not exist without Sigmar Polke. Julian Schnabel must be the most original of the group, even if one is only sledgehammered into bemused awe by the sheer macho device of huge canvases covered with smashed plates bonded together and skewered with antlers. His work has been described as 'holocaust chic' and, more spitefully, as 'poor man's Pollock'. Overwhelmed I may be, but I do not feel the authentic frisson which I do in front of a great work of art.

If pluralism was the name of the game in the 1970s, it has now changed its rules and is called appropriation. The avant-garde in New York would seem to have lost its collective marbles if it is judged sufficient to make an oversized car mascot and call it a

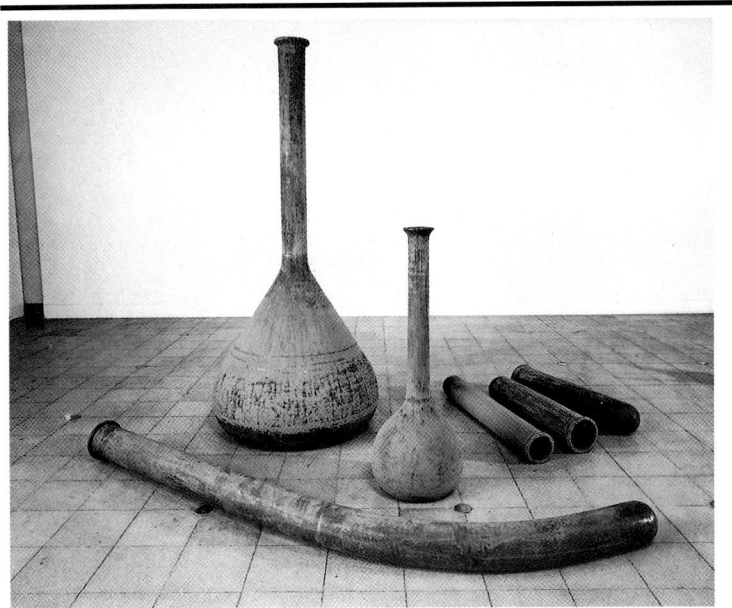 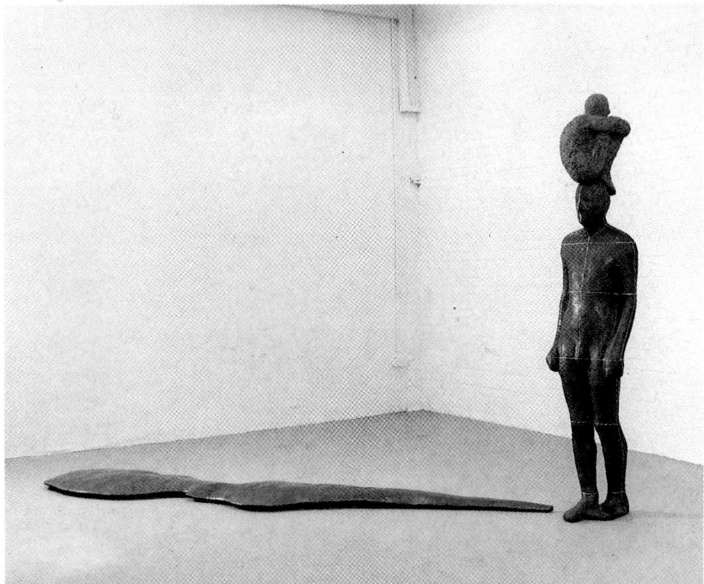

L to R: Tony Cragg, *Instinctive Reactions*, 1987, cast steel; Antony Gormley, *The Beginning, the Middle, the End* 1983-4, terracotta, lead, fibreglass, plaster, air

wrestled with his own inner vision, distorted and tortured as it sometimes appears, and come up with an honest alternative vision – his memorable gift – a personal demonology successfully visualised and made available to an audience hungry for intensity.'

Intensity is one of the key attributes of Expressionism, and we have here in Britain an artist who has never, since his years as a student at Edinburgh College of Art, deviated from the intensity of vision which distinguishes him. I refer to John Bellany, who was born and brought up in a fishing village on the east coast of Scotland. His father was a fisherman and from an early age he was aware of the fragility of life for seafaring folk. His paintings are imbued with the imagery of the sea, and many a seagull or fish has been metamorphosed into a surrogate human being. Like Ensor he uses masks as metaphors. Christopher Le Brun marries a Northern European intensity of *matière* with a classical Mediterranean subject matter. Stephen Campbell, the young Scottish painter who rocketed to fame in New York, is expressive rather than expressionist. His paintings are rambling narra-

sculpture (Jeff Koons) or put a brand new Hoover in a plastic vitrine and exhibit it in a gallery (Haim Steinbach). Worst of all are the Neo-Geos, who are like children aping their elders; the comforting thing is that they come off decidedly second-best. When you see Peter Taaffe doing a Bridget Riley you think longingly of the original which has been so lovingly and skilfully executed. Nostalgia is not enough when invention and passion are missing.

Mary Rose Beaumont is a freelance critic and lecturer

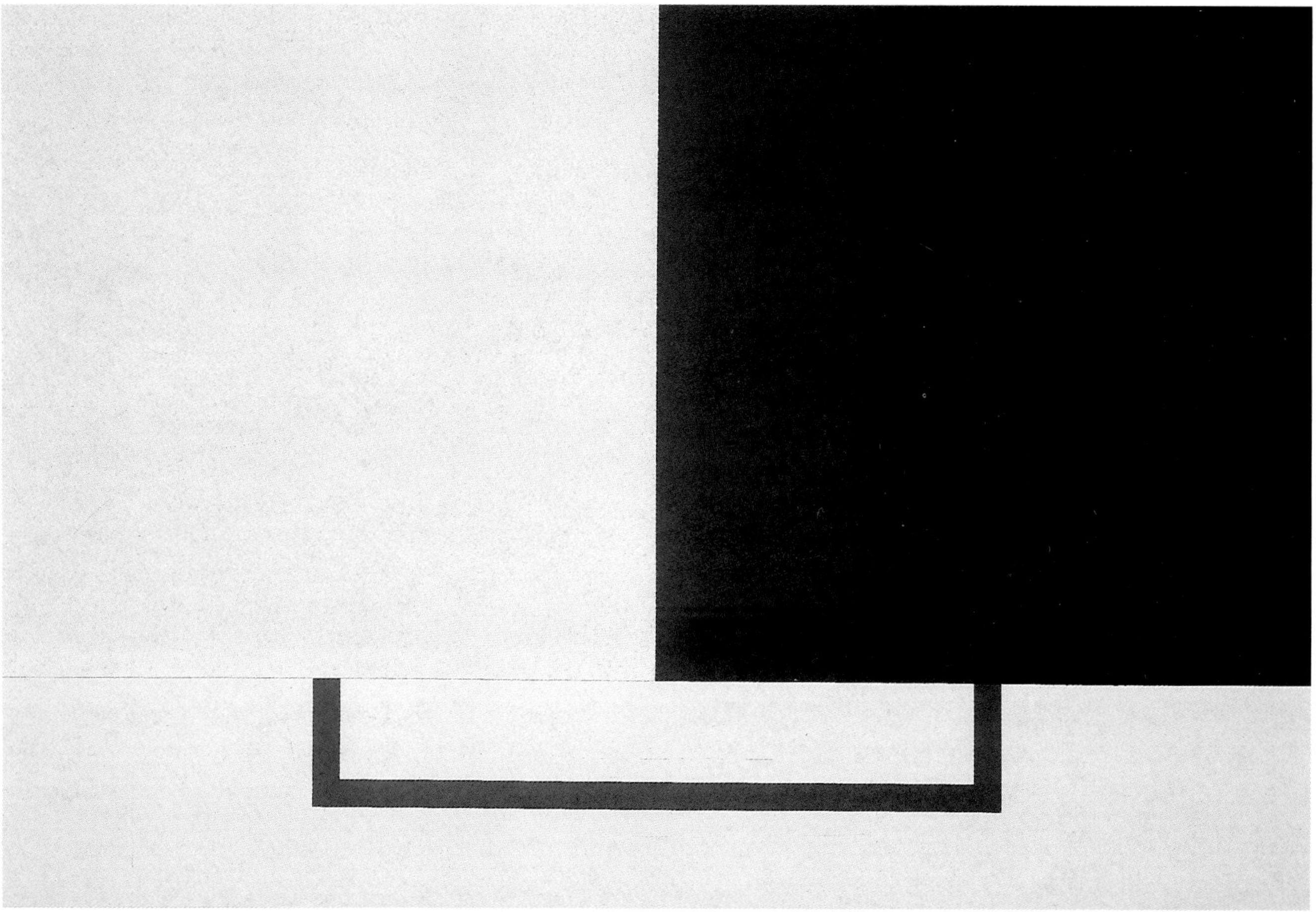

Peter Halley, *Yellow and Black Cells with Conduit*, 1985, acrylic, day-glo acrylic and roll-a-tex on canvas

Peter Halley, *Two Conduits*, 1987, day-glo acrylic on canvas

NEW AMERICAN ART
Dan Cameron

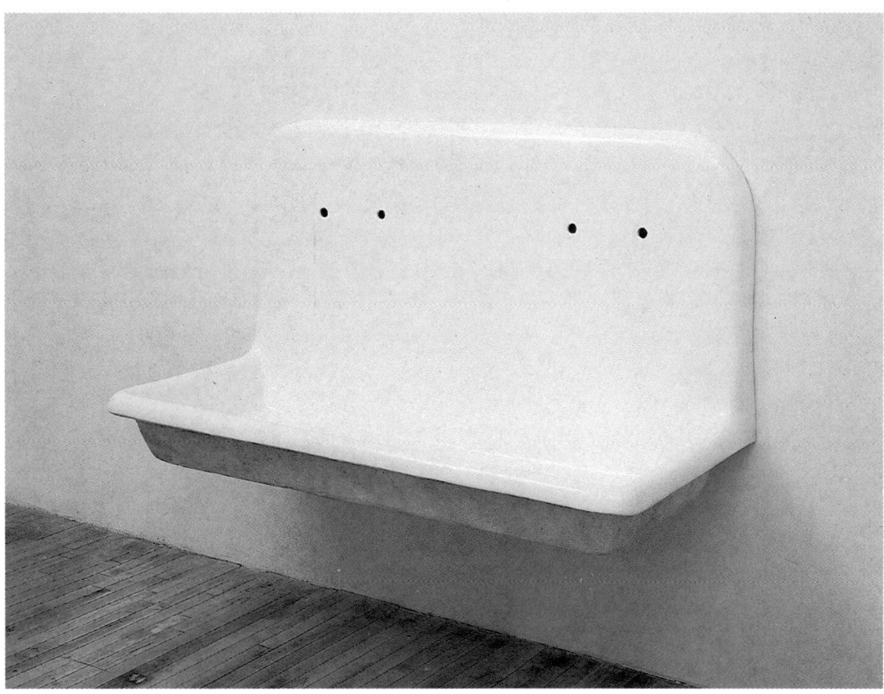

Robert Gober, *Double Sink*, 1984, plaster, wood, wire lathe, latex and enamel paint

A new generation of contemporary American artists are reinterpreting the themes and images of the heyday of American abstract, Minimal and Conceptual art. In the Post-Modern era such an explicit concern with forms of Modernism may seem anachronistic, but when a major collection such as the Saatchi Collection includes their work it cannot be ignored.

Two non-theoretical factors have played a considerable role in shaping the stylistic principles exemplified by the art currently under consideration. One is the tremendous surge in the international market for contemporary art in the 80s, a surge that has reinforced the significance of Manhattan as world capital for the creation, display, purchase and exchange of recent works of art by artists from all over the world. Today, successful artists are international celebrities of a sort, with the ability to command staggering prices for works barely released from the studio. It is the painter's role that has changed most radically since the era of Abstract Expressionism, when American art was first presumed to have international significance. At that time major figures such as Willem de Kooning or Robert Rauschenberg were still practically unknown outside their tight-knit communities. The size of the audience for a successful contemporary artist may have only increased tenfold since the late 60s, but the ability of that audience to enrich and empower its heroes has magnified exponentially, permitting younger artists an unprecedented opportunity to feel they may indeed be bringing painting and sculpture back into the mainstream of world culture for the first time since the heyday of Picasso.

Another factor with strong repercussions on current American aesthetics was the ascendancy of European art, particularly from Germany, Great Britain and Italy, in the early 1980s. Far from achieving a merely nationalistic spirit, this recent art from Europe strived to attain an unprecedented degree of universal expression, while articulating the presence of the individual spectator with an equal degree of generosity.

Most of this generation of Europeans had, in fact, been working in this vein since the 60s, but the impact of their work on a younger generation of American artists made it seem as if they had appeared overnight. As a stylistic response to European art, Julian Schnabel's strategy was to return to the example of Pollock and de Kooning as a point in recent history when American art had tried to achieve the same universality. Schnabel's re-definition of the large-scaled canvas as an arena for the artist's confrontation with elemental forces sparked an entire movement of American Neo-Expressionism (just as New York was beginning to celebrate a second wave of Europeans: Georg Baselitz, Enzo Cucchi, Malcolm Morley, Jorg Immendorf, Sandro Chia, Francesco Clemente, Sigmar Polke and others). It also triggered a crisis among a still younger group of Americans, who came to believe that recycling the ambience of Abstract Expressionism in response to European art was a less than challenging prospect for a generation weaned on the accomplishments of the Pop and Minimalist generation.

The immediate artistic roots of so-called 'neo-conceptual' work can be found in the explorations into photography begun in

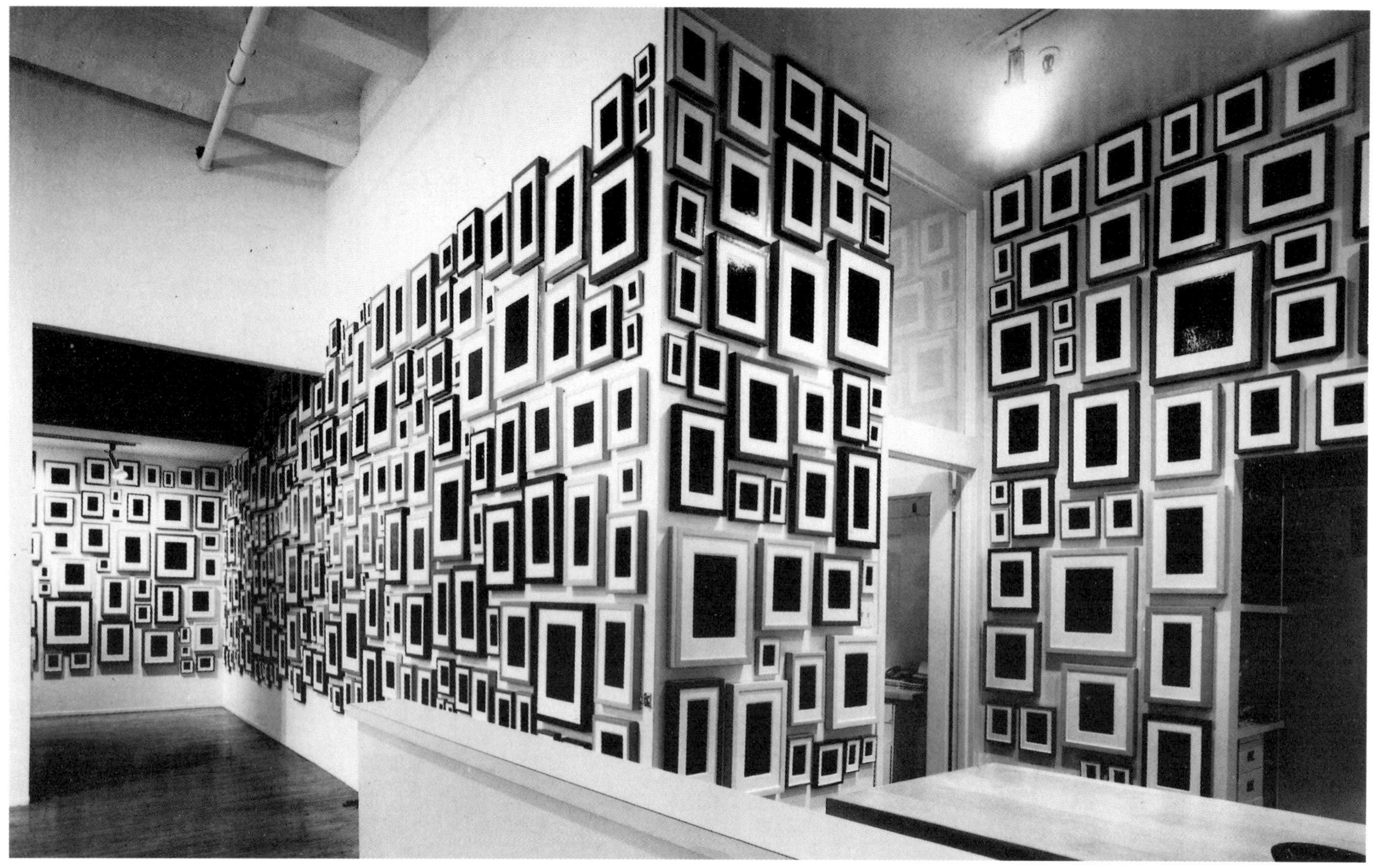

Allan McCollum , *Plaster Surrogates*, 1984, enamel on Hydrostone

the late 70s by artists such as Barbara Kruger, Richard Prince and Sherrie Levine. Beginning from the premise that fine art had become stifled by its emphasis on unique artworks and the mythic individuality of the artist, these artists began to explore the radical possibilities of photography as a means of re-presenting the world of images territorialised by the media, especially in magazines (Kruger, Prince), and books (Levine). Their venture was, on the surface, a critique of high culture which was grounded equally in Duchamp, in Walter Benjamin's influential essay, 'The Work of Art in the Age of Mechanical Reproduction', in Pop art (especially Warhol), and, finally, in the photo-documentation procedures of Conceptual art (John Baldessari and Bruce Nauman being the most conspicuous forerunners of this practice).

While this work took issue with the unquestioned assumptions about originality and uniqueness as primary goals of the avant-garde, certain other artists were devising a parallel investigation of the same or similar questions. Allan McCollum has been making work since 1967 that explicitly denies the primacy of the unique object, relying instead on techniques adapted from the performance and writing of the Fluxus group, specifically those which emphasised repetitive and task-oriented gestures. Both McCollum and Ross Bleckner were included in the last truly populist Whitney Biennial (1975), a collective that presented Bleckner's work shortly before he embarked upon his exploration of the simultaneous use of multiple styles. Although Gerhard Richter (and before him, Picasso and Picabia) had pioneered the practice of painting in a multitude of variant styles, Bleckner's

1981 exhibition of canvases that directly quoted the Op art movement from the mid 1960s was an unprecedented intiative. This show would have a lasting impact on a younger painter, Peter Halley, who would not show in a New York gallery for another four years, but who at the time championed Bleckner's work in an important essay for *Arts Magazine*.

By 1980, the work of two very different sculptors was beginning to coalesce around the twin principles of object and display. Rather than extend the art object as sign (like McCollum) or as slippage (like Bleckner), Jeff Koons and Haim Steinbach chose to substitute one kind of experience for another. In Koons' work, the object serves as an abstraction of the display of cultural value that art is meant to represent, while Steinbach's arrangements of standardised products function as representative cross-sections of what the artist believes to be the archetypal cultural location in society. The abstraction becomes symbolic (appliances encased in plexiglass, stainless steel locomotive-decanters and travelling bar, basketballs suspended in aquariums), while the representation becomes linguistic (lava lamps, Star Wars masks, digital clocks, detergent boxes).

Two years prior to this, McCollum had embarked on his first set of plaster 'surrogates' – multiple, mass-produced objects that seemed to be paintings but were only meant to suggest pictures in the loosest way: their 'frames' surrounding white 'mattes' which surrounded black 'images'. The 'surrogates' were installed in hundreds, extending the viewing space to its farthest limits. The austere blankness of McCollum's pieces seems the complete reverse of Carroll Dunham's paintings, where the imagery is

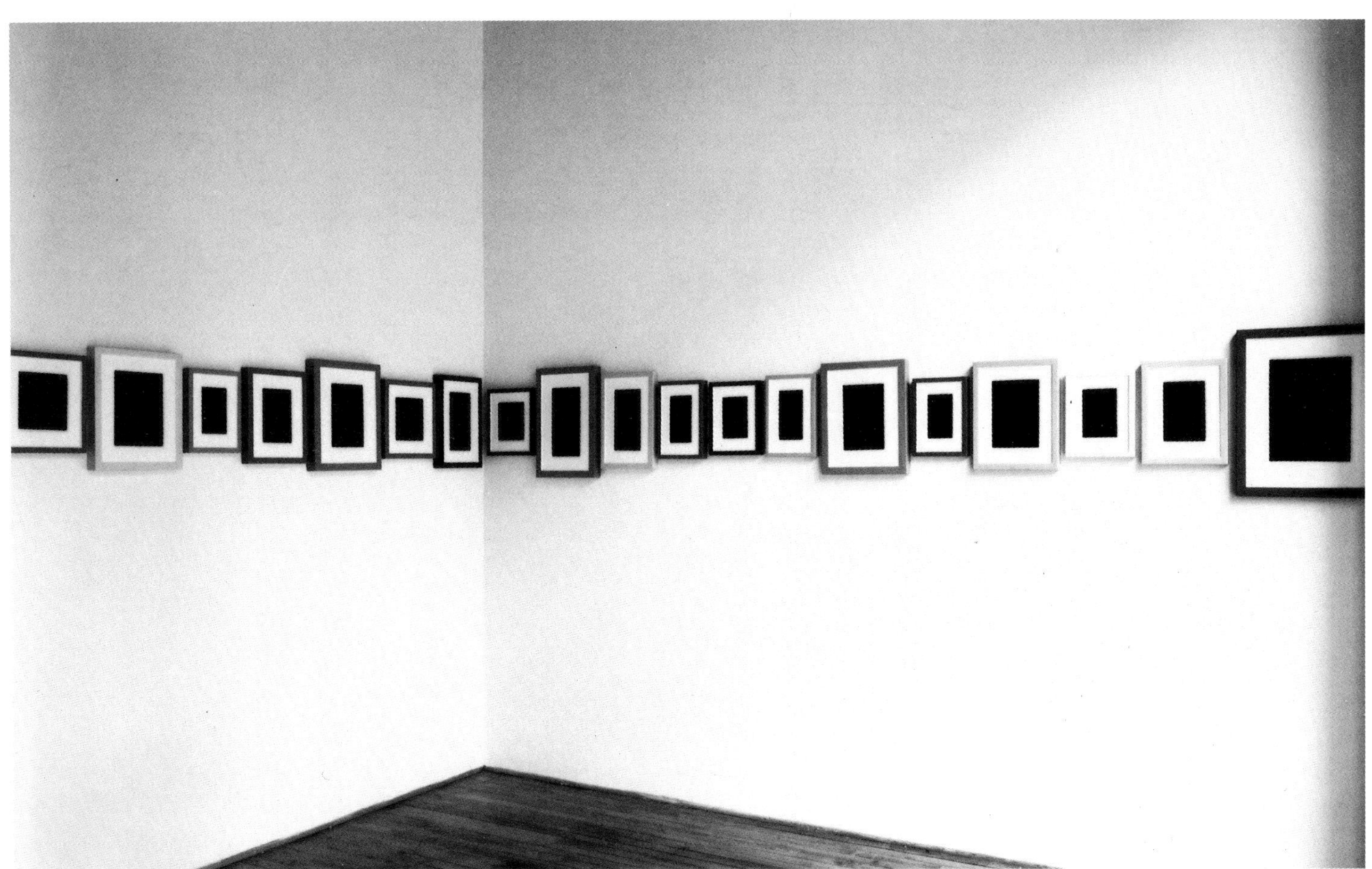

Allan McCollum, *Plaster Surrogates*, 1983, enamel on Hydrostone

laboured over extended periods of time. Dunham's antecedents are the so-called 'epistemological abstractionists' from the early 1970s such as Mel Bochner, Barry Le Va and Dorothea Rockburne.

Another painter who was greatly concerned at this time with the idea of process in his work was Tim Rollins. Inspired partly by Joseph Beuys, Hans Haacke and other artists who addressed art's possibilities as an agent of social change, Rollins pursued an education degree after he finished his art training, and began teaching at the pre-high school level in a troubled South Bronx neighbourhood. In 1980 he co-founded Group Material, a loosely defined collective of artists whose primary concern was the production of collaborative artworks; in 1982, he formed an after-school workshop called 'Art and Knowledge', which brought his students into a fulltime studio situation, where, with Rollins as only partial intermediary, they would disseminate works of literature into a series of visual motifs that would slowly be transformed into large-scale works of art. In so doing, Rollins was challenging the primacy of the single artist as sole author of the artwork, letting the innumerable hands and minds of the later-dubbed KOS ('Kids of Survival') have an equal role.

Robert Gober started by using traditional materials (primarily plaster and wood) to fabricate oversized, non-functional sinks that appeared to be both isolated from their functional context, and yet ripped away from a non-art environment. Because of the central place of craft in Gober's work, his sculptures convey a presence that is inescapably anthropomorphic, even to the point of suggesting a biographical fiction, the pieces seeming to have been through years of familiar use before being claimed as art.

Through the mid 1980s, as the issues in Bleckner's work became more widely disseminated, his influence on two younger painters became an important means for their establishing a theoretical base to their own practice. Philip Taaffe, whose earlier work suggested an affinity between geometric space and the technique of collage, became well known for his appropriations of works by Bridget Riley, Ellsworth Kelly, and Myron Stout. Rather than establish a relationship of complete dependence on his sources, Taaffe became interested in mixing imagery from unrelated painters, adapting a Kelly ground, say, to a form derived from Barnett Newman. In Taaffe's work, in fact, there is meant to be a perfect equilibrium between the 'borrowed' forms and the images which he invents himself. Meyer Vaisman's art commenced by establishing a greater emotional distance from his viewer than Taaffe, whose interest in optical effects recalls Bleckner's desires to visually seduce the viewer through the heightened painterliness of his pictures. Vaisman, in contrast, established a technique of silkscreening an enlarged fabric weave across his canvases to simulate their materiality, then laminating the surface to make them appear pre-fabricated. Across this field, Vaisman began to organise certain biological images, many with distinctly erotic overtones, which appeared to contradict the largely impersonal nature of the overall objects.

Vaisman's interest in suggesting emotional alienation through his art was perhaps more related to Peter Halley's work, although his emphasis on absence and on the diagrammatic presence (or absence) of colour are qualities present in both Bleckner's and Taaffe's paintings. Halley, on the other hand, was

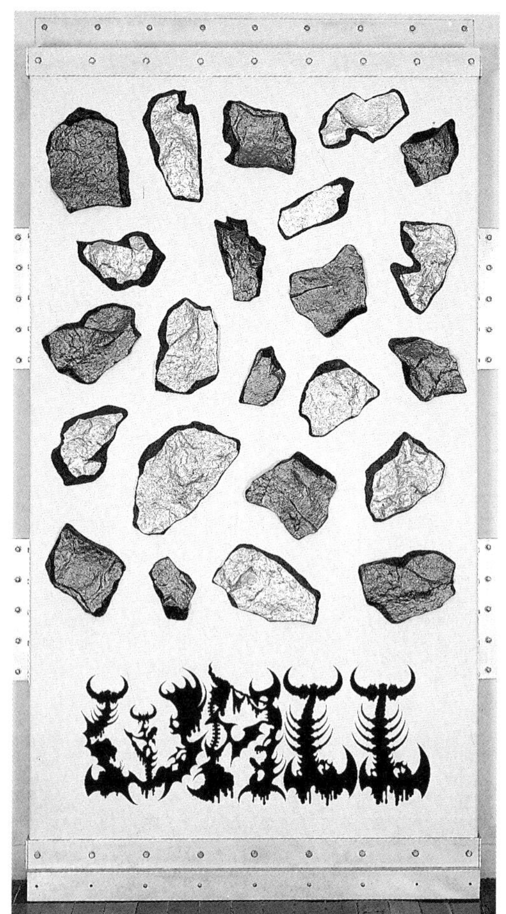 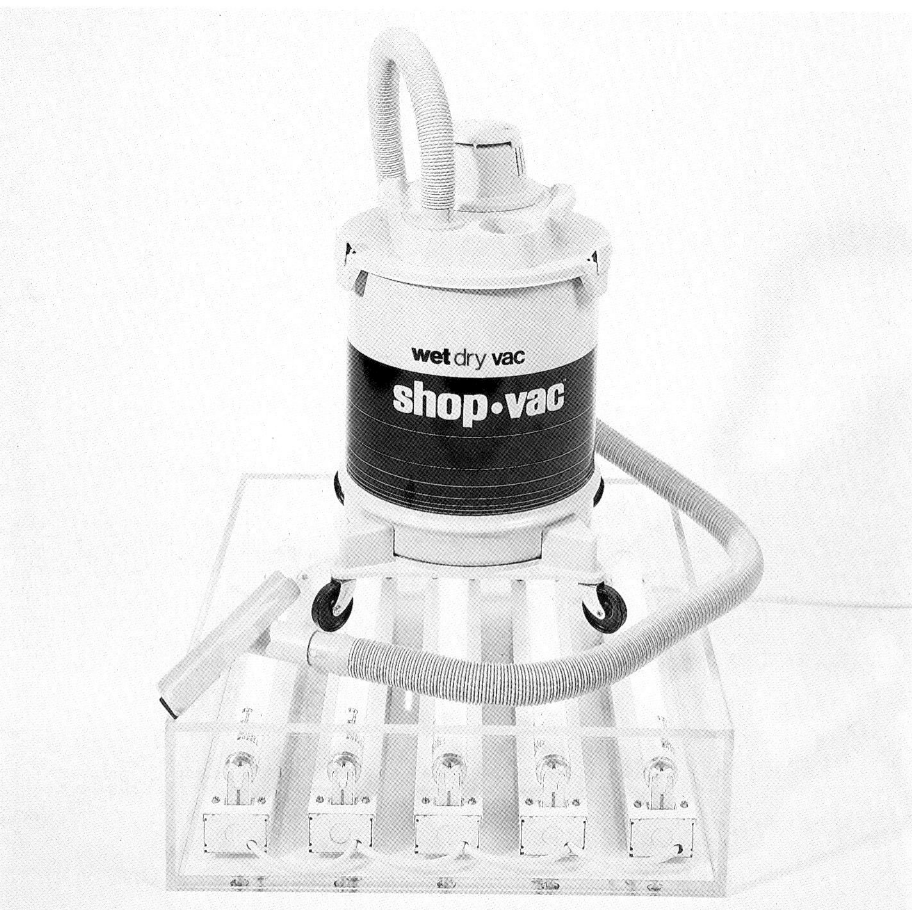

L to R: Ashley Bickerton, Wall Wall 7, 1986: Jeff Koons, New Shop Vac Wet/Dry, 1980, both mixed media

extending the possibilities in his art of geometric abstraction as a form of representation by depicting a structural reality that existed throughout the technologised world. His use of the square, of industrialised colours and synthetic stucco are meant to suggest a critical interpretation of reality, one that brings the viewer into close confrontation with certain hidden conditions of the manmade environment.

In Ashley Bickerton's painting-objects, the viewer is continually reminded that the work is a present-day artefact, complete with exaggerated frontality, framing edges, futuristic imagery and mock-signatures. For Bickerton, the aesthetic is at once exotic and banal, and he is hoping to address art's entry into the world of reality as a process which strips it of all illusion, leaving only beauty and self-consciousness behind.

In offering thumbnail sketches of these artist's activities, it is important to point out the recent developments of several of the artists who have been producing mature work since 1980 or earlier. McCollum's newest objects are identical vase-like forms, painted in bright bands of high-keyed colours, which are arranged in long rows with almost military precision. Koons' forays into stainless steel castings have recently included such borderline objets d'art as an inflatable bunny, a statuette of Bob Hope, a large bust of Louis XIV, and even a full-scale replica of a life-sized allegorical figure from the plaza of a German town. In Steinbach's current work, objects from antiquity and nature have been brought into the arrangement process, opening the viewer to an awareness of culture as the process by which man brings all objects into the immediate scope of his world-view.

Dunham's paintings from the last few years have utilised more complex juxtapositions of imagery, combined with a spatial sense that offers multiple perspectives while achieving a less crowded field of vision. In Bleckner's work since 1983, there is a more palpable emotionalism, often taking on commemorative forms and a dark, sinewy light. One painter appears to be typifying a pictorial state of pure active energy, while the other depicts a palpable state of absence and loss.

As audiences become more familiar in coming years with the works of these artists, it is possible that allowance will be made for the degree to which issues of artistic practice become synonymous with broader cultural perspectives. At present, when an artist claims to be addressing the commodification of the work of art, it is all too easy to leap to the conclusion that he or she is more interested in its role as commodity than as an artwork. This false dichotomy, by which some would cling to an inherent 'purity' in artistic practice, denies artists the liberty of manipulating the reality of their situations in order to add greater complexity to our experience of their work. This is a privilege that artists have enjoyed for centuries, but it is perceived at the present moment more as a restraint than as an opportunity.

We would like to thank the author and the Saatchi Collection for permission to reproduce this article and the works illustrated in it. A fuller version of the essay appears in the book accompanying the NY Art Now exhibition at the Saatchi Gallery.

AMERICAN ART AFTER 1945

Almost abstracted female forms persist alongside abstractions proper. Though he is classed as an Abstract Expressionist, his randomness, multiple viewpoints and seemingly arbitrary gestural marks are contradicted by the essentially nodal structure of the works.

MILTON AVERY
1895-1965

Colour dictates form, but the interest in the adventitious is strong, as the large number of monotypes shows. Areas of thickly applied colour become strangely translucent. He never wholly abandons figuration, but all representational pattern is subordinate to colour pattern.

ABRAHAM RATTNER
1895-

A strong colourist among Abstract Expressionists and one of the few to design stained glass. The emotional emphasis is directed into suggestions of traditional religious imagery.

JACK TWORKOV
1900-

The 'false-Impressionist' version of Abstract Expressionism. The shimmering colour and seemingly accidental gestures are arrested in perpetual yet perpetually threatened grid structures. Some of the best essays in unexpected equilibrium in the Abstract Expressionist school.

FRANZ KLINE
1910-62

An almost naturalistic agrarian tendency gives way to movements of heavy monochrome forms, sometimes projected to help the sense of alienation from reality. The winter landscapes of earlier works have been discerned in these large non-objective panoramas but, if anything, it is the encounters of cosmic bodies hurling through infinite space that these and the last, coloured works suggest.

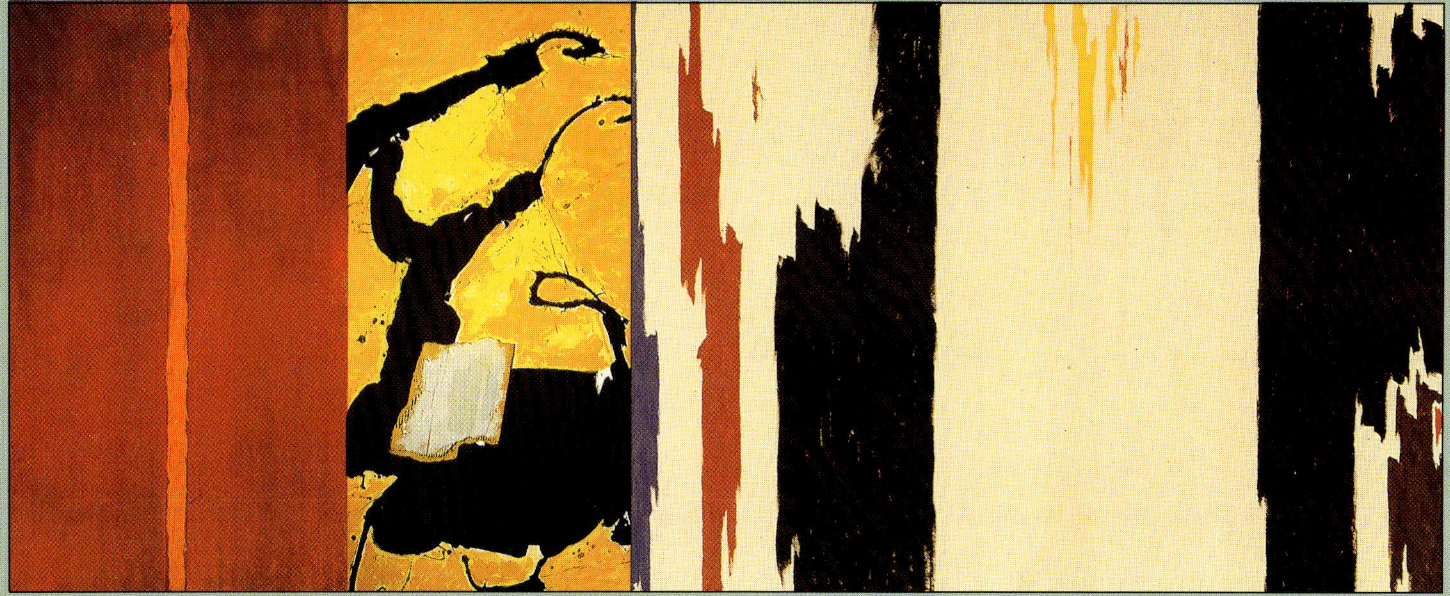

L to R: Barnett Newman, *Onement*, 1948, oil on canvas; Robert Motherwell, *The Irish Troubles*, 1987, acrylic and paper on canvas; Clyfford Still, *Untitled*, 1960, oil on canvas

BARNETT NEWMAN
1905-70

'Biomorphic' (or primitive biological) shapes derived initially from Surrealism are used to unite the unique high seriousness of the artist with that of the evolving universe. Newman embarked on an ambitious search for the principle of living form among primitive peoples – the key for deciphering universal chaos and discovering some kind of way through the unknowable. Titles are clues to the meaningful confrontation between artist and numen – the local or presiding deity. Stripes, bars and other vertical devices are portentous; series such as the *Stations of the Cross* proclaim Newman's ultimately religious intention: a non-figurative art of hope for a century whose countenance is too horrific and whose destiny is too terror-stricken to portray directly.

ROBERT MOTHERWELL
1915-

Fluctuations of space and form used to provoke and explore the unconscious. The initial influence of Surrealism has remained strong. Large monochrome or coloured works with emphatic romantic left-wing or erotic references and a certain jokiness are gradually supplanted by large Colour-Field works with simultaneous expansion and contraction effects (the *Open* series), and by collages.

CLYFFORD STILL
1904-

Expressionist figurative work is transformed into Expressionist Abstraction, but the goal is constant: self-understanding. The artist's feelings are shone forth in scumbled, scratched, worked and treated surfaces from which great totems of the primal urges rise to threaten and declare the mystery within and without. Later, biomorphic whorls and bright colour taches or rough forms dispel the suggestions of a formal composition. Changes in the environment of the verticals reflect changes in the artist's psychic history.

ADOLPH GOTTLIEB
1903-74

French-trained Abstract Expressionist with a strong influence from primitive art, which has remained effective in his often semi-figurative works. His landscapes of the psyche (*Grids and Imaginary Landscapes*) offer interplays of closed and bursting forms all in the essentially Surrealist tradition of the act of painting revealing a supreme truth drawn from within the artist. Later works have a direct religious function.

CY TWOMBLY
1929-

Post-Surrealist gestural painting verging on calligraphy and searching for a meaning whose discovery is always deflected by careful manipulation of the evolving structure of marks.

AD REINHARDT
1913-67

An iconoclast of iconoclasms, searching for an ultimate purity of form. Fiercely angular works pass through collage to almost calligraphic patterning, and then to large forms and monochrome paintings devoid of any discernable counterpart in the world of human reference. His *Black Paintings* offer the slightest possible suggestions of variations from black square to black square: purity being the least movement on the face of primal waters.

RICHARD DIEBENKORN
1922-

He moves from sensitive Social Realism with a lyrical sadness to Abstract Expressionist works, and then again to a figurative lyricism now endowed with the lessons of abstract structure and surface play. His *Ocean Park* series is an imposing contribution to the large stripe-and-bar period of US abstraction. Diebenkorn's special feature is the delicate tensions he introduces into this austere fashion.

STUART DAVIS
1894-1964

Abstracted shapes in the 20s (*Eggbeater* series), and in the 40s a continually up-to-date rodeo Cubism, with clear-cut, pleasing, never nervous or doom-laden references to the jazziness and lyrical mechanisation of Amer-

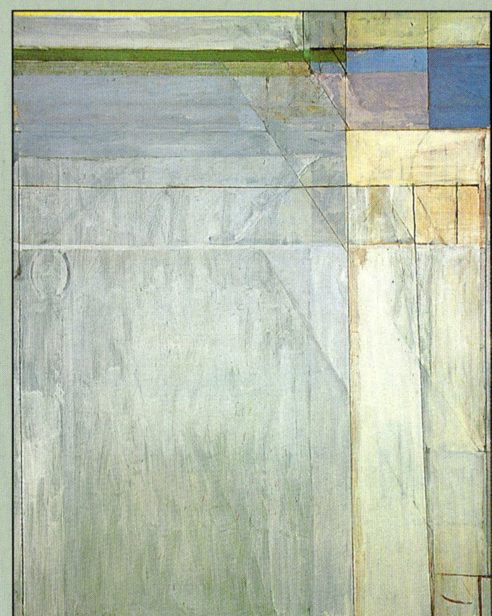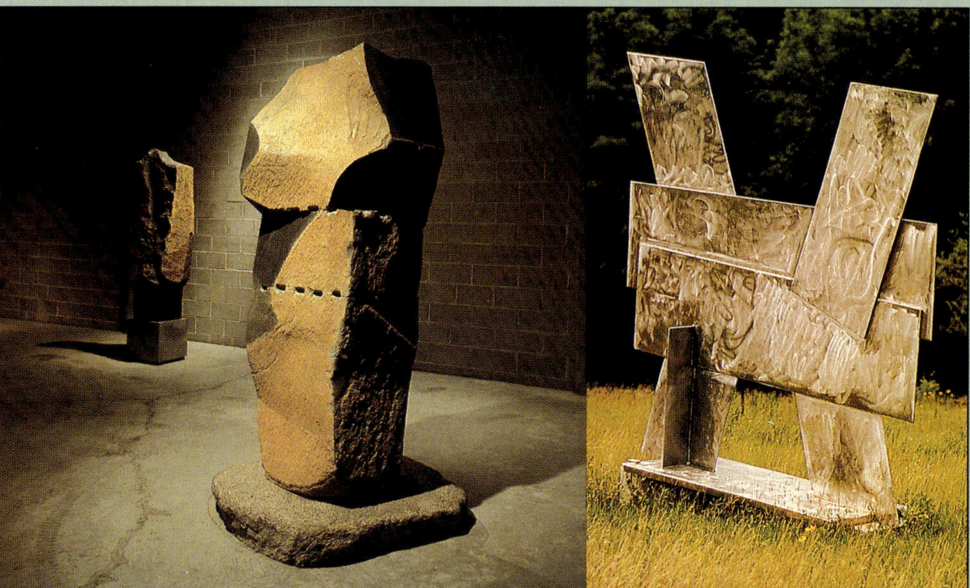

L to R: Richard Diebenkorn, *Ocean Park No 54*, 1972, oil on canvas; Isamu Noguchi, *Age*, 1981, basalt, and *Brilliance*, 1982, basalt; David Smith, *Becca*, 1965

ican life. The interplay of the chopped out, brightly coloured shapes of his later works are an important indigenous formal influence on Abstract Expressionism.

RICHARD LINDNER
1901-76

German emigré whose paintings are filled with an exotic cast of raffish types veering between a sinister erotic vaudeville and a circle of menace and absurdity. The echoes of pre-war German stage-sets, like their cinematic counterparts, are thoroughly Americanised – which means their European origins are ironically obvious in spite of the streetwise and media-aware references. Lindner's screaming, vulgar colours and caricature figuration have constantly, almost illicitly, redressed an equilibrium upset by the excessive austerity and good manners of Abstract Expressionist, Hard-Edge, Minimalist and similar schools.

ALEXANDER CALDER
1898-1976

Major US sculptor whose playful animal drawings, wire sculptures, mobiles, Surrealist references and ironies almost always obey an instinct and longing for essential form and fundamental structure in art echoing his belief in the basically ordered nature of the cosmos. His later stabiles and 'constellations' are important influences on Abstract Expressionism's universalist pretensions and on the tendency towards environments and total art works.

ISAMU NOGUCHI
1904-

Japanese-American sculptor whose eclectic references to Chinese brush drawing, for example, or to Mexican history, and contributions to much private and public art, from gardens to theatre designs, have echoed and advanced the richly various nature of modern American art. He is bound to no one tradition, yet is conscious of his responsibility to many traditions and anxious to create his own without obvious figurative hints of a specific extra-American allegiance. But his interest in surfaces, bases, textures, and formal relations is classical rather than Expressionist.

DAVID SMITH
1906-65

Sculptor whose work from Cubist, to Surrealist, to spatial calligraphic periods profoundly influenced painters throughout his career. His experiments in dissociating extremities of pieces from bases, or in establishing an explosive tension at the boundaries of welded sculptures, share the Abstract Expressionists' interest in art as a unifying exploration of evolution in the individual and in the universe.

ROY LICHTENSTEIN
1923-

The father of US Pop art. His references to American everyday and media behaviour are more obvious and mundane than Lindner's. His mature, 'programmed' painting constantly quotes and exaggerates the clichés and techniques of comic books. His quotations from Cubism, Op art, Art Deco and so on, and the cartoon bubble statements epitomising the American way of life, reverberate with ironies, sometimes so nicely stated as to isolate a work between critique and celebration.

DUANE HANSON
1925-

'Photo-realist' sculptor whose characteristic works veer between a critique of aggression and a satire of manners, while maintaining a humanist emphasis on human waste, alienation and solitary decay amidst mass consumption. His style is related to that of faux-realist painting and the photographer Diane Arbus, though it owes less to despair. His realistic resin, fibreglass and plaster figures are supermarket shoppers, sunbathers and trippers arrested in the stasis of the wholly banal.

JASPER JOHNS
1930-

Serene Pop art using emblems with nationalistic and other echoes, avoiding the Abstract Expressionist concern with the artist's emotionality, and aiming at a superior impersonality indifferent to the flags, numbers or maps displayed. An always strong interest in fine painting, in surface textures and in the medium's plasticity has produced many finely

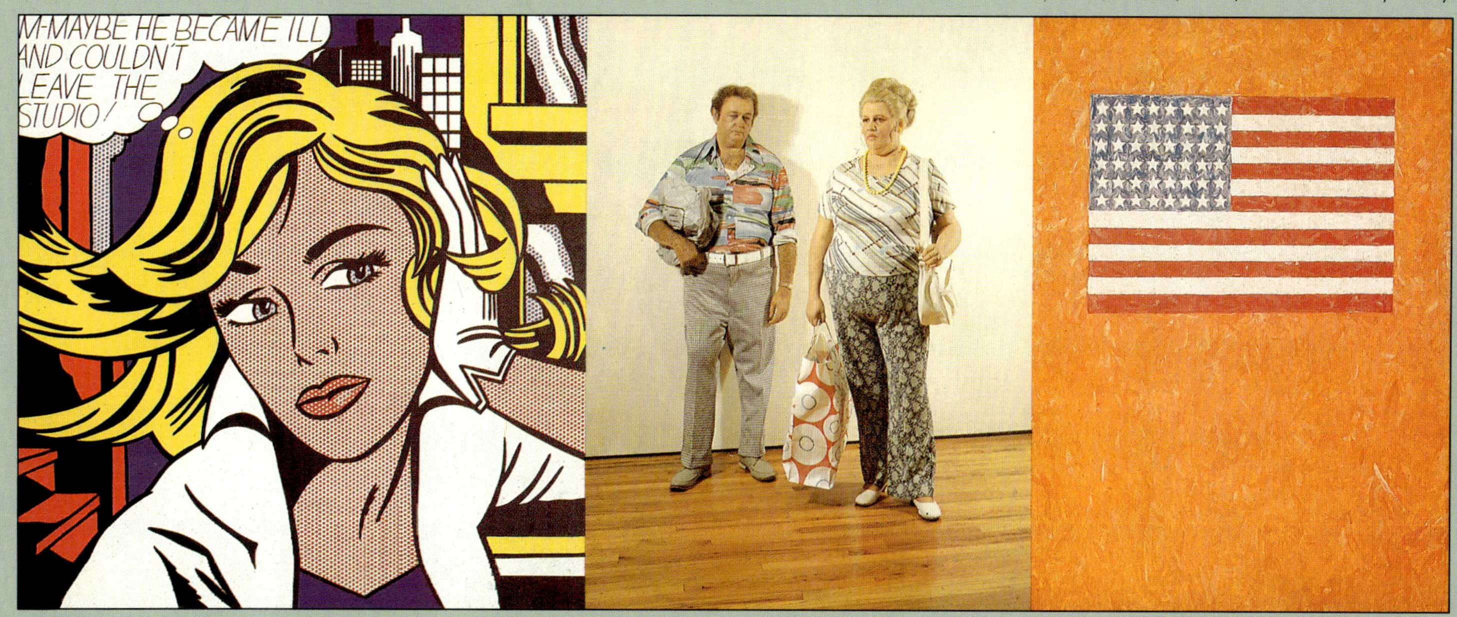

L to R: Roy Lichtenstein, *M-Maybe (A Girl's Picture)*, 1965; Duane Hanson, *Couple with Shopping Bags*, 1976, cast vinyl, polychromed in oil; Jasper Johns, *Flag on Orange Field*, 1957

honed objects which seem carefully weathered and even like museum objects fanatically restored.

CHUCK CLOSE
1940-

Pop and photo-realist painter whose stylised, sometimes menacing, figures are decidedly data-processed and set in a highly-structured, 'computerised' framework.

TOM WESSELMANN
1931-

Pop painter with predilection for large, mass-media-style female nudes presented (with some ambiguity of intention) as simplified sex machines. His foody collages betray a similar mixture of criticism and of painterly delight in a society which objectifies and commercialises its pleasures.

RALPH GOINGS
1928-

Photographic illusionism. A concentration on the raw, cheeky and immediate, on human beings as rough and tough, and on commercial and mechanical objects as precious as spaceships.

ALFRED LESLIE
1927-

Moves from Abstract Expressionism to full-length, full-frontal, all but photo-realist yet exaggerated representations of the self, and later to aggressive, etched-out religious paintings which recall Mantegna and Caravaggio.

LARRY RIVERS
1923-

Moves slowly from Abstract Expressionism to vague realism, and then to an austere Pop art with ironic references to the commercial environment.

JAMES ROSENQUIST
1933-

Abstractionist who changed over to a Pop art, employing commercial and mass-produced objects and fragments to make a wholly formal statement whose sole irony is the lack of social comment.

AMERICAN ART AFTER 1945

by John Griffiths

Leaving the old in search of the new is the quintessentially American experience. Since the 1940s, most important visual artists in the USA have abandoned traditional canons. One after the other, even enthusiastic borrowings from the European formal revolutions of the early years of the century have been questioned, and the terms of that very questioning have been interrogated in relation to the great myths of America, from Success and Openness, Eternal Youth, Classlessness and Perfect Sex, to Materialism as Paradise. Most of these big questions have been asked in abstract or quasi-abstract terms which defy translation into words. Recent US Post-Modernism reverts to styles of the immediate postwar years, but only to combine them in a new scrutiny of inherited myths.

ARSHILE GORKY
1905-48

Apolitical Armenian emigré. In the 1940s his long-favoured Cubism and Surrealism fuse with newly indigenised memories of folk-art to produce an emotively patterned, semi-figurative painting. In a single work, nervous inter-weavings and transitions, from Uccello through Ingres to Miró, and references to the American landscape and its mythic openness, uniquely proclaim the profound longings of the exiled and their inevitable bitter-sweet dis-appointment. Forerunner of Abstract Expressionism and its acceptance as the art form of the American dream and nightmare.

HANS HOFMANN
1880-1966

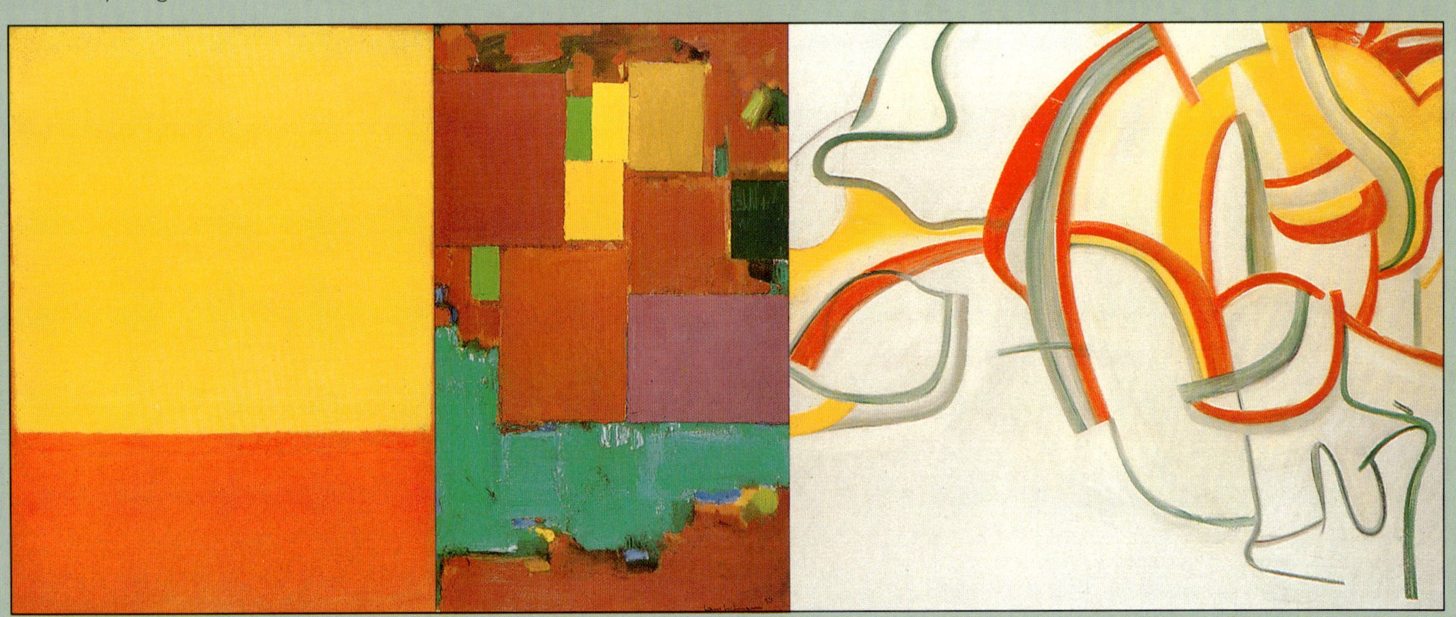

L to R: Mark Rothko, *Untitled*, oil on canvas; Hans Hofmann, *Pompeii*, 1959; Willem de Kooning, *Untitled V*, 1986, oil on canvas

German emigré with engineering background. Proponent of picture plane as field of expressive action, of forces born from a uniquely personal and emotive fusion of form and colour, of a 'push-and-pull' superior to a static representation of mundane reality. Art as existential action aiming — through angst-free fragmentation, spattering, boundary-defying colour sorties and other random devices — at a possible equilibrium which might happily astonish the artist-adventurer, who imitates no more than the evolutionary process itself.

JACKSON POLLOCK
1912-56

Automatism and other Surrealist practices for obtaining meaningful pattern from randomness, Jungian analysis and verse-writing, Mexican mural painting, primitive rituals and games, come together in a dab, spatter, drip-and-pour technique for conjuring outward-moving forms from the individual and collective unconscious. The pictures produced from such dull elements have an inexplicable grandeur and complexity that rival the effects of the greatest calligraphic and architectonic masterpieces.

MARK ROTHKO
1903-70

Co-founder with Gottlieb of 'The Ten', an Abstract Expressionist group. Deep interest in connections between individual and general psyche, between ideas of Freud and Jung on supposed unconscious mind of person and of race. Mural painting and 'automatic' or random techniques derived from Surrealism give way eventually to a search for means of portraying the most universal human and then pantheistic images: those which have to be purged of all finite representation in order to reveal the infinite in the very 'principles and passions of organisms'. Simple transitions of tone make huge rectangular paintings throb gently and suggest a primal pulsation of organism and cosmos.

WILLEM DE KOONING
1904-

Dutch emigré. Fragmentation and vague definition of human images in uncertain pictorial domains increasingly stressed over the years. This imprecision is made almost aggressive by fierce spatter-and-dash techniques. He makes an essentially impossible attempt to define male-female differences and conflict, and to analyse gender and sexuality simultaneously.

AMERICAN ART

colour is intended to carry a message about the reality underlying the technological environment.

DAVID SALLE
1952-

A Post-Modernist 'painter of modern life' whose extremely wide-ranging collages of film stills and quotations from earlier paintings, from fine art and/or visual pap for the masses, reach back, no holds barred, to Dadaist forebears in seeking to disorientate and disconcert the viewer to the point of dissatisfaction with all previous, too well-known codes and unique enjoyment of an experience that is wholly

novel because it consists only of what is already known.

TIM ROLLINS
1955-

Rollins has proffered a challenge to the individual artist by founding a form of collective endeavour – 'Group Material', created by the 'Kids of Survival' (KOS), whose collaboration in producing a richly varied texture and structure may have socially regenerative effects.

ROBERT LONGO
1953-

Spectacular Post-Modernist drawing, completed by assistants, intended to upset and disconcert by eclectic references to urban violence, riots, commercial ruthlessnes, calling on popular images of the erotic, aggressive and technological in startling juxtapositions and establishing a kind of ritual shock.

ALLAN MCCOLLUM
1944-

'Surrogates', 'perpetual photos' and 'perfect vehicles' are 'false pictures' which beguile the viewer, entice him or her to look at their central darkness, and then cease to function. After such easily comprehensible strategies,

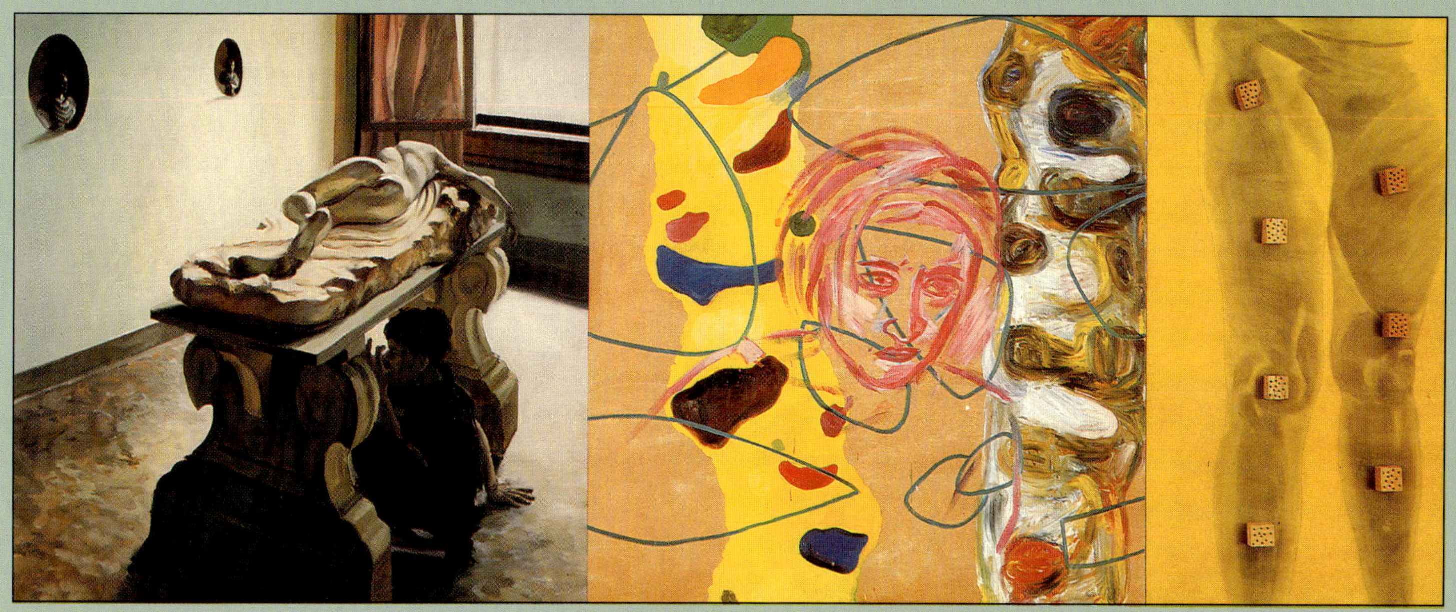

L to R: Eric Fischl, *The Sheer Weight of History*, 1982; David Salle, *Pure Difference*, 1982, oil, acrylic on canvas

these and the other modes of McCollum's work are dubiously founded on Lacanian notions and such suppositions as castration anxiety. For those, for example, who do not know that a vase stands for an 'exteriorised vulva', these and many similar works say nothing precise.

ROSS BLECKNER
1949-

Neo-Conceptual, multi-stylistic works citing a variety of art movements from Op onwards.

PHILIP TAAFFE
1955-

Quotations from unconnected painters are related to the artist's own novel contributions

in order to establish a new balance between 'tradition' and the new.

ASHLEY BICKERTON
1959-

'Painting-objects' manufactured for a state of cultural crisis. In them mock signatures are among the ironic devices which follow Dadaist forebears in refusing the viewer any illusion in the contemplation of a work of art.

MEYER VAISMAN
1960-

An art of multiple contradictions in which emotive and biomorphic themes suddenly arise to contradict an earlier notion of impersonality, and contribute to the viewer's healthy

awakening from a socially induced idea that there is one traditional way of looking at things.

ERIC FISCHL
1948-

Fischl deals with an explicit return to a form of social and psychological realism. His world is that of suburban America and he portrays the interiors, the environments, and psychological atmosphere of day to day disenchantment, longing, fantasy and ennui. Fischl looks back to the peculiarly American atmospheric realism of Edward Hopper, creating a unique sense of place and character. He is able to deal more explicitly with sexual fantasy, frustration and desire. His main theme is the American Dream: 'now we don't believe it, whereas then everything seemed totally possible.'

JIM DINE
1935-

Contributor to the rise of 'Happenings'. Paintings with objects and fragments attached move into and out of 'reality' with disconcerting indifference.

ANDY WARHOL
1928-87

The ultimate Pop artist whose self and social environment becomes his art. Publicity images, comic book characters, multiple commercial icons, and so on, are 'treated' by the artist and converted singly or as multiples into superimposed and juxtaposed, aligned and serialised art objects. Impermanence, the approximation of American man to American machine, the destruction of sensitivity through banalisation and repetition, and the artist as laid-back, turned on, decadent host and dandy, are themes for which silk screen is an apt medium of presentation.

GEORGE SEGAL
1924-

Initial paintings of large-scale nudes give way to a form of mummified sculpture in which plaster bandages are used to reproduce friends and the exteriors of figures are re-assembled and defaced in order to intensify the sense of alienation encountered among the familiar and the unknown.

PHILIP GUSTON
1913-80

Socially concerned 'Modernist muralist' who develops a private universe of strange, initially clumsy yet ultimately hieratic and stately figures with mythic pretensions. This phase is gradually undermined by an austere calligraphy, and once again abandoned for a ghostly presentation of alienated figures and distorted objects of menacing beauty.

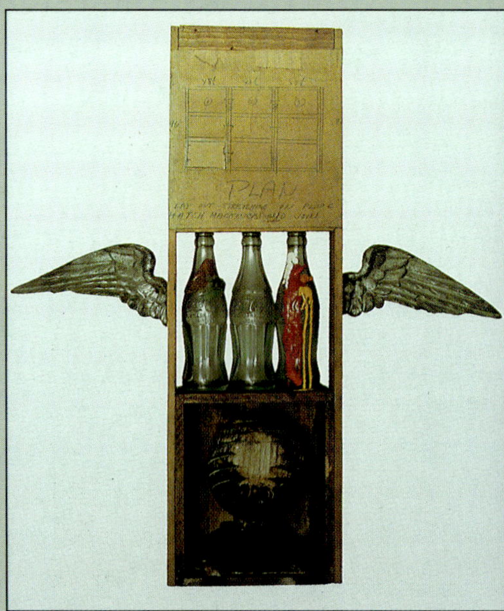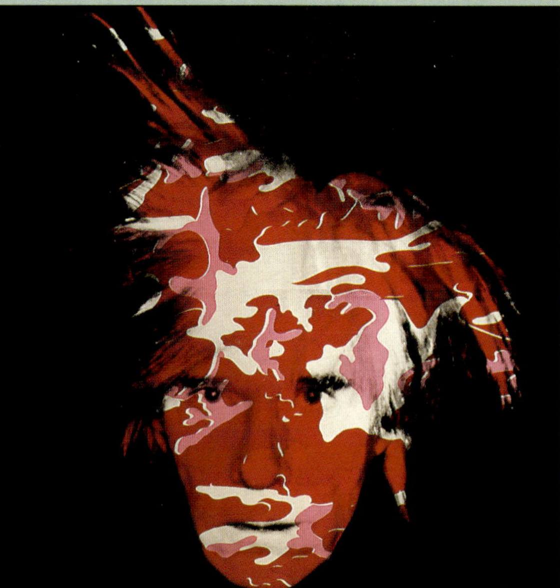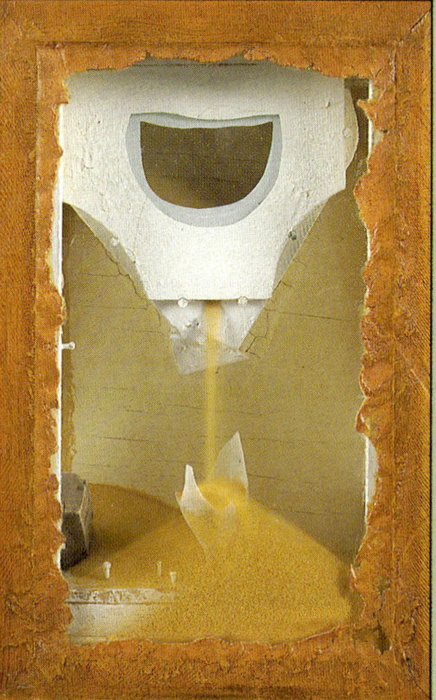

L to R: Robert Rauschenberg, *Coca Cola Plan*, 1958; Andy Warhol, *Self Portrait*, 1986, acrylic and silk-screen on canvas; Joseph Cornell, *Untitled*, 1959, box construction

LARRY POONS
1937-

Moves from grid abstraction to more random distribution of colour forms and then to poured and dripped surfaces.

JOSPEPH CORNELL
1903-73

Influenced by Surrealism and Dada, Cornell specialises in the creation of evocative boxes, with artistic and cosmic allusions, offering a toy theatre for meditation on shadows of one's own and the surrounding past.

ROBERT RAUSCHENBERG
1925-

Abstract Expressionist turned Pop artist, with interest in assemblage and the possibilities of ever-new materials. Austere backdrops for Cage's music, monochrome paintings in series, a post-Dadaist use of fragments of photographs and technological references, and of cardboard and fabric, switch from city to land, from the personal to the grand-political, so as to suggest that all citations of reality are of equal value in the assemblage.

CLAES OLDENBURG
1927-

The sculptor of American Pop art. His environments, happenings and assemblages are wry, gutsy comments on the tawdriness of the city, a violently emphatic visual slang of motels, stores, bars, giant plaster hamburgers, cigarette ends and crazy space-mixers, sometimes in more than one version, which puzzle about the reality of the Western urban world.

EDWARD KEINHOLZ
1927-

Maker of small to large assemblages which enhance a recreated environment or a commercial enclosure of the human with associated emotions and anxieties, especially the fear of decay, suffering and death.

BEN SHAHN
1898-1969

Lyrical Social Realist with a profound sense of the numinous. An implacable enemy of abstraction, he nevertheless incorporates in his postwar pictures and prints many of the devices thought proper to abstract and quasi-abstract art. His distortions of naturalistic reality serve to emphasise insults to the spirit of social justice, whether from poverty, war or nuclear fall-out. As his confidence in a comprehensive social answer to the bottomless heart of evil and to human distress fades, his themes become more personal, but also more consciously religious and even apocalyptic.

PHILIP PEARLSTEIN
1924-

Figurative Expressionist (post-abstract Realist) whose nudes are directly presented in a dry yet ultimately sad manner. They are so textured

and positioned as to deprive the viewer of easy comments on their or the artist's existence.

ANDREW WYETH
1917-

For the most part a tempera artist whose seemingly realistic narratives echo their 19th-century forerunners in general communicativeness and popularity. Inevitably ignored or patronised as tediously middle-brow by art establishment critics for some decades, the muted colour of Wyeth's pictures, the distressed condition of most of his subjects, the alienation and isolation of his figures and objects, and the subtleties of his

spatial organisation are now seen as related to the methods and concerns of his abstractionist contemporaries.

MARK TOBEY
1896-1976

From a strange combination of Oriental experiences and study of Chinese calligraphy and painting, his Baha'i faith, and practice as a fashion artist, Tobey derives a uniquely symbolic form of abstraction with an avowed goal of unifying universal space and disparate elements, and presenting the viewer with a visual equivalent of the idea that what is and what isn't are actually, and comfortably, one.

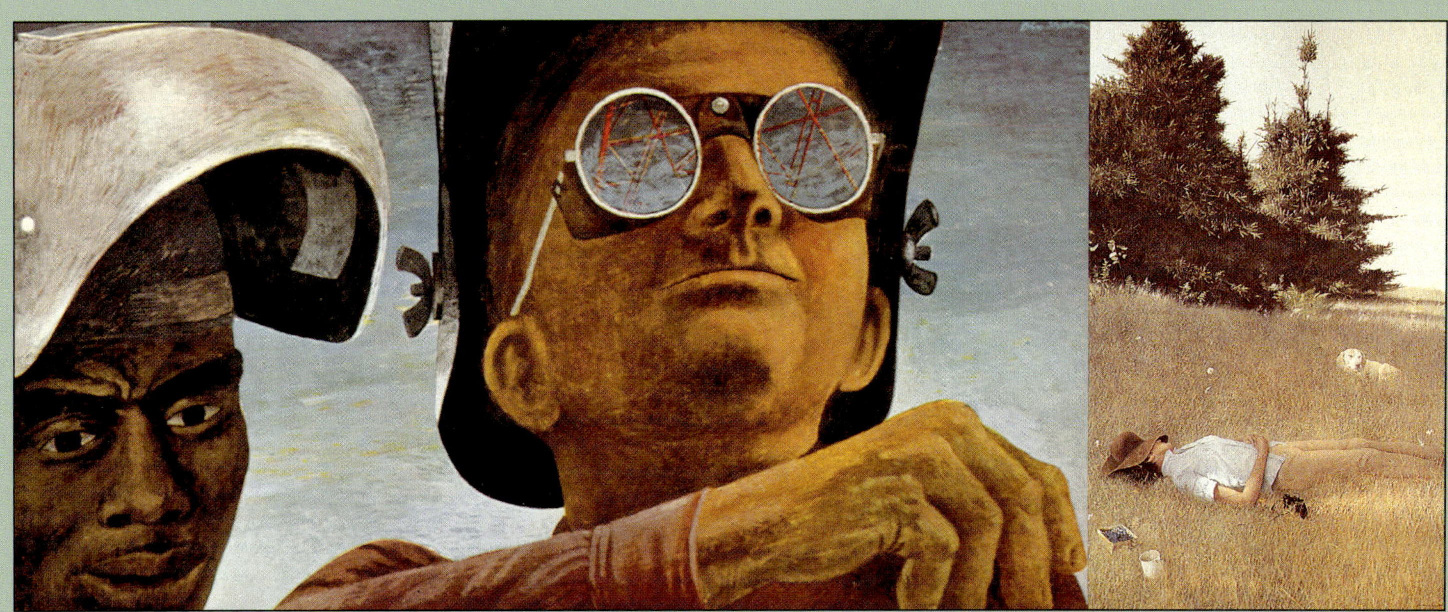

L to R: Ben Shahn, *The Welders*, 1944, tempera; Andrew Wyeth, *Distant Thunder*, 1961, tempera

GEORGIA O'KEEFFE
1887-

Austerely beautiful quasi-abstract landscape and still-life artist who continued to astonish with her individual studies of space, form and tonality right through the Abstract Expressionist era of the 40s to 60s.

BALCOMB GREENE
1904-

Prewar Hard-Edge abstractionist who evolves an oddly monumental yet distorted figuration suggesting unease.

JACK LEVINE
1915-

Highly painterly and wide-ranging critic who strangely enriches the texture of the low-life scenes he prefers. His commentaries are increasingly underpinned by traditional religious references.

LEONARD BASKIN
1922-

Above all a printmaker and illustrator. His humans and anthropomorphic animals are heroic victims portrayed with Expressionist devices that enhance and universalise both their suffering and their nobility.

SAM FRANCIS
1923-

Drip-and-trickle colourist with various modes

of 'empty centre' and stained-support painting.

HELEN FRANKENTHALER
1828

Follower of Pollock who transfers her attention to the canvas, and to intensities of blot and stain, and emptied and filled centres.

ELLSWORTH KELLY
1923-

Hard-Edge, Minimalist painter. Grid and uniformly patterned works and colour solids give way to monochrome and shaped canvases. The special achievement of Kelly's painting is to preserve a sense of order and uniformity while addressing the open-ended and chance nature of the whole, in colour and in form.

EDWARD RUSCHA
1937-

Pop and Surreal artist with unique interest in, among other devices, the evocative power of letters for the representation of commercial and mass-media trends.

MORRIS LOUIS
1912-62

An obsessive colourist using Abstract Expressionist and above all Pollockian drip-and-pour techniques in an attempt to make colour one with the support, and to achieve a pure depth-lessness: the ultimate flatness. *Veils* is a typical series title.

KENNETH NOLAND
1924-

Minimalist and 'colour painter' who draws from Abstract Expressionism an interest in the possibilities of colour gesture and structuration. Chevrons, stripes and other colour shapes are disposed so as to deprive the viewer of any sense of background.

AGNES MARTIN
1912-

Austere Hard-Edge painting with minimal colour. A special use of ruled lines said to express wilderness experiences and various states of mind, but impenetrable to the inevitably key-less viewer.

FRANK STELLA
1936-

Minimalist and archetypal 'stripe painter' concerned to make the canvas itself part of the work. Flat, neutral, highly serious essays in symmetry between boundary and inner 'content' give way to experiments with indented and unusually shaped canvases to see what interactions between overall shape and inter-

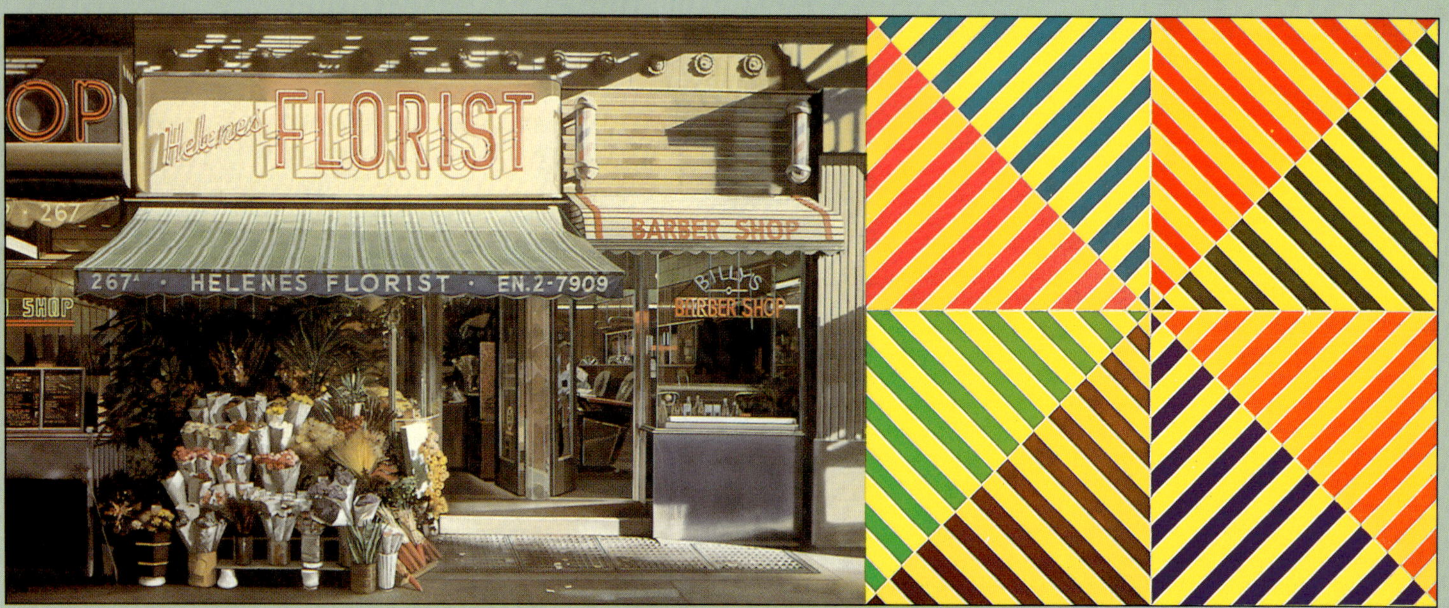

L to R: Richard Estes, Helene's Florist, 1971, oil on canvas; Frank Stella, Fez, fluorescent alkyd on canvas

nal elements may be evoked. To avoid any idea of development he banishes beginning, middle and end from his series of works, moving successfully towards variations of equal status.

JULIAN SCHNABEL
1951-

Painter who by the seemingly random attachment of fragments of objects to the support obtains a transiently beguiling pattern with a faint Dadaist element of order manufactured from chaos and destruction. The sense of showmanship and action is important for this trend.

RICHARD ESTES
1936-

Photo-realist who bases paintings (often of the urban environment) on photographs and produces the final work from a number of essays in colour. The final combination is as far as possible comment-free, and the means involved show extraordinary technical virtuosity.

SOL LEWITT
1928-

Conceptualist for whom the idea precedes the work, which is the product not of chance or of an indeterminate process, but of planning. So decided is the course of his work that apprentices can execute satisfactory LeWitts by following his directions.

ROBERT GOBER
1954-

Sculptor who follows Dadaist principles in detaching, for example, non-working sinks from their functional context in order to use them as 'suffering objects' and thus as symbols of human experience.

JEFF KOONS
1955-

Objects (for instance, a 'vest with aqualung') offer an art experience which stands in for our experience of standardised actuality.

PETER HALLEY
1953-

Geometrical abstractions with a realistic and even critical reference mediated through the choice of materials, for even the synthetic

NARRATIVE CLASSICISM

Charles Jencks

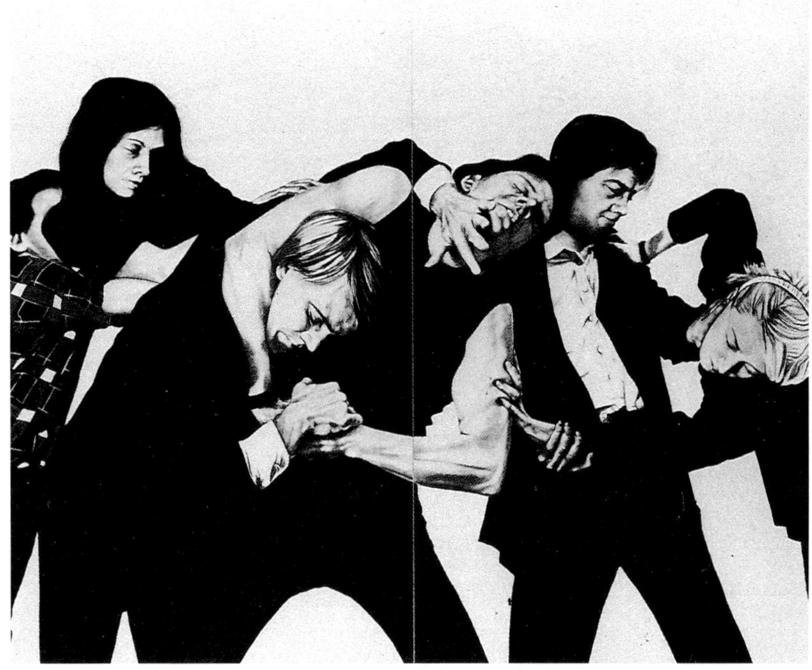

Robert Longo, *Untitled* (*White Riot Series*), 1982, charcoal, graphite and ink on paper, 95½×116″

For the longest time, roughly from 1480 to 1840, historical painting was considered the most elevated type of art within the classical tradition. Often it illustrated a significant event and pointed to a moral. At best it would show the great actions of leading statesmen, or their mythological representatives. Jacques-Louis David's *Oath of the Horatii and Death of Socrates*,

two of the best-known moralising paintings in this genre, show historical figures renouncing private duties for public virtues. Such paintings were meant to be read as uplifting moral sermons about the present, and so they were, especially just after the French Revolution when public virtue subjugated individual desires. The Reign of Terror, it is often said, was a Reign of Virtue engendered by the high-minded idealism of those such as Robespierre, Saint-Just and Jacques-Louis David.

The Aesthetic Moralists and Suggestive Narrative

Perhaps all narrative painting has an implicit moral goal, since in any recognisable plot there lurks a potential parable. In the late 18th century this implicit meaning became more explicit as artists and writers insisted on the *exemplum virtutis* — the work of art intended to teach a lesson in virtue. Historical events, usually taken from the Graeco-Roman past and filled out with classical dress and architecture, might illustrate the ideal of the chaste mother's worldly sacrifice, the uncommon charity of a Roman general, or, like Socrates taking the hemlock, some unyielding dedication to abstract beliefs.[1] These scenes should, in the ringing phrases proclaimed during the Revolution, '*Faire haïr le vice, adorer la vertu en charmant les yeux*'.[2] This elevated purpose took art above and outside aesthetics — although it was still supposed to 'charm the eye' — and set it against the decadence of Rococo

and art for art's sake. The major way it could do this was by illustrating 'the virtuous and heroic actions of great men, the exemplars of humanity who showed generosity, courage, disdain for danger, a passionate zeal for honour and the well-being of the Nation, and above all the defence of its religion'.[3] These lofty sentiments, expressed by La Font de Saint-Yenne in 1754, might appear embarrassing today to anyone apart from the 'moral majority' — and they have yet to inspire great art in this century. Patriotism and organised religion, like the belief in myths and heroes, have succumbed to moral relativity and social pluralism, at least when it comes to art. Serious artists have not tried, except in rare instances, to portray public virtues, and those few who have — the Social Realists, the WPA artists or, today, those involved in protest and mural art — have come dangerously close to creating illustration or propaganda. The social *imagination* seems either to be seduced by power or dwarfed by events such as Hiroshima. In either case it is deflected from the classical goal of imagining great men involved in noble actions. There are however some good paintings of ignoble men involved in questionable deeds, and these *do* have a didactic purpose.

Paul Georges, who has been patiently engaged in modern narrative since the 1950s, painted *My Kent State* (p 50), 1971-72, as an imaginative comment on a significant event: the brutal killing of Vietnam protestors at Kent State University. He uses here a figure of the 'muse', a strong feminine personification of freedom and the arts, which was to inspire his work for the next decade. The muse tries to flee evil, rendered explicit in the gas-masked paratrooper, while Georges holds her back; Nixon washes his hands of the whole affair over the bloodied corpse of one of the students. This combination of realism, the depiction of an important event that catalysed Americans, and the imaginative representation of artistic inspiration as a central actor in the plot – all three work to lift the painting above illustration. In *Return of the Muse* (p 50), 1969-70, Georges shows this same sexual and poetic power coming back to the artist in the midst of New York skyscrapers, and he has continued to transform this presence in a series of classical allusions: *The Mugging of the Muse*, 1974, *Venus and Cupid*, 1984, etc.

Alfred Leslie, a realist who is explicitly committed to the moral purpose of art, again makes use of Christian and classical iconography. In a cycle of paintings devoted to the death of his friend, the poet/critic Frank O'Hara, he has used traditional prosaic situations. *The Butcher Shop*, for instance, portrays a Jewish New Yorker's shop. The ethnicity is indicated by the spare lettering, but the rest of the environment is portrayed in fundamental shapes and abstract contrasts, mostly black and white. This abstraction, or generalisation, gives to the frail characters a classical dignity which they sometimes lack in Leslie's work. Often, as in the *Two Bathers*, 1983, figures and background are reduced to a Minimalist white on white, before the Greek polychromers have arrived, and the work is set in an architectural context. Poses and expression are 20th century, but distanced by generality while the foam of the water is both a particular sexual sign and an abstract set of swirls and drips.

Jack Beal, also committed to merging opposite traditions of narrative and abstraction, is not always entirely successful. His *Prudence, Avarice, Lust, Justice, Anger*, 1977-78, could be a Mannerist allegory of card-players in modern jeans who have imbibed too much Schlitz beer. The subject is plausible both as a timeless parable and a modern illustration of these traditional

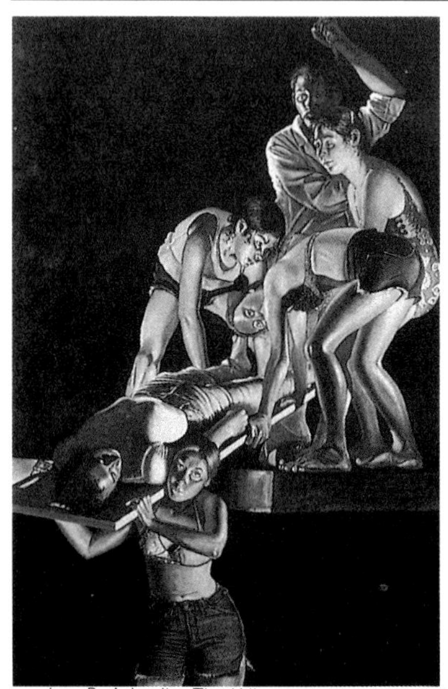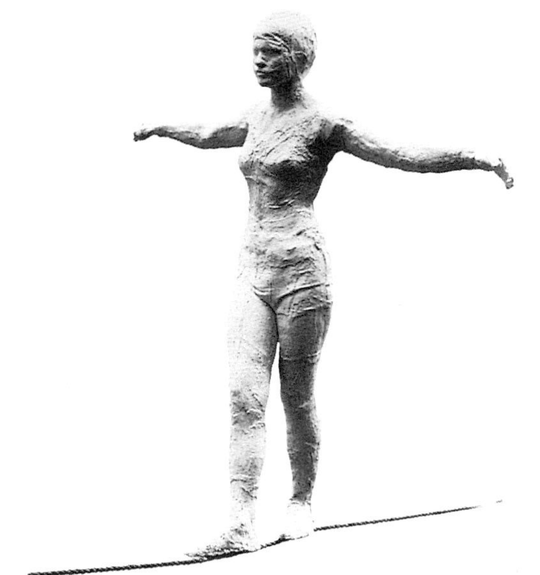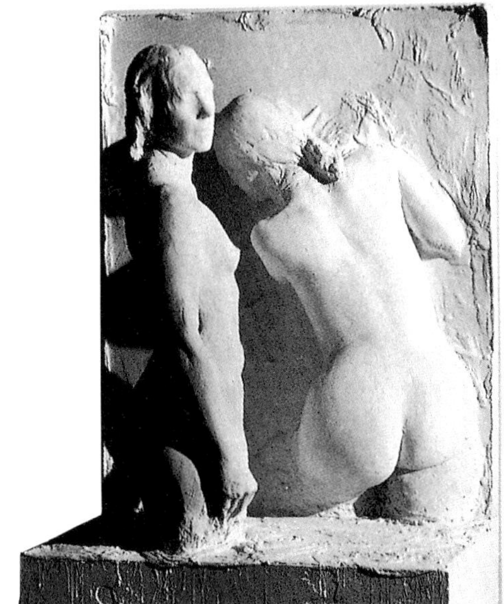

L to R: A Leslie, *The Killing Cycle IV: Loading Pier*, 1975, oil on canvas; G Segal, *The Tightrope Walker*, 1969, plaster, metal and rope; and *Two Bathers*, 1983, plaster and wood

themes – such as the deposition of Christ – in a modern context. Here young girls in bathing dress and jeans help lower the body in a compositional grouping that recalls so many Mannerist depositions from the Cross. The dramatic lighting is reminiscent of Caravaggio and is also a realistic portrayal of the night-time lighting when a beach taxi accidentally hit the poet. The other paintings in the cycle show the variety of people involved – Leslie believes in portraying all conditions of people – some of whom are reminiscent of Paul Georges' muse: that is nude women acting in a quasi-allegorical role. The problem with some of Leslie's realism is that the particularity can overwhelm the idea. When the sharp-focused eyes of his teenagers stare out from the canvas, as if caught by a flash camera, the event suddenly looses its classical *gravitas*. Leslie's intention, however, is to find a straightforward realism that can dignify democratic, ethnically diverse, everyday life.

The same intention can be seen in George Segal's plaster sculptures which often take everyday people and put them in virtues and vices. The problem is, however, that Beal's characters do not portray the depth or complexity of the classical types, but remain a dramatic, even melodramatic, illustration of the very real American models. Realism has always been one of the classical armoury's double-edged swords, respected as the ultimate goal of verisimilitude but attacked for its endless empiricism. If a painter becomes too involved in the details, colour and chiaroscuro, for instance, he will lose sight of the overall idea, the *concetto* that should guide selection.

Sometimes Jack Beal aims for generality through the illustration of details, and this is particularly true of his *Danae* (second version), 1972 (p 54). Danae, the mythic heroine who conceived Perseus in a shower of gold as she waited by the window, has been a subject for several Post-Modern Classicists, perhaps because the archetypal figure of a nude in a room full of sunlight is a natural subject for painting.[4] Beal has completed many such portraits since the mid 1960s – *Nude with Suitcase, Nude on a Red Sofa*, etc – that contrast the intimate view of a woman's body caught in raking light with a strongly textured bed cover and quilt. The build-up of richly coloured details which fold and undulate equate the skin with its surroundings and, since a strong orange glow suffuses everything, the theme of Danae is successfully suggested in terms of painting. Exaggerated and tilted perspective (a device often used by Beal) makes the room and mattress as much a part of the narrative as the musings of the two women and the supposed miraculous act of conception. One imagines that the classical subject and title were found by Beal during the process of painting; that they resulted from his commitment to realism.

James Valerio also adopts this open-ended approach towards subject matter. Some of his narrative paintings such as *The Card Trick*, 1980, are premeditated genre scenes which tell a story, but more often their plot is suggested and discovered slowly. *Studio Figures*, 1982, (p 55), came from a fascination Valerio had with a photograph he took of a man on a tightrope. This led to a drawing which suggested a Thomas Eakins painting of a modelling

statement' because the alarm clock shows four minutes to midnight (where we are according to the Committee of Concerned Scientists). One can see why this interpretation makes sense and Valerio has admitted its point.[5] There's a black (nuclear?) submarine on a glass table, a cube with a falling aeroplane, a torn photograph, the telephone (about to ring?) and Valerio's look of profound dismay as he reaches up to his staring face – again with uncertain gesture. His impotence as a painter in a nuclear age is suggested by the adjacent easel and his floating presence placed against a black void. The green velvet chair and cashmere sweater suggest how luxurious are our last four minutes.

This is perhaps as close as a painter has come to giving us 'the man of the 1980s': concerned, distracted, anxious, well-off and waiting. Although Valerio denies didactic intentions and explicitly distances himself from painters such as David, his paintings gravitate in this direction because of their lay-out and control. Even such an erotic work as *Reclining Dancer*, 1978, (p 55),

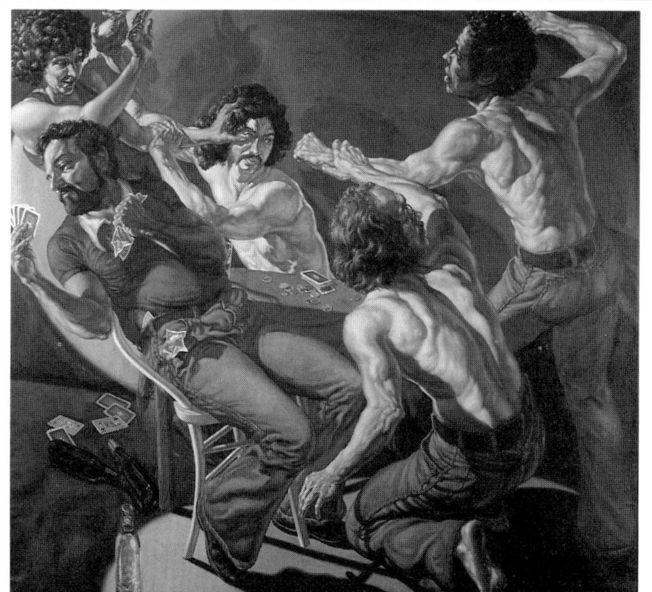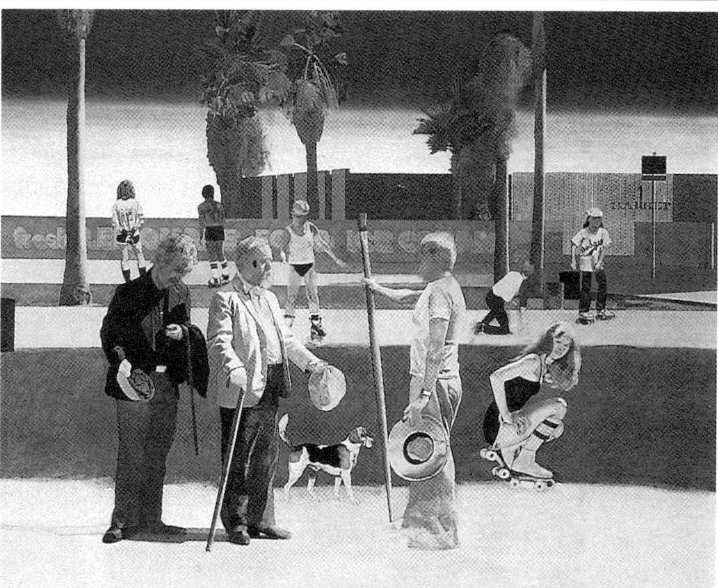

L to R: Jack Beal, Prudence, Avarice, Lust, Justice, Anger, 1977-8, oil on canvas; Peter Blake, The Meeting or Have a Nice Day, Mr Hockney, 1981-3, oil on canvas

class. Further photographs of figures that fascinated Valerio – the head emerging from the body of a swimmer, a crouching nude – were drawn and added to the composition. Slowly the narrative was built up with other figures, artist-friends, posing for the art class and Valerio himself looking tentatively out from behind a canvas. The subject remains caught between the painter's uncertain gaze and the other artists' intense concentration. A black painter wears a Mickey Mouse shirt; the kimono of the model, and the dress and faces of the female painters suggest further diverse viewpoints, both of ethnicity and purpose. The three easels are set at discordant angles and no one is paying attention to the model swimming on the floor.

We are close here to the category of Enigmatic Allegory, but the title *Studio Figures* and the realism of details, a form of Photo Realism, verge on what might instead be called the Suggested Narrative. We can guess that the story is of Valerio's uncertainty in a time of valid pluralism. He has painted a haunting *Self-Portrait*, 1981, which some critics have read as a 'closet anti-nuclear

suggests the Neo-classical tradition through the spare background, frontal layering and one-point perspective. What is the narrative here? A jumping cat suggesting the danger of the woman's fickle libido? The afternoon light and her stretching towards it suggest that she is about to act. No doubt Valerio wants to suggest many scenarios and consciously loads his canvases with meaningful details that spin the viewer from plot to plot. Some of the elements are actually called 'decoys' and are meant to pull in the mind's eye as much as the different easels and paintings within paintings.

Michael Mazur in *Incident at Walden Pond*, 1978-79, (p 54), has produced one of the great narrative paintings of our time. Again, imaginative suggestion is used as a very positive aspect of the context. Has there been a rape or murder? Is the fleeing figure towards whom the runners gesture the criminal, or has he disappeared into the space of the viewer? The violence and heat of the drama are increased by the punctuation of trees and light, the way streaks of colour fall across the contorted faces, the way the calm of the pond is broken by the staccato of tree trunks. Indeed, the extremely wide-angle view and the fact that there are three stages of this painting increase our pursuit of the solution and the heat of the chase. And then there are the extraneous details, so real in everyday tragedies: the panting dog, the unconcerned jogger, and the domesticated suburban landscape of Walden Pond. These dramatically gratuitous elements remain in the background to give added weight to the foreground event, to give it that odd psychological twist which Dostoyevsky has shown to so often accompany criminal acts. Finally, the combination of elements from traditional iconography (for instance the pietà scene to the right) adds a resonant mystery to this unnamable crime.

The master of Suggested Narrative on a public level is certainly David Hockney who has managed to evolve a sad, accessible gaiety with which many people can identify. Few artists could attempt such pretty painting without becoming trivial, but Hockney has managed to give this taboo genre a special wistful

anything of importance concerning Michelangelo. Of more substance, and more direct classical lineage, are *A Bigger Splash*, 1967, *Mr and Mrs Clark and Percy*, 1970-71, and *Contra-Jour in the French Style*, 1974. All three are frontally layered, well-proportioned paintings which owe much to the classical tradition, especially its use of architecture to frame action and give it a noble permanence. The action may be absent (the splash) or private (Mr Clark's vulnerable nervousness) but the scene and geometrical harmony are reminiscent of Piero and the classical sensibility in general.

Hockney might not claim this pedigree for himself as he was hardly trained in the full academic tradition. His subject matter remains modest and sometimes provincial, but it is a provinciality nourished on the Western tradition. As if to show that he is a self-trained amateur in the classical tradition his debts are often explicitly acknowledged with a written label, or title of a book. Thus one can find small quotes in his work alluding to Picasso, Michelangelo or, in one of his most moving series, *My Parents*,

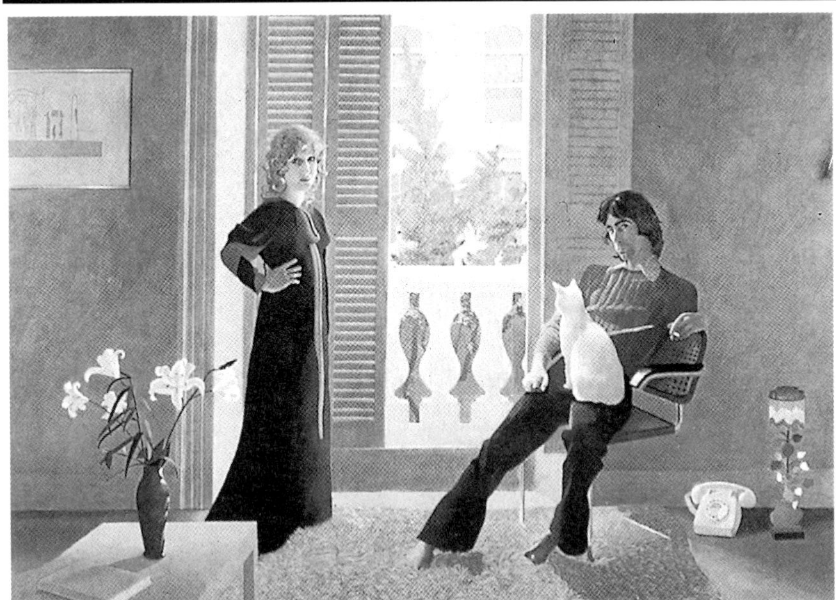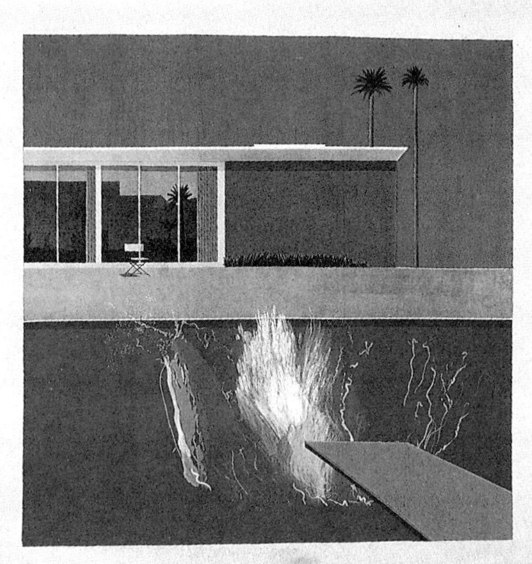

David Hockney: *Mr and Mrs Clark and Percy*, 1970-1, acrylic on canvas (*left*); *A Bigger Splash*, 1967, acrylic on canvas (*right*)

stamp. Prettiness, like quaintness, has been a term of opprobrium for Modern artists since before the First World War. However for Hockney, and some other painters who were connected with Pop art, an ornamental prettiness is a natural part of one's mental environment. Many of their narrative paintings take place in beautiful settings, whether Los Angeles, Provence or cleaned-up studio bedrooms. With Hockney such settings have become so conventionalised that even restaurants have started incorporating the look: it might be called 'Habitat-Hockney' after the formula made famous by Terence Conran, Design Research and other purveyors of minimalist good taste.

There is a lot of room for Suggestive Narrative in this environment and occasionally it is even literary and classical. In *Homage to Michelangelo* two similar women cross paths while T S Eliot's lines are scrawled near Michelangelo cartoons drawn on the wall: 'In the room the women come and go / Talking of Michelangelo'. The drawing is just as evocative and daunting as Eliot's lines, especially since these women are not about to say

1977, (p 58), to Piero and Chardin. The humble atmosphere of this portrayal – the spartan A-frame of the furniture, the bent figure of his father attentively and awkwardly reading, the resigned repose of his mother, the carefully tidy trolleyscape – are all ironic and timeless images which fall somewhere between the heroism of David's revolutionary figures and the realism of Courbet. One can see why Hockney is the heroic subject of Peter Blake's *The Meeting*, 1981-83, and the sometime mock-heroic subject of Ron Kitaj's brush. He has again discovered that modesty and prettiness can be as real as austerity and ugliness. However, if his Suggestive Narratives remain domestic, then their moral and political purpose also remain underdeveloped.

This is not true of Ron Kitaj's work, which is the most deeply serious of the Post-Modernists' on a moral and political level. Here, such issues are dealt with imaginatively and in all their complexity. Kitaj avoids treating historical events either as illustration or private myth, two of the most obvious failings of so much narrative painting, and he can insert a personal and moral figure into a historical situation without becoming banal or simplistic. For instance his epic *Juan de la Cruz*, 1967, which concerns a negro helicopter pilot flying in Vietnam, suggests violation, passions and destruction without making them melodramatic. Thus the pilot is allowed to convey a classical dignity even though surrounded by acts of outrage committed on women – an ambiguous and powerful allegory of war.

Much of his later painting also deals with serious issues, both domestic and political, and such significant figures as Walter Benjamin and the poet Cavafy. His first ambitious attempt at a synthesis, *If Not, Not*, 1975-76, (p 59), is based on *The Wasteland* of T S Eliot not only in part of its subject matter, but also in its fragmentary references. Survivors of war crawl through the desert towards an oasis, survivors of civilisation (Eliot himself) are engaged in quizzical acts, some with representatives of an exotic culture. Lamb, crow, palm tree, turquoise lake and a Tuscan landscape, consciously adapted from the classical tradition, resonate with common overtones. They point towards a

suggested in Kitaj's *Rise of Fascism*, 1975-79. Three women, hardly the classical Three Graces, display attitudes to which the title of the painting points in different ways. The central figure, a fat, false blond reminiscent of the fascist types depicted by Grosz and Beckmann, strides menacingly towards the dark beachline. The bodies and sea immediately recall classical prototypes including Titian's *The Rape of Europa*. But here the violence is ambiguous and coupled with an attractive sensuality. A middle-aged figure, a model or prostitute, looks up in a dazed lethargy, the frame of mind that allows fascism, while the suave, rich vixen, exposing her sex, seems to be part Egyptian sphinx, part whore. At the upper left a phallic bomber, presumably another fascist presence, looms out of the sky threatening the three women. The sensuality of the paint and pastel nicely underscores the shape of the bodies. One's eye is led from area to area, rather like a lapse-dissolve in film, in search of the meaning. And, in so far as this is public, it concerns the archetypes which may lead to fascism: sensual decadence, inattentive passivity, explicit display

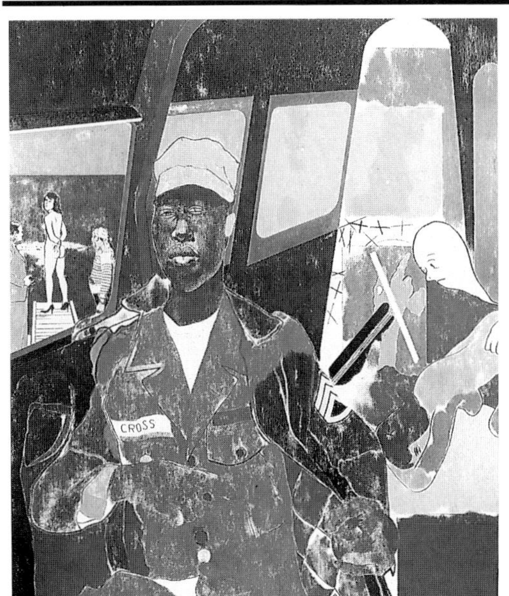
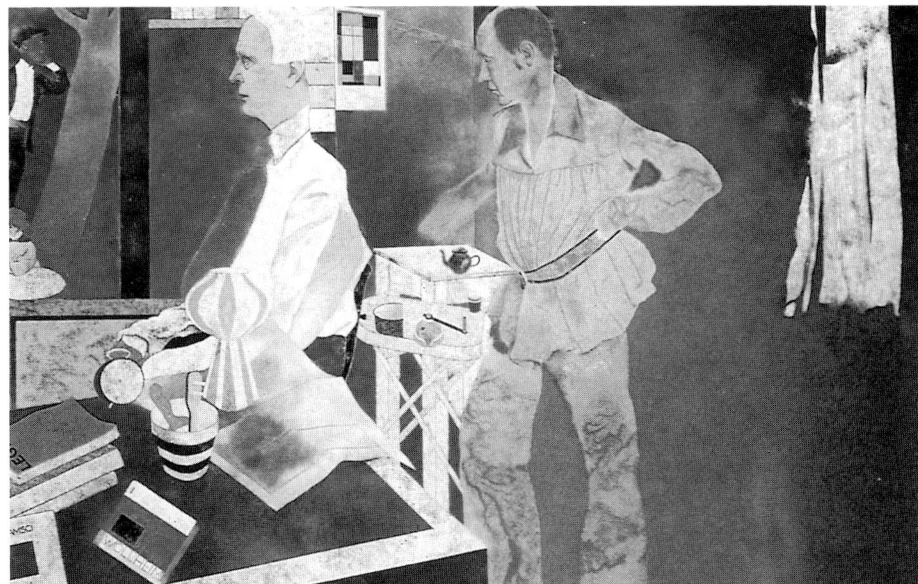

R B Kitaj: *Juan de la Cruz*, 1967, oil on canvas (*left*); *From London (James Joll and John Golding)*, 1975-7, oil on canvas (*right*)

Western and Christian background overlaid by Modernism – the cult of primitivism and disaster. The classical barn/monument at the top, so reminiscent of the work of the Italian architect Aldo Rossi and of other Post-Modern face buildings, is suggestive also of death camps. Indeed, the burning inferno of the sky, the corpse and broken pier, the black and truncated trees all suggest life after the Second World War: plural, confused and tortured on the whole, but containing islands of peace (and a search for wholeness?). The title, with its double negative, was taken from an ancient coronation oath: 'We who are as good as you swear to you who are no better than we, to accept you as our King, provided you observe all our liberties and laws; but if not, not ...'[6] This curious oath, combining the opposites of monarchy and democracy in extreme contrast, underscores the tentative nature of the artist's commitment to society. If the State or its representatives break the rules then the artist, and we, can break our allegiance.

This double negative attitude towards leadership is also

and power.

This interpretation is inferential rather than public or conventional, as didactic, historical painting would have been in the Renaissance. But the work has both dignity and monumentality: it conveys a grandeur of decadence with a high moral purpose – however much the latter may be obscured by intentional ambiguities. Kitaj characterises the intellectual's moral dilemma in the 20th century when confronted by oversimple alternatives which demand total commitment. In refusing to simplify, or to back away from depicting the dilemma, he produces the most suggestive of narratives which allows competing readings.

The Autumn of Central Paris (After Walter Benjamin), 1972-73, is ambiguous in title and make-up. The Jewish writer Walter Benjamin is shown sitting at a café not long before he committed suicide. Other archetypal figures can be inferred: a fascist in black leather, the caricature of 'reds under the bed' in the foreground, a gangster and an intellectual. All these figures press into a tight space which also appears to hold the broken windows of Notre

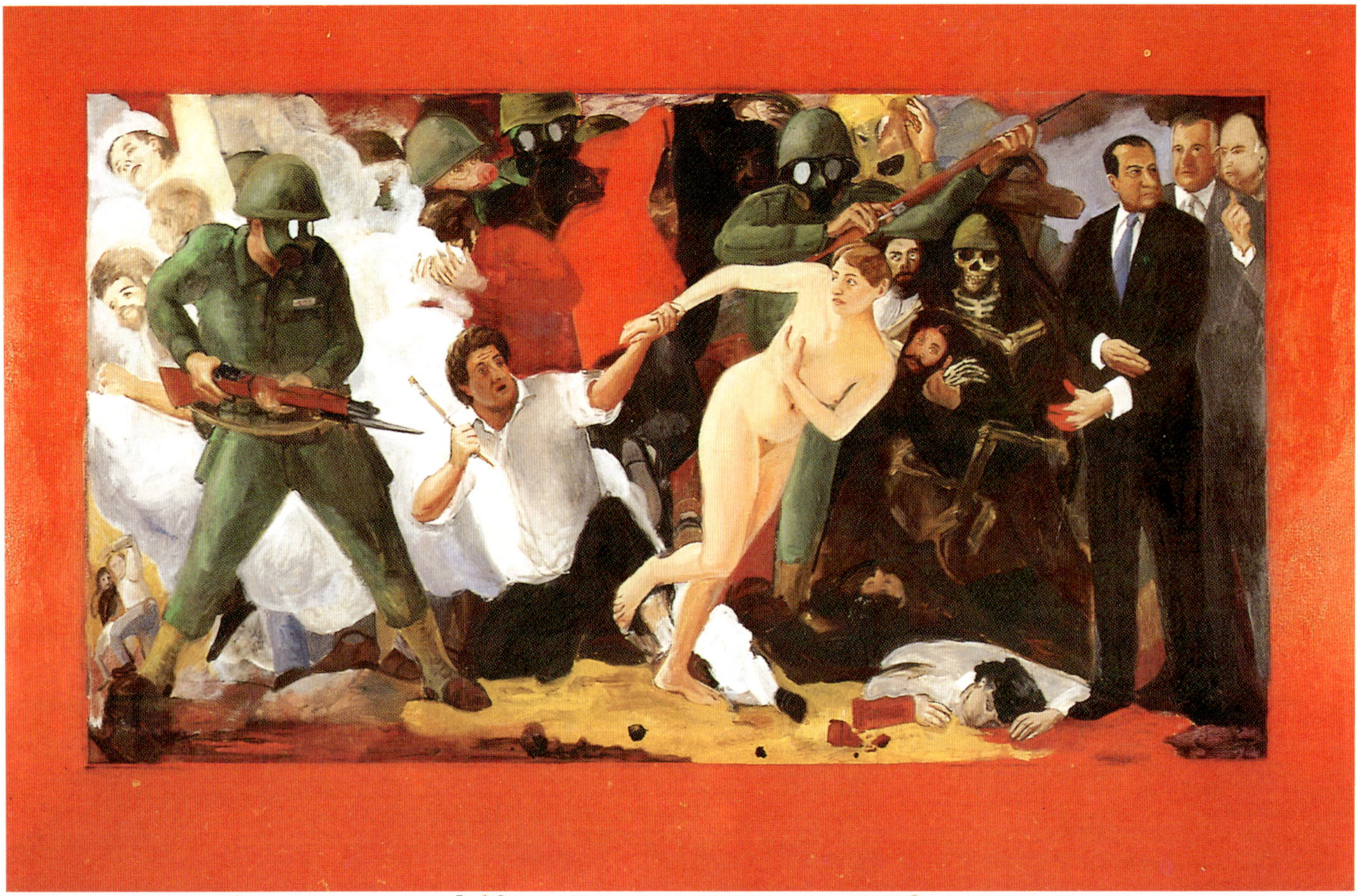

Paul Georges, *My Kent State*, 1971, oil on canvas, 92×104"

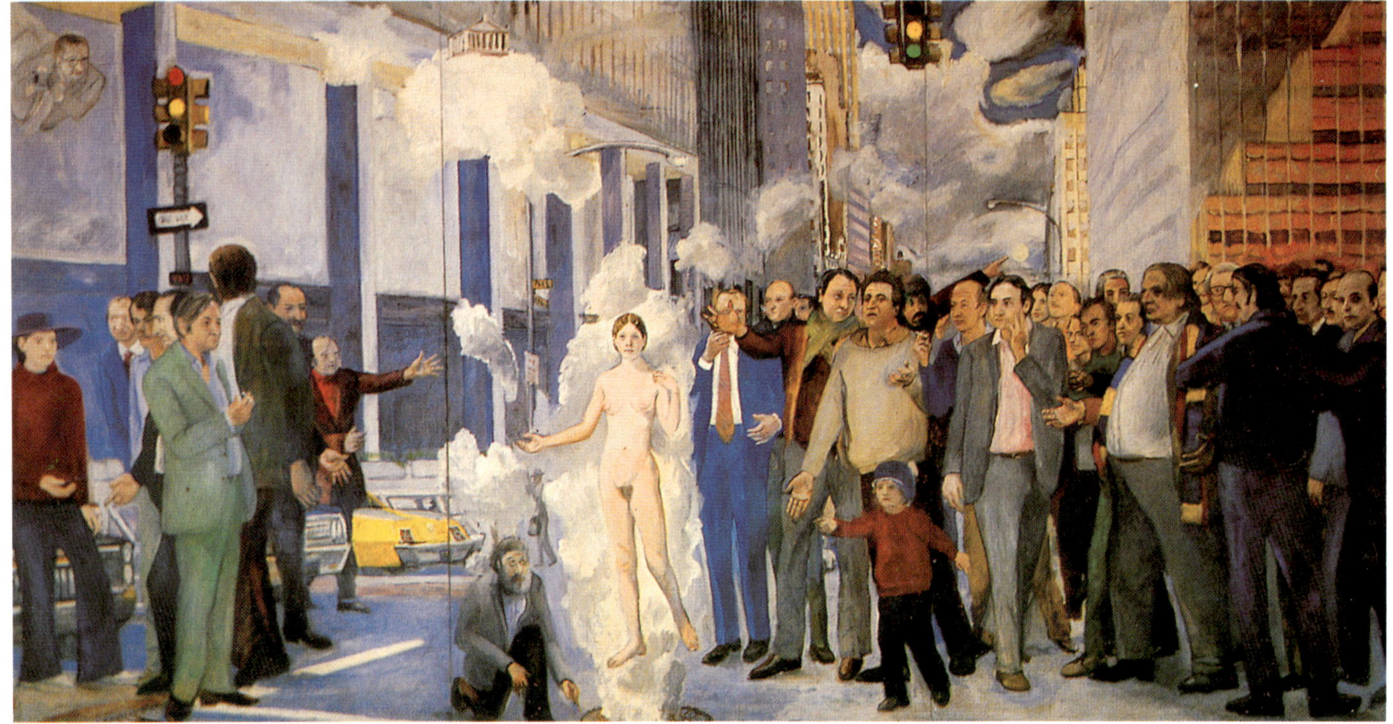

Paul Georges, *Return of the Muse*, 1969-70
oil on canvas, 10×20"

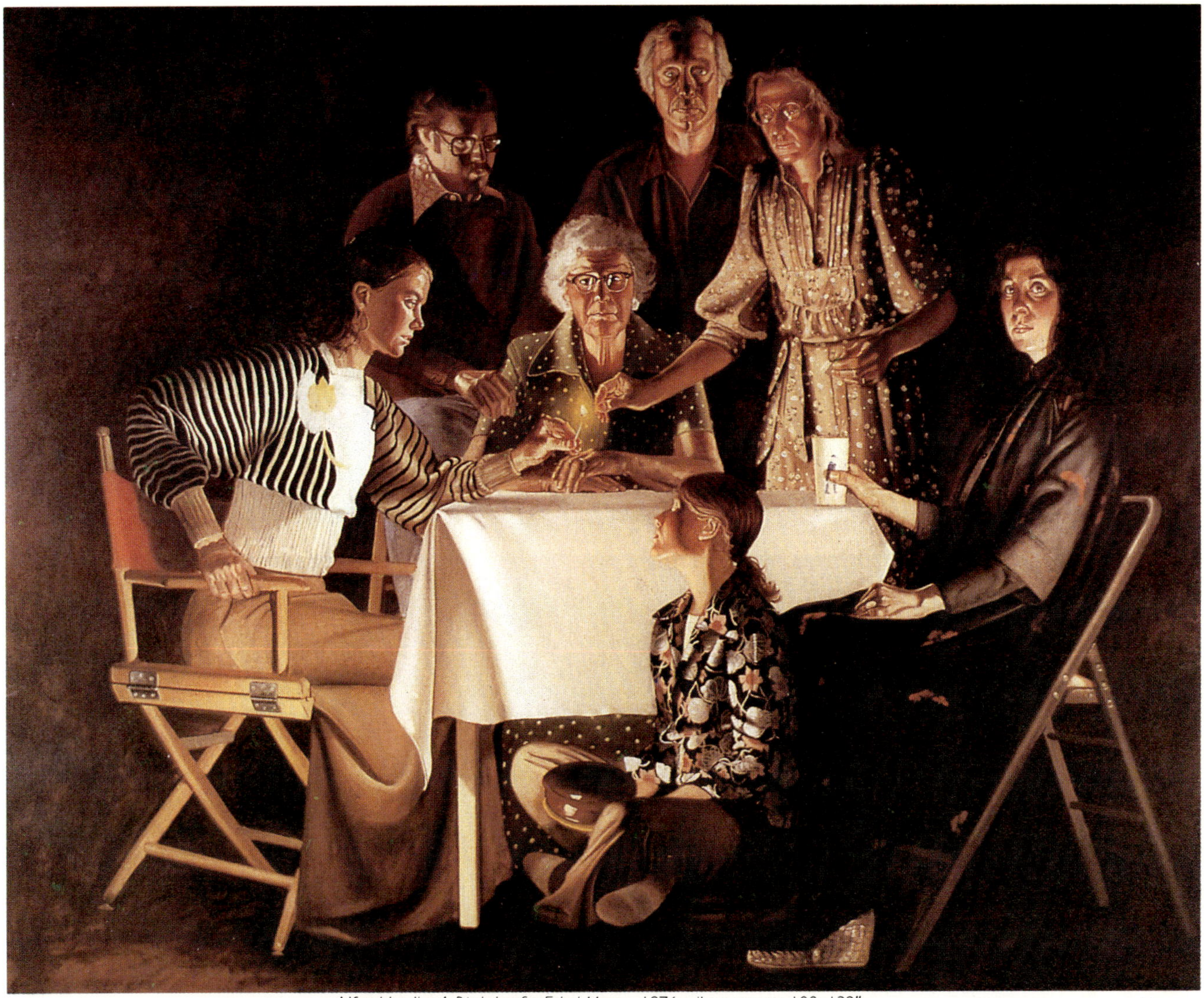

Alfred Leslie, *A Birthday for Ethel Moore*, 1976, oil on canvas, 108×132"

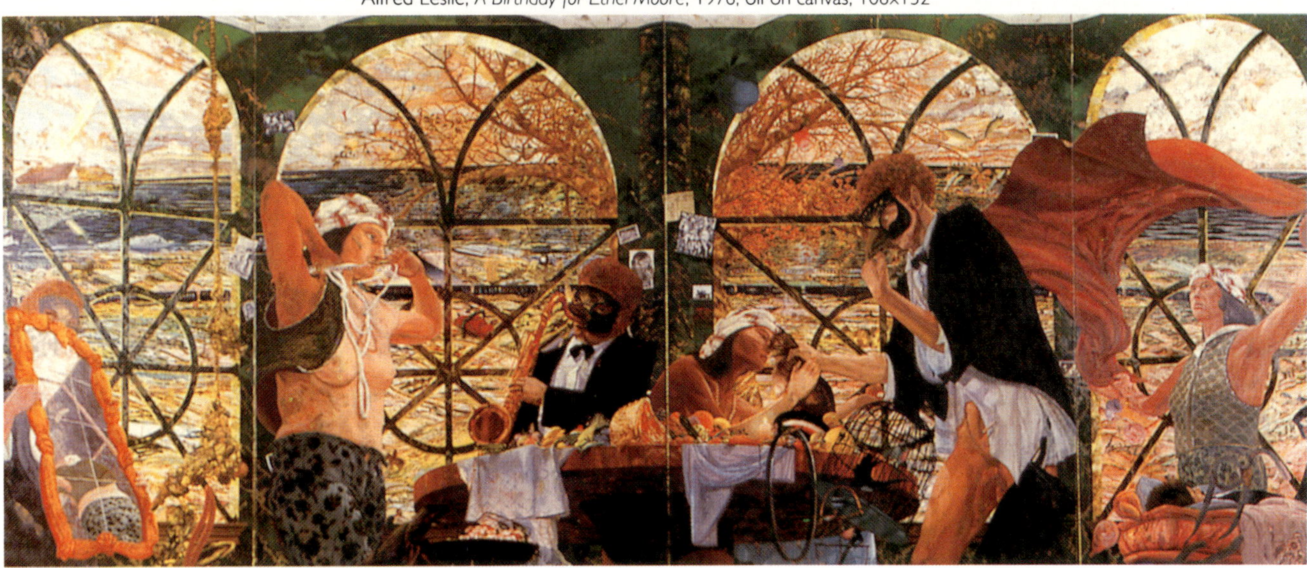

James McGarrell, *Travestimento*, 1980
oil on canvas, 96×226"

Dame (?) and a café awning. The montage technique is used with flat graphic boldness, loud colours and a subtle, blurred *sfumato* which together create a violent mixture of moods. The eclectic, politically charged café life of Paris 1940 is reflected in the clash of styles. Just what is going on in this Suggestive Narrative is not clear beyond the general confrontation of the intellectual with rising European thuggery. Kitaj presents his view of the world as a struggle between 20th-century heroes (the writers and philosophers in exile) and villains (the leaders of organised violence). As with Paul Georges, or Ian Hamilton Finlay, the good and bad are clearly cast. Kitaj does not have recourse to classical mythology, but the consistency and depth with which he presents the implicit allegory place him closer to the great tradition of historical painters, to Raphael, Poussin and David, than many of those who use the classical style. Kitaj revives its spirit while bending its language in an Expressionist direction.

Erotic and Subversive Classicism

and taboo as forms of Subversive Classicism to challenge conventional notions of art and morality.

James McGarrell, a Midwestern artist in his fifties, has painted an elaborate narrative of 20th-century debauchery. *Travestimento*, 1980, has so many allusions and layers of narrative that one can read it as a meticulous detective story about art history and affluent society. Men, half-dressed in black tie and masks, play music and sport with women. The tuxedo finds an echo in the tiny photograph of Max Beckmann stuck on the pillar to the right, *Self Portrait in Tuxedo*, 1927: the artist is here the detached, tough, urban dandy. Above this is another photograph, this one of the Dionysian initiation ceremony in the Villa of Mysteries in Pompeii. The Roman figure who drops her veil in apprehension as she dances (?) or flees (?) from flagellation finds an echo in McGarrell's figure who spreads her flowing red cape over the central action – an orgiastic last supper where women in pearls caress a cat or expose their unhealthy sunburns. The Pompeiian frieze, representing a marriage ceremony or mystic ritual, is the classical

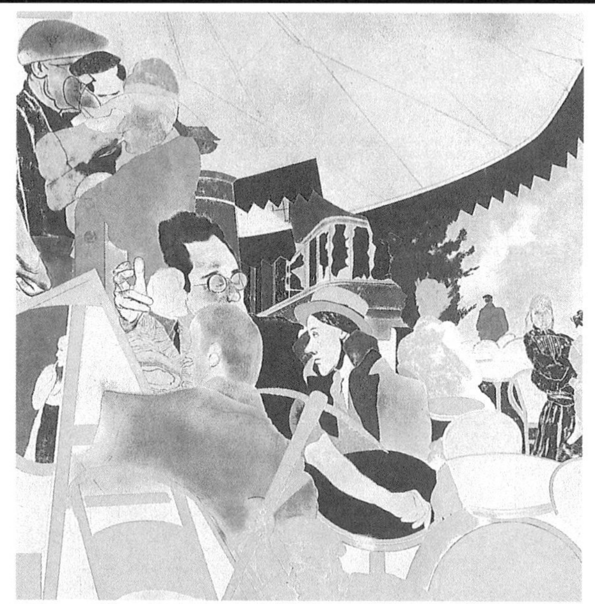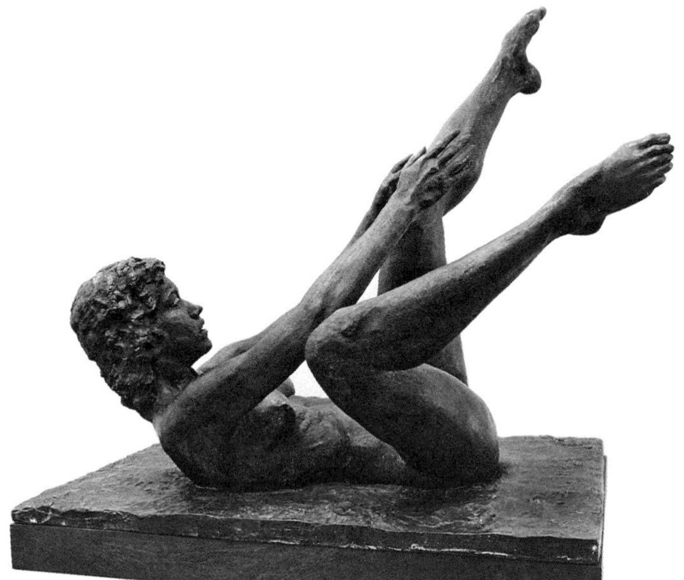

L to R: R B Kitaj, *The Autumn of Central Paris (After Walter Benjamin)*, 1972-3, oil on canvas; William Crozier, *Marilyn*, 1975-8, bronze

If the subject of narrative painting often poses a problem in an agnostic age there is one issue which remains eternally real and attractive: eroticism. The painter's muse is often personified as an appealing woman, as Paul Georges reminds us, and the human body is a perennial metaphor for investigation, as current architects have shown us.[7] When all else fails there is sex and gossip, as the tabloids prove. This would seem to be rather arid territory for classicists to investigate, but they have always kept an eye on it. Not only have erotic situations been portrayed in almost every period of classicism, but in some eras, notably the Pompeiian, sexual appetites in the ordinary burghers' houses are celebrated and lampooned as a matter of course. Classicism and sensuality have been willing partners since the Egyptian ithyphallic Min gave his fertility blessing to the Pharoahs of the Old Kingdom and it is only relatively recently, since the 17th century and the French Academy, that they've gone separate ways. Thus their present reunion, especially in an eclectic manner, is bound to cause a double resistance. Some artists even use sexual innuendo

counterpart to McGarrell's work with its similar subject matter and similar objects of mirrors and masks. For instance to the far left of *Travestimento* a masked figure holds a mirror revealing the dancer's back and a phallus suspended on a string. In the background are further postcard references to erotic and religious themes, also taken from the wider classical tradition.

The density and disturbing juxtaposition of so much colourful detail remind one of those traffic jams in hell that Hieronymus Bosch loved to paint. Here too the mind and eye can rove into the far distance finding one horizon after another, cars bigger than cypress trees, trains and boats travelling irrationally over each other, the whole pastoral landscape so rich with produce as to drive the inhabitants mad. Red and blue apples float miraculously through the window towards the viewer, the malachite green arcade and floor seem to fall away as the ground outside rushes up. These disorientations and the multiple horizons work effectively to heighten what is already a very disturbing and raucous orgy.

This is not exactly an *exemplum virtutis*, an example meant to teach a lesson in virtue, yet one can read into it moral attitudes towards consumption and play; after all the party is hellishly overripe, in its second day perhaps, and the pleasure is beginning to become a torture. We could call this the Suggestive Ethical; a counterpart to the Enigmatic Allegory on the moral plane. Even Erotic Classicists intending to promote a more open sexuality have an ethical strain to their work. William Crozier's bronzes, for instance, show women on bed-like plinths aggressively offering themselves to men in a way which could be interpreted as insisting on feminine sexuality. Such frank expression of desire has not been seen often since Roman sculpture, and the few examples usually portray male lust. Crozier's work, somewhat reminiscent of Rodin, is usually explicit in its narrative of sexual desire and intercourse and, as a result, somewhat limited in its range of meaning.

The artist who has been criticised and even attacked by feminists for his portrayal of women's sexuality, Allen Jones, is in

Dancers are always falling into embraces or bent over in a provocative pose, or tied up in a corset to accentuate their shape; some wear phallic masks, as with McGarrell, and the men seem to be having a pretty miserable time. For the most part they crawl around on the ground with dunces' caps pulled over their eyes, or play a banjo, like Father Time, as they gaze longingly at the happy, voluptuous women in their prime. In fact Jones' women are eternally twenty-five and beautiful, a race of robust Amazons taken from the pages of *Vogue* and undressed, never at a loss for dominating men's desires. The enigmatic figure in *Night Moves* of the crucified mermaid in a green rubber suit is one of the few victims of pleasure. More often the moral of a Jones party is that women rule society by manipulating male desire. Although the message emerging is ambiguous and not didactic, it may be that these are then, on the whole, 'examples meant to teach a lesson in virtue', which is one reason why their sensuality has proved so provocative.

There are two younger American artists who use sexuality in a

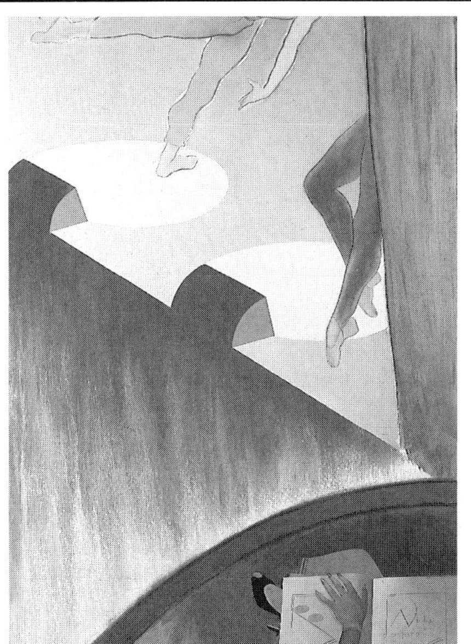

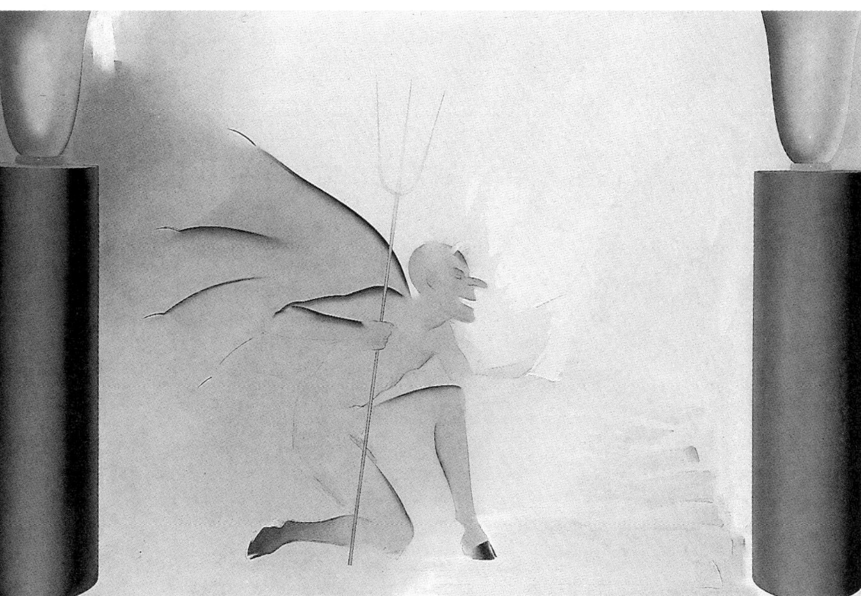

Allen Jones: *Counterpoint*, 1980, oil on canvas, (*left*); *Enunciation*, 1978-9, oil on canvas (*right*)

fact much more subtle and complex in his narrative. It is true his women still show the stylisation of a fetish – the curvaceous and shiny leg ending in an ultra high heel – but these are now absorbed into a greater narrative which includes men. Jones' series of party paintings and lithographs done in 1984-85 show a development in his work towards a richer handling of paint and subject matter. In *Night Moves*, 1985, one can see the iconographic motifs built up from several different sources including Poussin, Kitaj and Jones' own past work. Here the kneeling waitresses and dancers of previous paintings are blended together into the synchronic space of colourful dreams. Flat graphic forms merge into decorative patterns, outlined caricatures and then modelled, three-dimensional shapes. The notion of the artist as the outsider, the voyeur at the party, is suggested by the draughtsman and the man with the flashlight crawling on the floor. What is the typical Allen Jones party – is it like McGarrell's frenetic and unhappy orgy? On a painterly level it is much more sensual and involving, if less detailed and precise.

similarly provocative manner: David Salle and Eric Fischl. Salle has cultivated a very urbane way of representing stereotypes, taken from the mass media and the world of art, which has affinities with Jasper Johns' early classicism, such as the *Target with Boxes*. Parts of the human body, usually the erogenous zones, are fragmented and recombined in a diptych as part of an enigmatic collage. *The Cruelty of the Father*, 1983, (p 62) shows poses taken from 'How to Draw' manuals and mass-circulation magazines like *Penthouse*, overlaid with splotches of abstraction and a nervous map outline; this is then contrasted with the representation of a Joan Crawford head stuck unnaturally on top of the water, as if left there by an absent-minded swimmer. What cruelty is this? What father? To understand any one of Salle's paintings one has to understand their overall meaning since, like the film techniques they use and comment on, they are slices from a larger narrative.

The basic text concerns middle-class life as seen through television, newspapers and glossy monthlies. This is a nonsensical life as Salle portrays it; full of glamour, disjointed sex and violence.

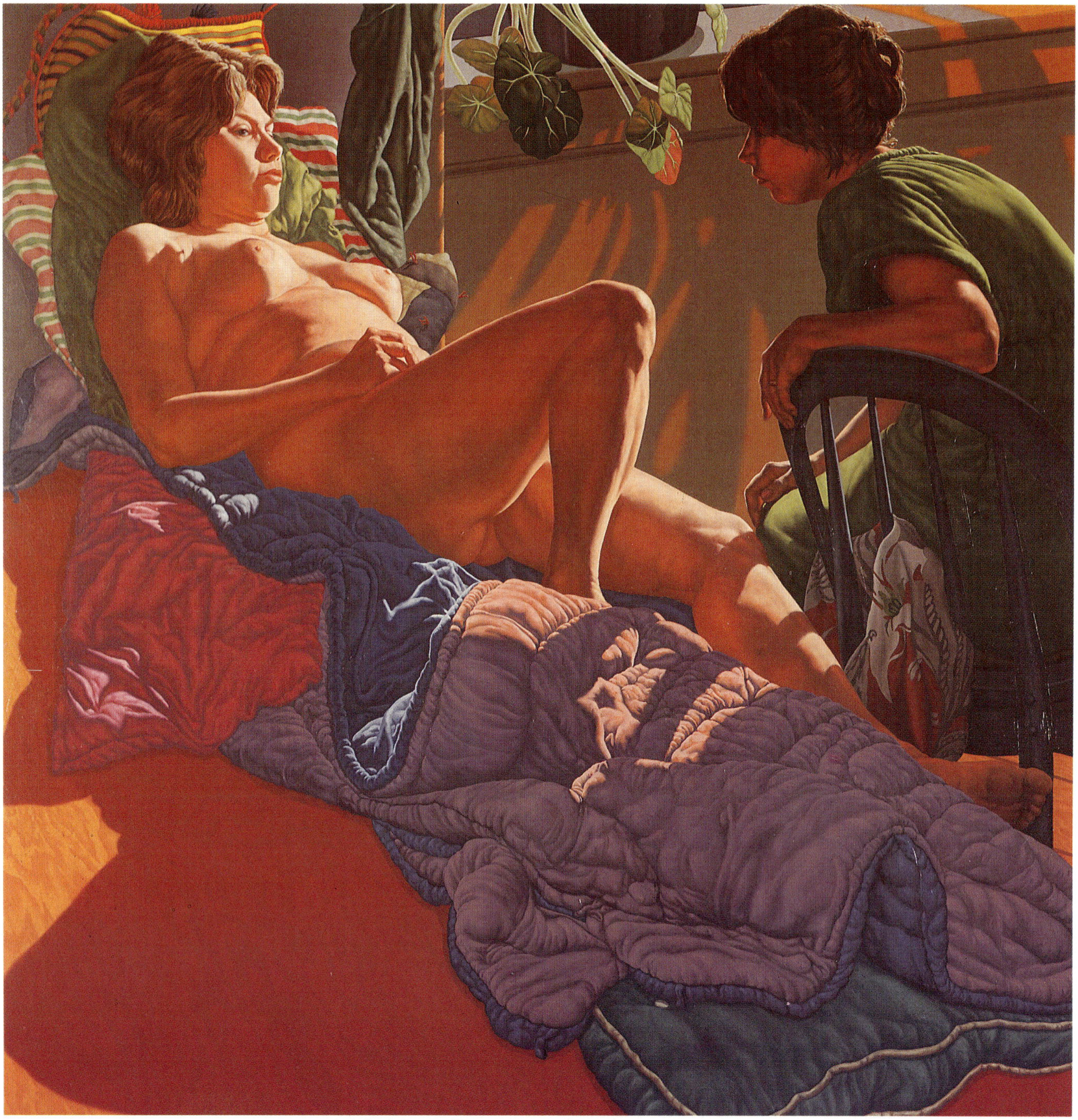

Jack Beal, *Danae, (Second Version)*, 1972, oil on canvas, 68×68"

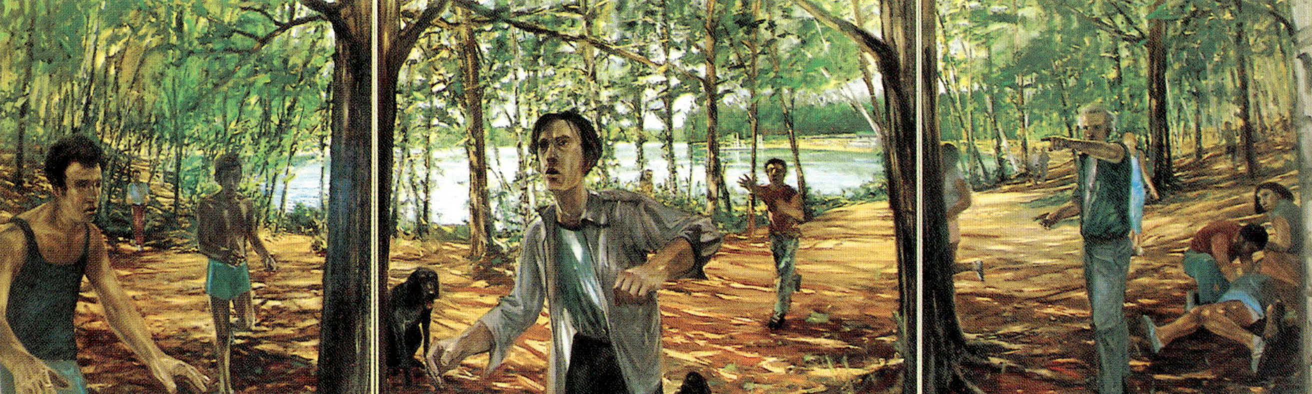

Michael Mazur, *Incident at Walden Pond*, 1978-9, oil on canvas, triptych, 48×150"

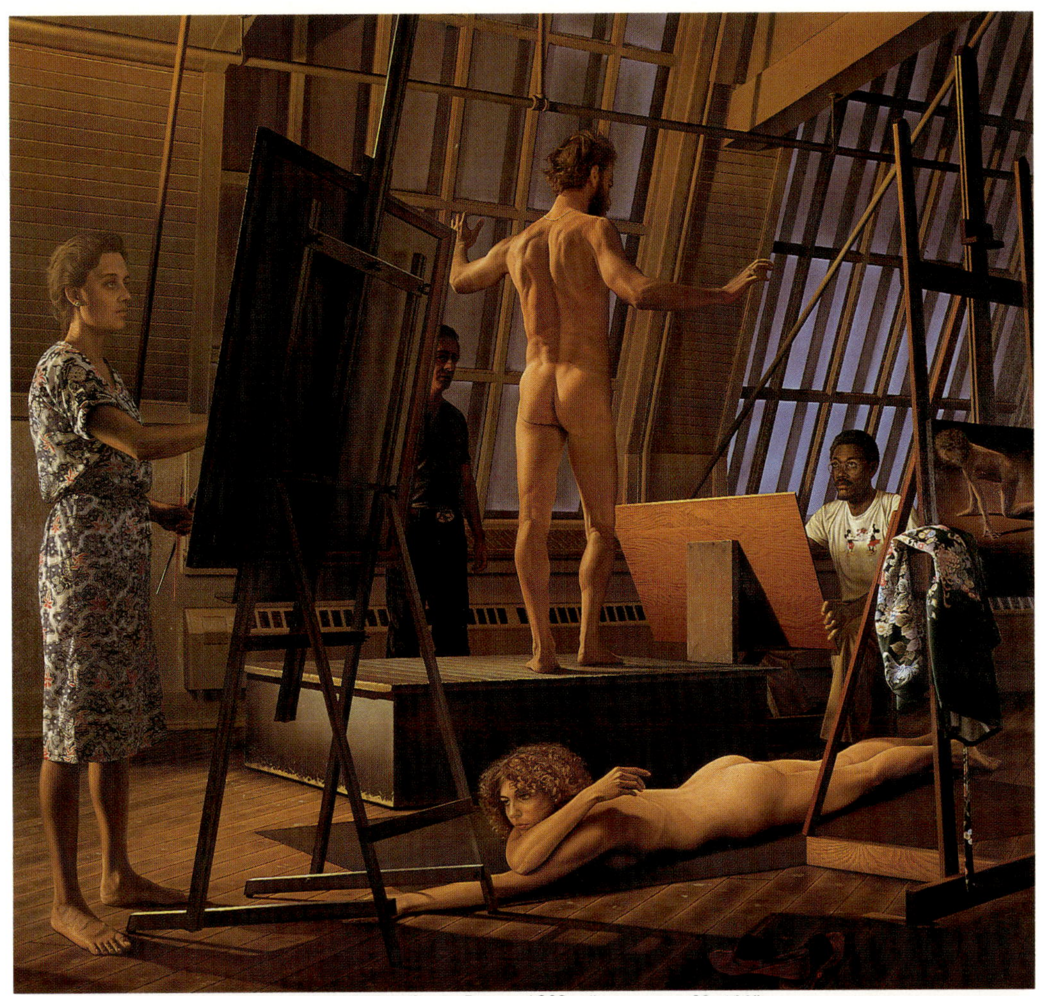

James Valerio, *Studio Figures*, 1982, oil on canvas, 92×100″

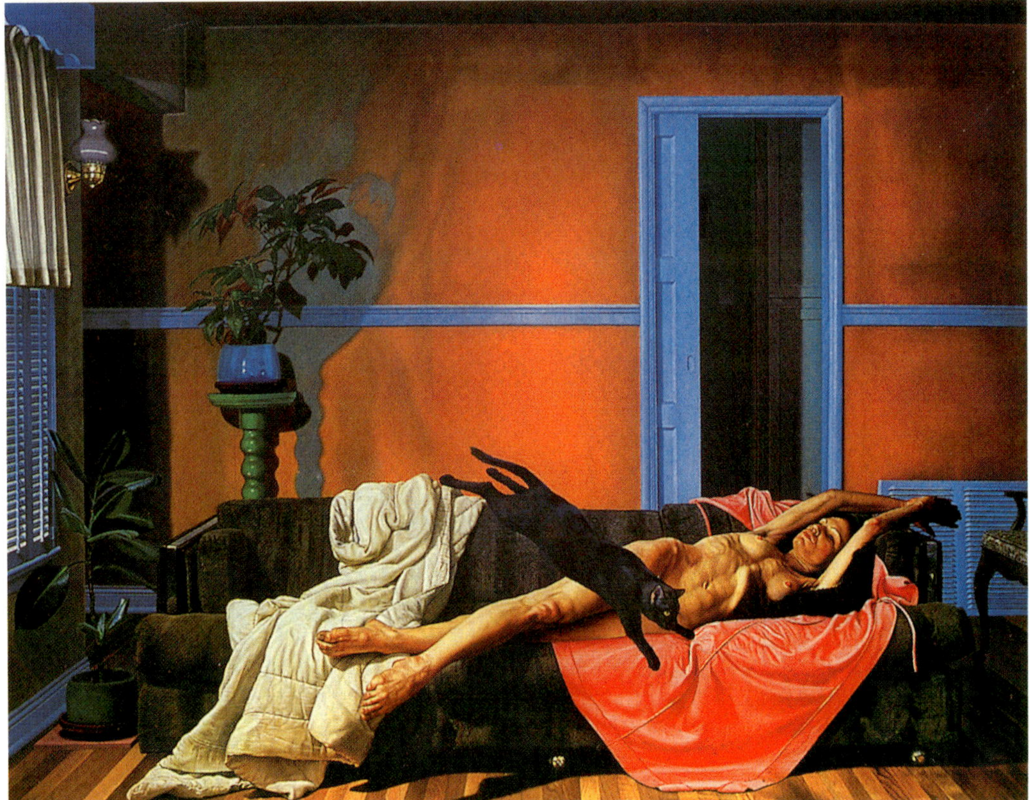

James Valerio, *Reclining Dancer*, 1978, oil on canvas, 84×100″

These three elements, as reduced to the media image or sometimes a comic strip, are the characters of the story. Disparity is the key, as in *Burning Bush*, 1982, (p 62) where two pornographic images contrast with a political cartoon and burning bush (?) of abstraction. The implication is that they are all the same at the level of imagery. We make no sense of the First World War caricature fleeing with his loot of clocks; nor of the girl peering at the viewer from between her legs. What does give pause is the way these images jump back and forth in successive readings. No sooner has one finished decoding the outline cartoon than one is off chasing a three-dimensional girl with a headache (and he · aspirin relief at the top of the canvas?). This is mildly amusing, as are Salle's wry juxtapositions.

His deadpan approach has been considered by some as a form of subversion, the 'deconstruction' of habitual categories of perception.[8] Since 'meaning is intimated but tantalisingly withheld' and its 'obscurity is its source of strength', 'Salle follows a strategy of infiltration and sabotage, using established conven-

cancels out each side of his equation: high art questions low art, abstraction negates representation, male attacks female, depth is set off against flatness, impulsive scrawl against academic realism, and so on in a series of mutual negations. Ultimately the meaning of middle-class imagery itself is cancelled as the narratives lead us to zero, or nihilism – a meaning Salle would probably also reject as being too explicit and singular. Like the Dadaist works of Picabia, which were based on similar techniques of overlaid contradictions, we have the choice of reading both erotic imagery and its cancellation.

By contrast Eric Fischl's eroticism is more seductive, less cancelling, but still disturbing. Again, the subject is middle-class eroticism, but now it is not the media, but the viewers who are put on stage to be shown in all the ages of concupiscence. Again, taken as a whole, the work implies a morality which is ultimately ambiguous, implicating the viewer of the painting as a voyeur, as well as a character caught in the act. The self-conscious irony of this exposed hypocrisy is positively Stendhalian: to be seen

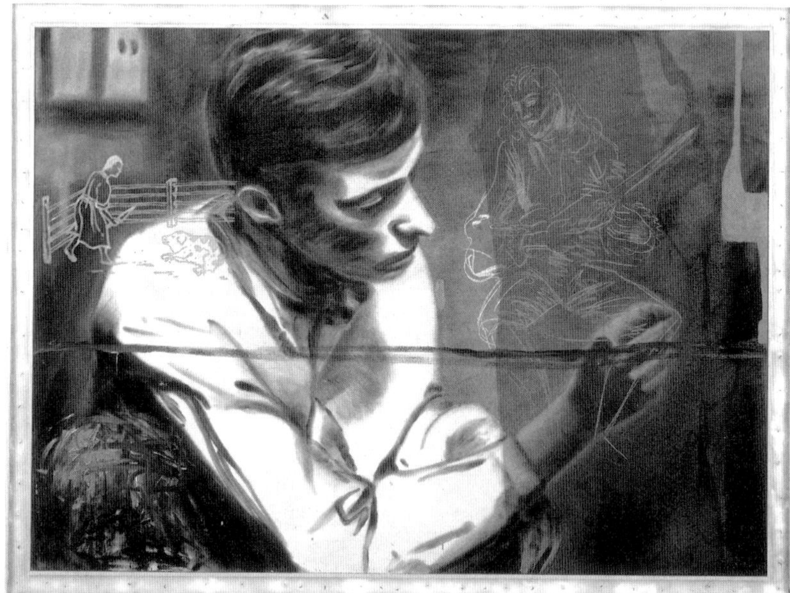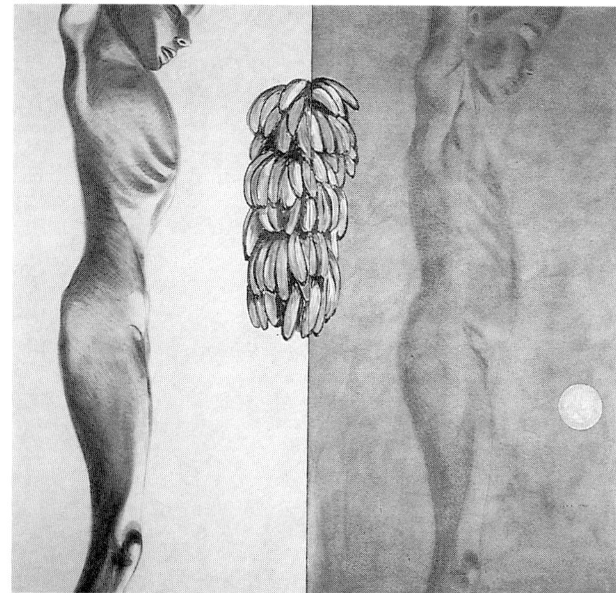

David Salle: *An Agreement*, 1984, oil and acrylic on canvas (*left*); *The Wild Bunch*, 1982, oil and acrylic on canvas (*right*)

tions against themselves in the hope of exposing cultural repression'.[9] The avant-garde military metaphor has this 'deconstructor' blowing up 'ideological institutions' by using the conventions of classicism against classicism, the Pop image against the assumptions of TV, the pornographic still against *Penthouse*. On a certain level this subversion is probably effective: anyone coming to Salle's work with the assumptions of an authoritarian classicist, or the values of a suburbanite, is bound to feel betrayed. They are enticed into the painting by the use of seductive imagery and then slapped in the face by its obvious nihilism. On the other hand, its ambiguous aesthetic approach can be, and has been, criticised for precisely the opposite reason: for exploiting debased imagery for personal gain.[10] This reading, although contradictory at one level, is also correct inasmuch as Salle's own strategy, in his career, is quite calculated. But he wouldn't be the first artist in history to make a fine living out of subversive, seductive satire.

What Salle's art shows as a whole is an effective dualism that

enjoying a Fischl, as one should, provokes adolescent guilt. This helps explain why the most moving paintings concern young boys or girls trapped in the snare of adult sexuality. One rather innocent work, *Father and Son Sleeping*, 1980, shows two males on a clean Hockney-like bed in exactly the same curled-up pose, presumably having the same dream. They are identical in every way but age, Fischl implies, engaged in the ultimate stereotypical act of sleeping. A corresponding work is *Mother and Daughter*, 1984, which portrays them as engaged in the typical suburban activity of sunning themselves in a garden while they peruse *Vogue* and gossip. Their concentration on developing a sexual suntan is positively aggressive. Beaches, parks and homes are full of this animal activity every summer, but it took Fischl to bring this social convention to our eyes for psychological inspection. 'The animal in the home' could be the title of the overall narrative, the depiction of the desires which are so ordinary and legitimised that we overlook their subversive fetishism. Every suburbanite strokes his dog, cuddles his children and spends a significant part of his income on improving his body, cosmetically and physically. These everyday actions have a dark, illicit side which Fischl expresses through obsessive concentration on a psychologically revealing detail – a quality he admires in the work of Max Beckmann.

The Old Man's Boat and the Old Man's Dog, 1982, suggests in its title a menacing, Hemingwayesque plot. Knowing in Fischl's universe that dogs are the acceptable subjects of suburban libido and seeing the position and expression of this animal over the 'odalisque', we have the inference of some bestial act. The 'old man' is of course an American euphemism for the father of the family (as well as a reference to *The Old Man and the Sea*) and he's seen here sipping beer in an unconcerned way. In back a storm is brewing and 'off canvas' as if 'off stage' something has disturbed the two adolescent males, while the daughter raises her finger as if to say 'Haven't you forgotten the tiller?' Somehow this innocent fishing party has gotten out of hand and the family is threatened with destruction. Or so it seems. The best work of Fischl has this

undermine accepted values allows us to speak of a common 'media style' running through this work. Like Salle's, Fischl's paintings have an archetypal quality that relates as much to TV as to classicism. The titles – *Dog Days, Birthday Boy*, etc. – read like entries in a TV guide, although TV does not show the explicit sexual acts of these works, or deal with their complexity of attitude. But the bodies and poses, even the sky, water and lawns are well known to us through the media. It is to Fischl's credit that he can move through this world of cliché and give it some meaning and mystery. *The Women*, 1982 (p 63), again shows some indeterminate but disturbing act. Women of different ages warm themselves by a fire, or are lost in ecstatic reveries or contemplation. One walks towards another as if to rouse her from sleep. The night-time light reveals the suburban furniture and ordinary car, and gives this enigmatic scene a frightening reality. This is an average American beach scene, but these night-time Amazons, reminiscent of Gauguin's Polynesian women, are about to engage in some menacing action. Or are they innocent

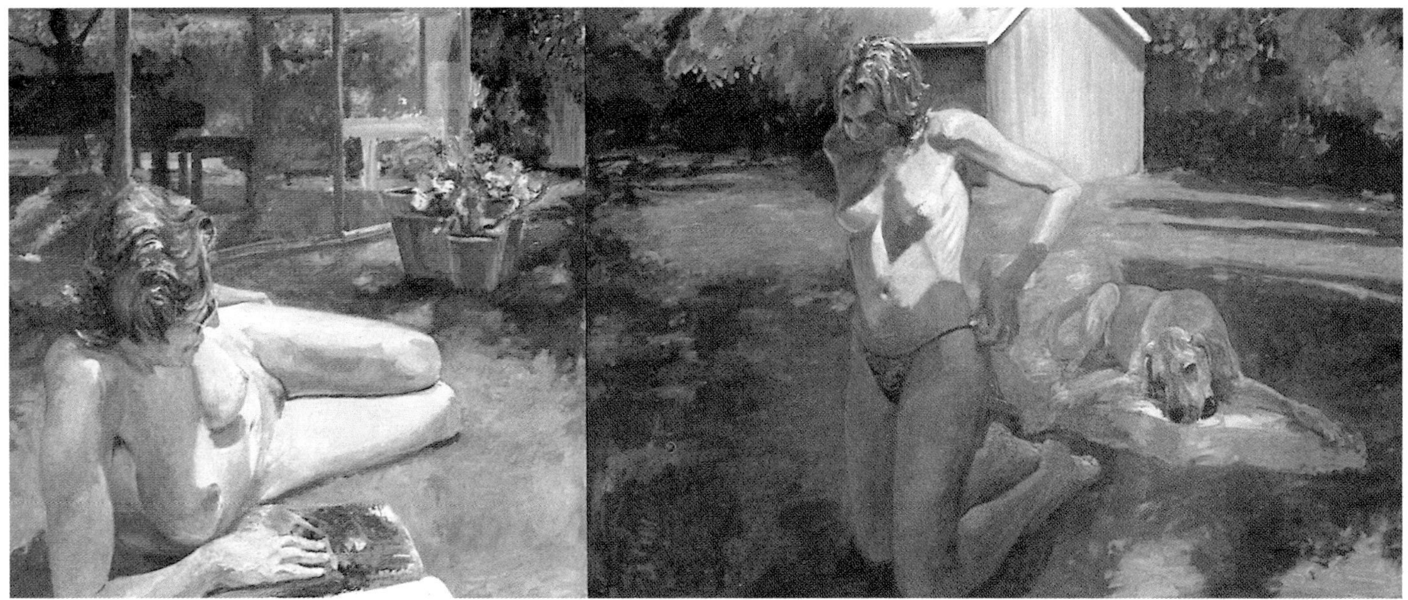

Eric Fischl, *Mother and Daughter*, 1984, oil on canvas, 84×204"

dramatic implication which we've seen Michael Mazur use to such effect. Something unspeakable or bestial has just happened and now a train of action is set off – which cuts through the heart of the family.

In *Bad Boy*, 1981, (p 63) an adolescent watches his mother (?) stretch and reaches into her purse while illicitly peering at her sex. Clearly she knows what is going on, just as we, the viewer placed behind the boy, know that she knows. Implicating the audience in this kind of compromising situation is similar to what Manet did with *Olympia*: exposing the hypocrisy of the distanced perceiver, the objective aesthete. If we become the 'bad boy' by looking from his position, we also recognise in the Hockney-Hollywood bedroom the stereotypes of this situation. Here is that attention to psychological detail which makes Fischl's comment on the media and its stock images so compelling. The soap-operatic quality pulls one in to reveal what often happens, but is rarely shown, on the other side of Sitcom Land.

Using this formal language in a subversive way, like Salle, to

mothers and daughters? And if they are suburban innocents, has the camp fire kindled some forgotten instincts, some ancient feelings that no amount of televised behaviour can suppress? Fischl has described the psychological states he conveys as partly the result of living in an inadequate culture. 'Central [to his work is] the feeling of awkwardness and self-consciousness that one experiences in the face of profound emotional events in one's life. These experiences, such as death, or loss, or sexuality, cannot be supported by a life style that has sought so arduously to deny their meaningfulness, and a culture whose fabric is so worn out that its public rituals and attendant symbols do not make for adequate clothing . . . Each new event is a crisis, and each crisis . . . fills us with much the same anxiety that we feel when, in a dream, we discover ourselves naked in public'.[11]

Awkwardness and a feeling of crisis pervade his work and as he gets older (Fischl was born in New York, 1948) his limited suburbanite cosmology might expand so that his very real gifts are applied to a wider subject. As it is now, his compelling view

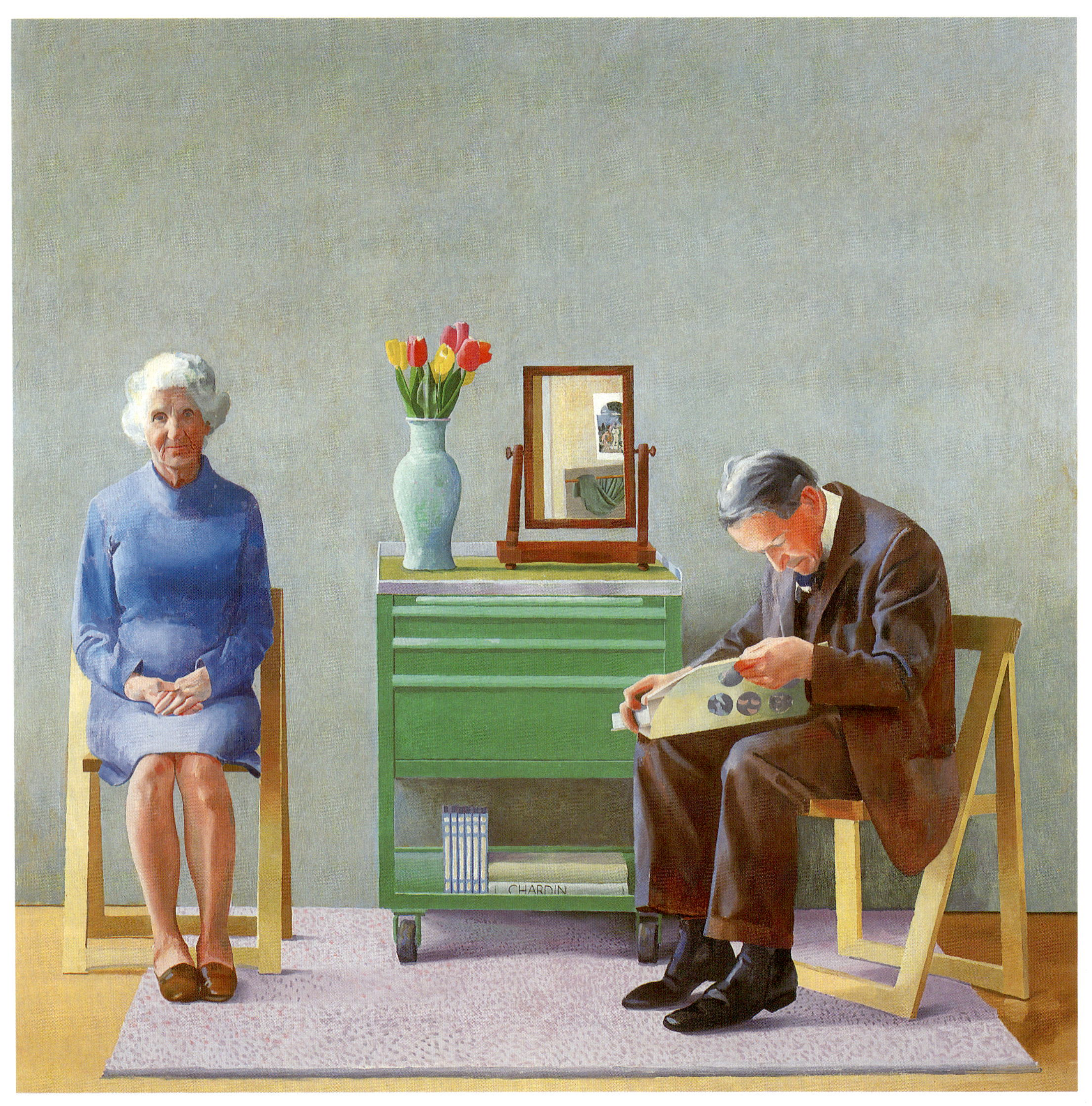

David Hockney
My Parents, 1977
oil on canvas 72x72"

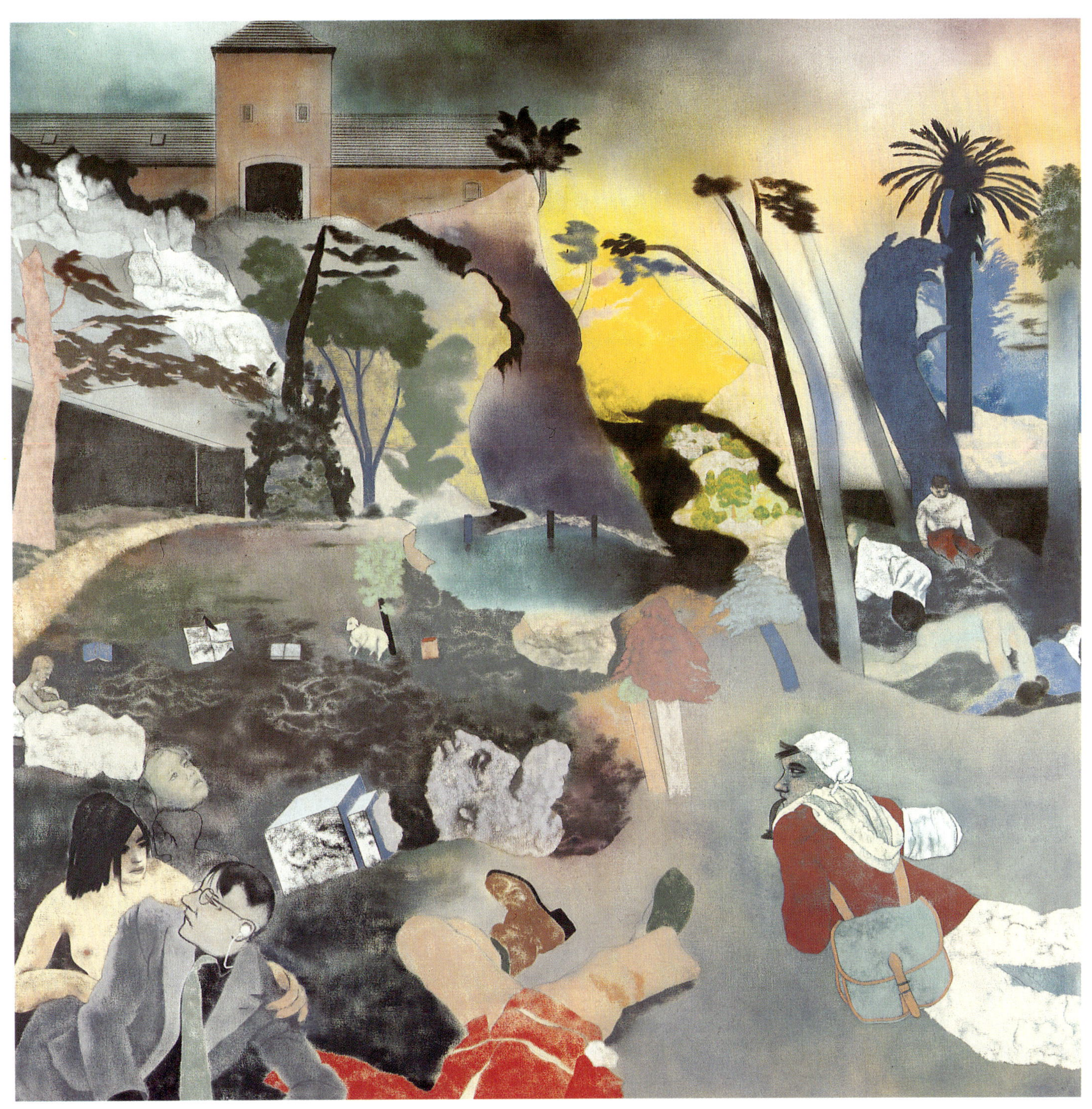

R B Kitaj
If Not, Not, 1975-6
oil on canvas 60×60"

has shown us some truths behind the upper-middle class American dream and the truths appear as astonishing as they are normal.

Robert Longo, a contemporary of Fischl and a fellow New Yorker, is also instrumental in evolving a 'media style' to deal with everyday life, but here it tends to be urban. *Men in Cities*, 1980, shows well-dressed executives jumping, falling or twitching about as if shot or pushed onto a strong current of electricity. *Corporate Wars, Wall of Influence*, 1982, reveals what life is really like when one multinational takes over another. The Brooks Brothers' jackets come off and everyone gouges and pummels each other just as they do in a spaghetti western or a Last Judgement of Jan van Eyck. As with Salle and Fischl, low and high art are mixed. Indeed, *Corporate Wars* is, characteristically, a triptych of mixed media: a cast aluminium relief depicts the battle scene, and two black, alienating Art Deco buildings stand to either side. The impersonal sophistication of this piece catches the cruel professionalism of New York corporate life where blood is spilled, and

Rauschenberg in the 1960s. Like them, Longo is interested in performance art, mixed media and producing films, and, again like them, he keeps a cool distance from all his material, refusing to take a stance beyond a tense and ambiguous presentation. On the other hand he sees his role as pointing up the power and violence of American life – an authoritarianism he often considers as worse than that of Nazi Germany. Responding to this he casts himself in the role of policeman or guardian. 'The artist has to . . . be like a policeman. A great deal of my art, particularly the relief *The Sleep*, is about blowing the whistle on society. I made the piece right after Jonestown [massacre] and right before the Phalangist murders. Here they are selling the image of genocide in family sportswear [the image is actually taken from a family leisure-wear ad]. *The Sleep* is the perfect example of the artist serving as the guardian of culture'.[13]

Here again we are close to the moralist role of the artist and the *exemplum virtutis* except that it is vice – aggressive sex, brute power, the macho personality – which is being celebrated in

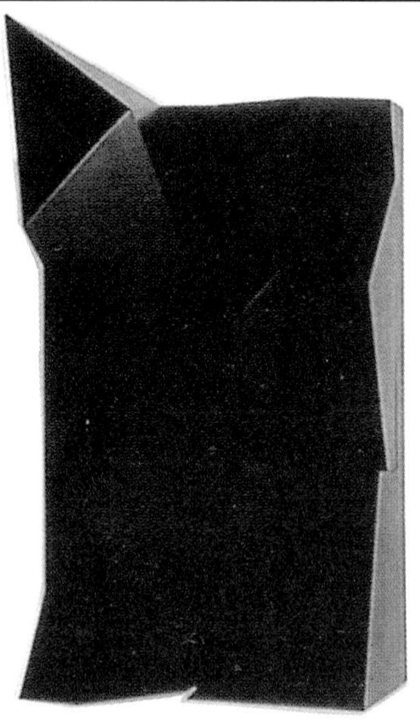
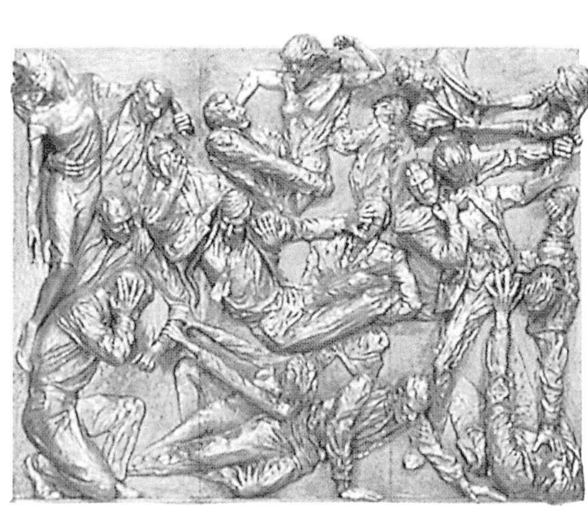
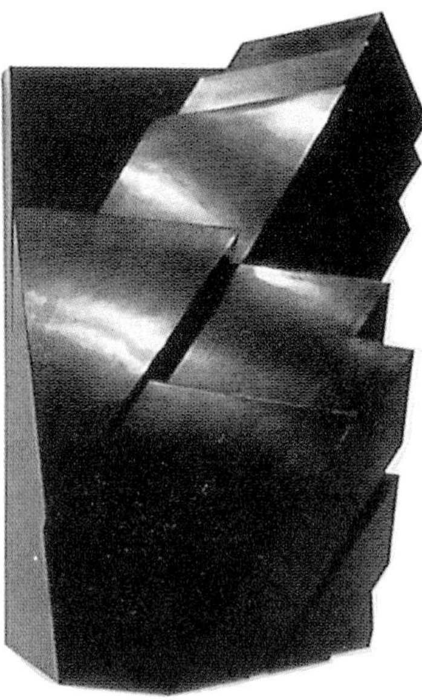

Robert Longo, *Corporate Wars, Wall of Influence*, 1982, mixed media, 9x26x4"

cleaned up, with consummate style and disinterest. All the legs and flailing arms are as stylised and posed as the faces. Although death is here, it's a suave generalised death of executives without names, reminiscent, as Robert Hughes has pointed out, of a Roman battle sarcophagus.[12] Even the glistening suits resemble classical drapery.

If Longo is right in his depiction of the business world, it is as seedy and cruel as the suburban family life of Fischl. Constant struggle, with no heroes or winners, is the implication of the 'White Riot Series', 1982 – a ballet of hammerlocks, half-nelsons and dislocated necks. The abstract beauty of these darkly suited professionals is a wry comment on their selfish activity, as is the implicit equation with a black riot in Harlem. Is the yuppie as vicious and stereotyped as he looks, is life-on-the-way-up at IBM really like this?

The idea of displacing one convention, a TV gangster film, with another, a man in a grey flannel suit, is a rather interesting formula that reminds one of the ironic combinations of Warhol and

order to chasten the viewer. Ultimately, like a dramatist, Longo wants to present the truth of society in a sequence of acts to produce a catharsis, not a parable. It's Aristotelian poetics without the metaphysics.

Still, 1984, mixes all sorts of images and materials in a staccato five-part sequence like a series of movie stills. This ordering is a good example of a widely used technique – 'non-sequitur juxtaposition' – which leaves the working out of connections up to the hard-pressed viewer. In the first frame a fist squashes a tomato-like heart; second, a muscular red-coloured woman engages in some unspeakable act; third, a black fascist (American?) eagle strikes down; fourth, a soulless panel of black granite implies an urban skyscraper; fifth, a stereotyped knight engages in battle. This is another enigmatic allegory about 1. the violence of today's surgery (?); 2. the media; 3. the State; 4. the corporation; and 5. ideas of warfare. The five-part organisation and near symmetry are fundamentally classical even if it's a Mannerist Classicism of violent juxtaposition and suppressed centre. In the

Los Angeles installation, 1984, the whole piece acted as the embracing 'arms' of other mixed media intended to represent the whole body and all its appetites.

Occasionally Longo delivers Warholian boasts: 'I make art that's going to kill you either way, mentally or physically'; 'I'm like the revenge of the media'. And the monumental scale of his work, the sculpted reliefs, the references to Albert Speer show a love of megalomaniac classicism of the terrorist sort. This sado-masochism is ultimately ambiguous, being a subversive form of art in one context and a heightening of bombast and careerism in another. It's tempting to say of Robert Longo, as of the Post-Modern Classical architect Ricardo Bofill, that the megalomania is quite salutary as long as it isn't catching and the monuments remain singular. Rather like the Pompidou Centre in Paris – one is invigorating, two a disaster.

An artist who bears comparison with Robert Longo, and who would no doubt be surprised to hear it, is the Scottish poet Ian Hamilton Finlay. His works, although not erotic or bombastic, are

Finlay, called 'Scotland's greatest concrete-poet' in the 1960s, combines writing, conceptual art and sculpture into an effective and amusing whole. In his picturesque garden, for instance, is one small memorial stone, a Neo-Classical slab placed under a tree with a double-entendre cut into the surface: 'Bring Back the Birch'. Allusions to Poussin and Claude in his landscape designs get the stone inscriptions 'See POUSSIN *Hear* Lorrain'. Where one comes across configurations of reeds and trees that resemble an Albrecht Dürer, Finlay hangs on a branch in front of this view a stone with the artist's monogram *AD*, 1975. This art of labelling and writing captions, out of fashion in an aesthetic age, is as much in the tradition of the Chinese garden as the classical one. The visual arts aren't really 'finished' until the captions are written; or at least they remain necessarily ambiguous without such strong conventions.

Some of the most provocative captions are those Finlay wrote for *The Third Reich Revisited*, 1982; graphic works that he and Ian Appelton realised together. These show, for instance, the

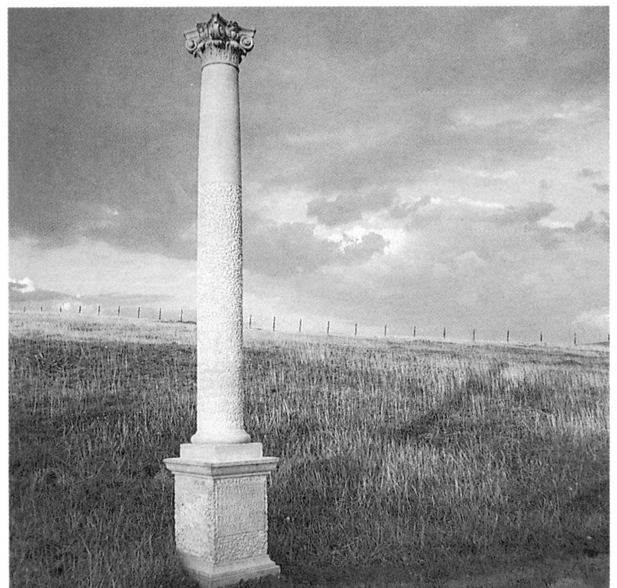
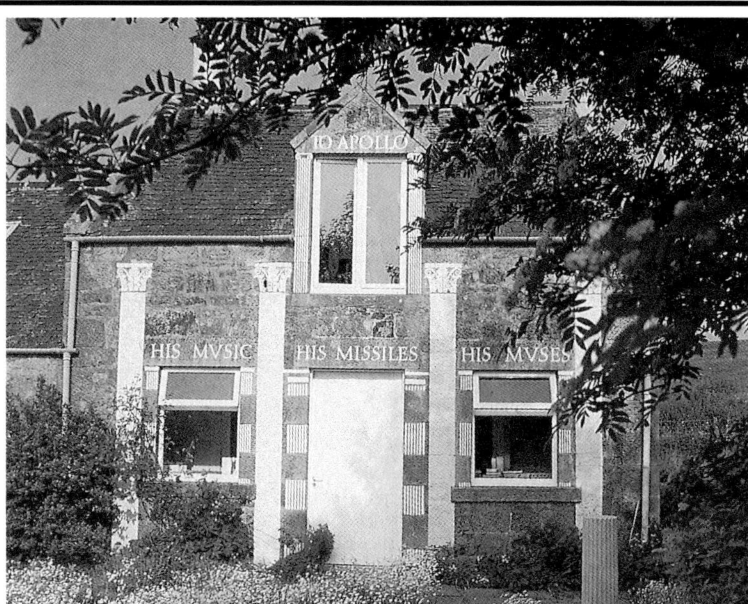

Ian Hamilton Finlay: *Rusticated Column*, 1983, cement; *Temple of Apollo*, Little Sparta, 1978-84

good examples of the current Subversive Classicism. Like Longo's, his work is very autobiographical and he creates it with other artists and helpers, including his wife Susan Finlay. Instead of being based on performances, its location is the political and media event itself. And the media is so mixed – including photos, pamphlets, sculpture, gardens, art works, model battleships and engraved stones – as to defy any simple marketing strategy New York City might come up with. When the time comes to collect Finlay's classicism, it's going to take a grand gesture from the National Monument's Board, or an Act of Parliament, because it will involve declaring a previously desolate Scottish hillside an important national treasure. What Finlay has been doing, systematically since 1978, is turning this windswept moor into a rural Acropolis while, at the same time, showing how recalcitrant are the official powers of law and culture. Finlay has declared 'war' on these powers and although he is losing the legal battles, he is winning the fight of ideas: 'The Battle of Little Sparta' as he has termed this long-term art/political event.

elevation of Albert Speer's *Reichskanzlei* in Berlin – the ultimate piece of fascist classicism – with the central lintel inscribed 'Small is Quite Beautiful', and a revealing, witty comment below the image. Another drawing shows the National Monument on Carlton Hill – the unfinished Parthenon of Edinburgh's unfinished Acropolis (Edinburgh used to be known as the 'Athens of the North'). Finlay describes the reason for the chiselled lettering 'EVENTS ARE A DISCOURSE', and tells how his 18th-century vigilantes would have managed to inscribe this polemical slogan. 'Working overnight with muffled chisels, Saint-Just Vigilantes letter-carvers have added lettering to the frieze of the unfinished classical monument ... The classic Roman letter-style harmonised with the architecture to the extent that the aphorism went unnoticed by citizens and city authorities for several weeks. Once it was discovered, there was little the authorities could do but accept the fait accompli; to *restore* an embarrassingly uncompleted, historical monument would have been too much ...'[14]

A wonderfully mad but just and creative idea this. 'Events are a

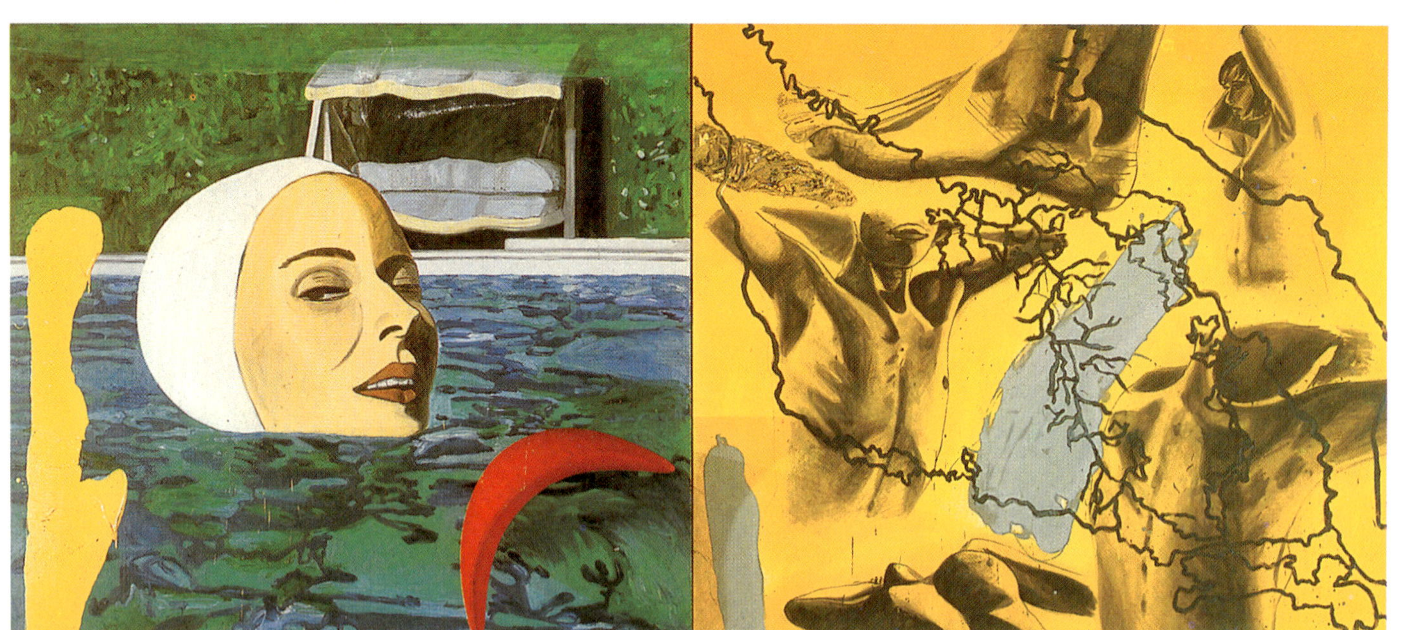

David Salle, *The Cruelty of the Father*, 1983, oil and acrylic on canvas, 75x100"

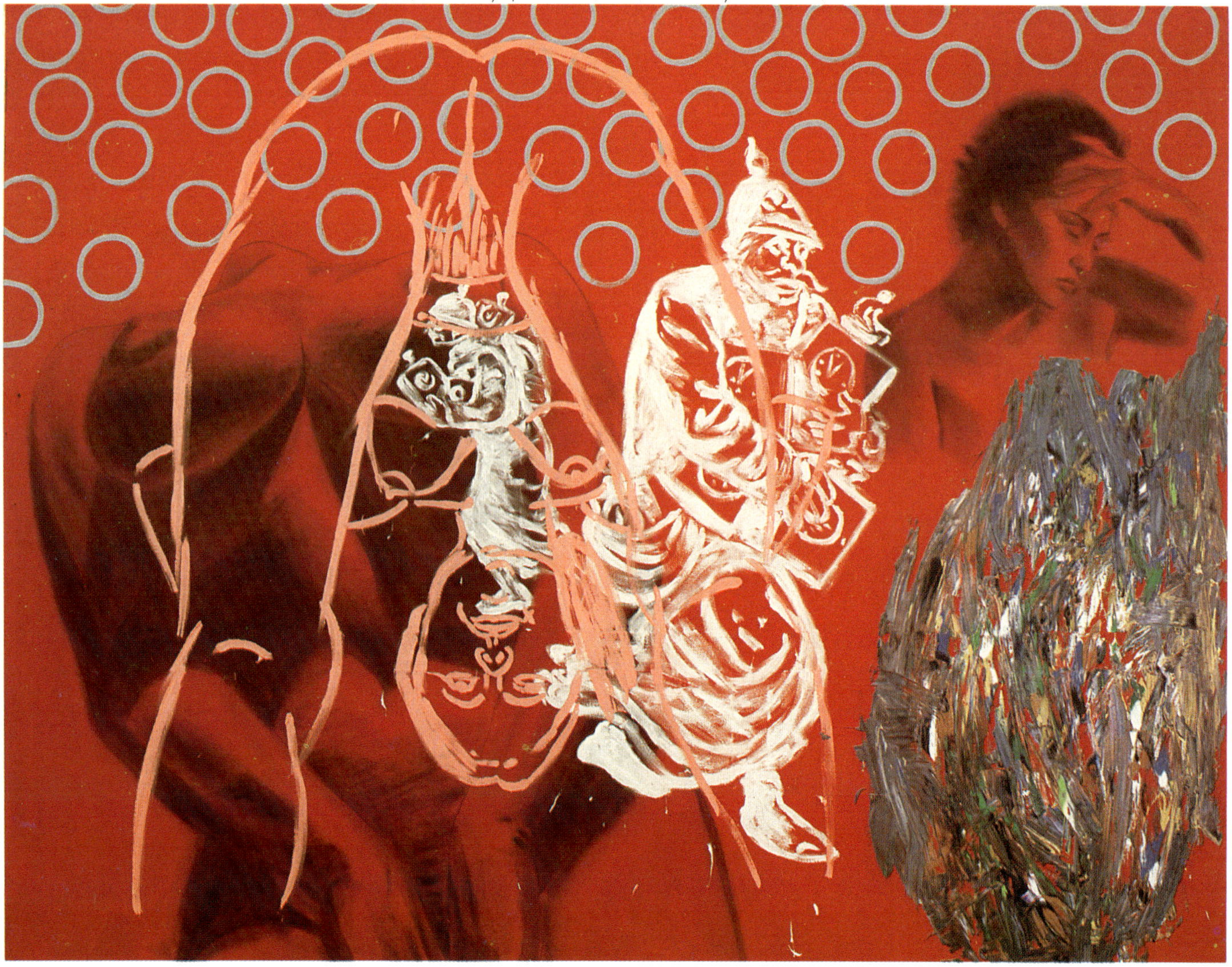

David Salle, *Burning Bush*, 1982
oil and acrylic on canvas, 92x118"

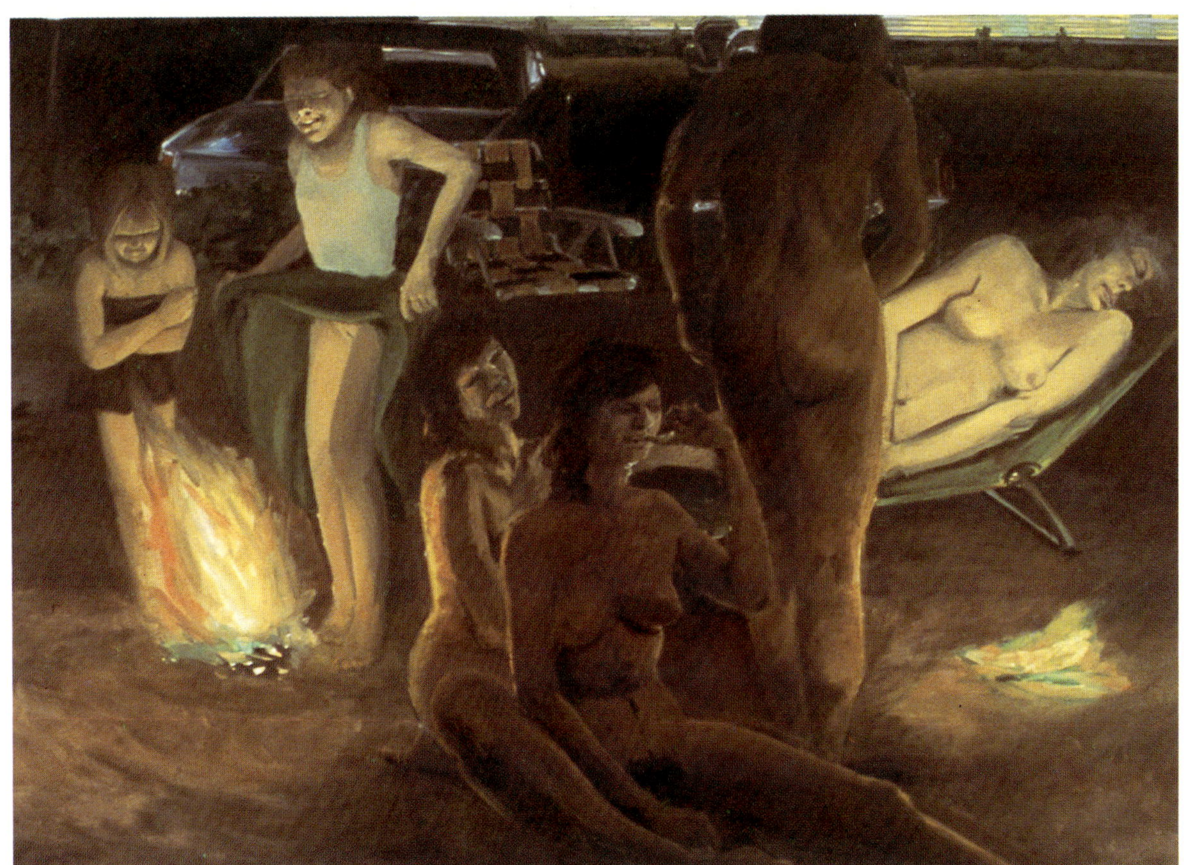

Eric Fischl, *The Women*, 1982, oil on canvas, 66x96"

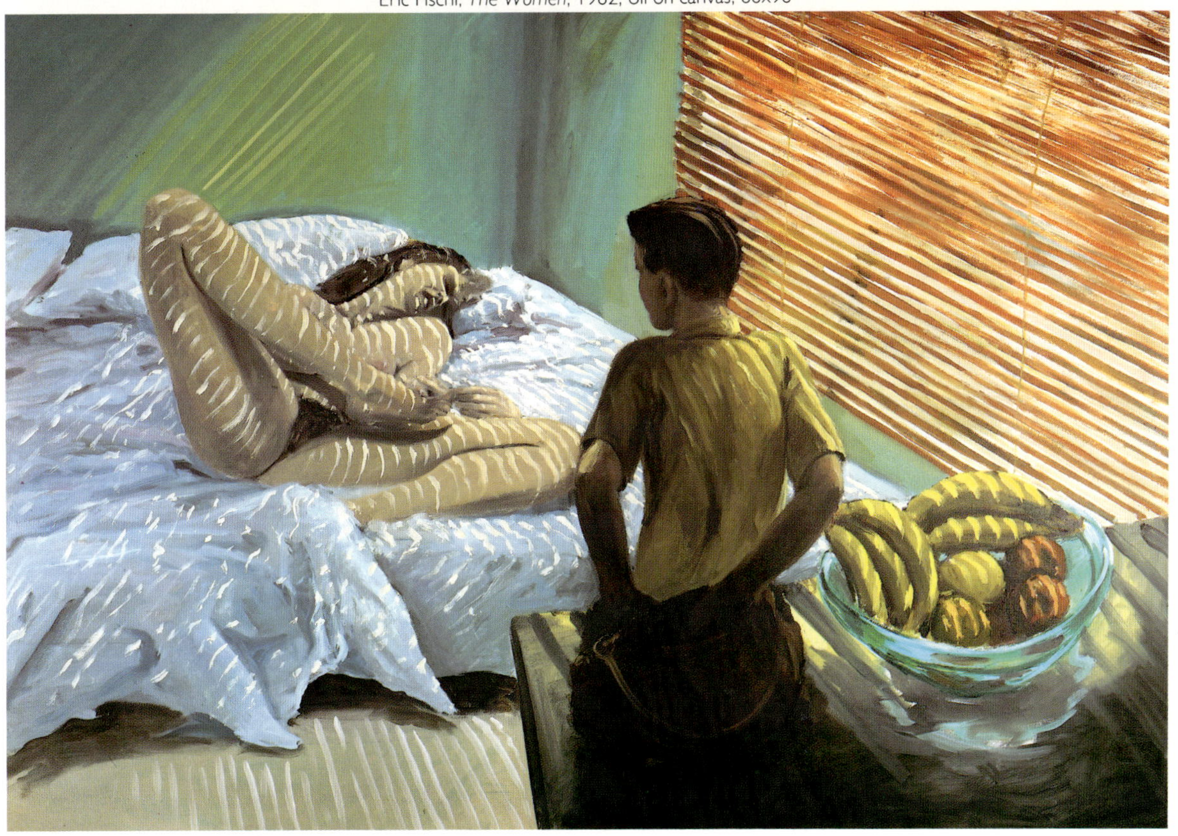

Eric Fischl, *Bad Boy*, 1981
oil on canvas, 66x96"

discourse' is Finlay's basic point and he is tireless in creating events. Another, slightly manic intervention is *Apollo in George Street*, 1982, in which the Greek god is given a machine gun and the following explanation. 'The statue is stone, the sub-machine gun is only plaster. It was added by disillusioned Abstractionists, as a protest, but *looked* so acceptable that it remained unnoticed till the plaster was damaged by frost and the addition fell off. Apollo's emblems are the bow-and-arrow, and lyre; the gun is only the former, appropriately up-dated (though unlikely to be approved of by present fashion).

One of the enigmas of the 1970s and 1980s is the failure of pluralist democracy to produce a public art for itself. Where (except possibly in the new Sculpture Parks) is there any public celebration of radical secularism? Of ecological utilitarianism? Of caution-at-all-costs free conformism? Of Benthamite pacifism?'[15]

This query explains Finlay's use of Nazi Classicism as a critique: by changing its labels and meanings it becomes a challenge to the present. The classical work and buildings that Finlay builds around his *private* home should be seen as a lyrical lament for the loss of the *res publica*. But it's also funny and mad. In fact, if one considers Finlay's continuous 'war' with the authorities then three historical parallels come to mind. First is the high-minded civil disobedience of Henry Thoreau and other figures now sanctioned by history as the heroes of democracy; the mythic protagonists of the French and American revolutions (whose real tawdriness Finlay is prepared to admit). Second there are the bitterly funny polemics of Jonathan Swift. And finally there is Monty Python's low comedy – the mad-cap antics of Finlay and his Saint-Just Vigilantes in setting up their 'panzer' divisions to repel the onslaught of the Scottish authorities (this battle was documented for the media in the style of a Python cartoon). But it would be wrong to think 'The Battle of Little Sparta' is just amusing, it's also very serious; like all good satire it brings out truths about everyday life. What his war has proved (if it needed proving) is that 'the law has been treated as the property of the class which holds power'.

This is not the place to recount the 'tempest in a cow-byre', which has been done many times and at length.[16] But the principle events are these. The Finlays had a semi-ruined cow-byre next to their modest cottage which they converted into a 'Canova-type temple', a 'garden temple'. Finlay contends that as a quasi-religious edifice, based on the precedents of 18th-century Neo-classical garden temples in Great Britain, the building should not have been taxed as a commercial building even though works of art were contained in it. Since 1978 Finlay and others have been trying to get the powers-that-be (The Scottish Arts Council and the Strathclyde Regional Council) to enter into a discussion of what a 'garden temple' is and whether it is liable for tax. This they have refused to do with a bureaucratic indifference that proves Finlay's major point: the law is used and defined most effectively by those who have power. Works of art have been confiscated from this temple by the authorities and the only time they took note of Finlay's objections was when an American owner of one of the pieces – the Wadsworth Athenaeum of Connecticut – asked the assistance of the US State Department to have it returned. The work was promptly released.

Clearly there are two sides to this story, but as told by Finlay and his supporters the Strathclyde Regional Council will never state its position on garden temples and their rating assessment: they just hold onto the confiscated art. As this 'war', or from Finlay's view 'legalised violence', drags on, he continues to build Little Sparta and it has now become quite an idyllic landscape of temples, votive columns, inscriptions, primitive huts and small lakes. It could almost be the Roman campagna of a Poussin or Claude except for the relentless Scottish mist. But it is a fitting, if modest, successor to 18th-century classical gardens, those at Stowe and Stourhead, which have their Temples of Ancient Virtue in the garden: quasi-religious structures intended to instil an *exemplum virtutis*. And the whole is dedicated to 'the neoclassical triumvirate of Robespierre, Saint-Just and J L David'; those who fought for a public, moral art. The last words in Finlay's booklet *Liberty, Terror and Virtue*, put his larger case succinctly: 'The war has produced a quantity of art; what it has not yet produced (in Britain as opposed to Europe) is serious didactic *thought* on its *causes* – the chief of which is, that where the Arts once overlapped with Religion, they now overlap with tourism and entertainment, and there is no form or mode for the non-secular in our society.'[17]

Embattled in his little patch of windy moor, which he never leaves, Finlay seems destined to prove his point even if it makes his life unpleasant. He has made Everyman's gripe over income tax into a larger cause, a question of religion and cultural definition. It might not be Solzhenitsyn fighting the Politburo, or Martin Luther King taking on Washington, but there is a public point to this battle and it gives his classicism a focus more defined than Robert Longo's: the definition and place of the 'non-secular' in our culture. We are here back to 18th-century didactic art.

Notes

1 See Robert Rosenblum, *Transformations in Late Eighteenth Century Art*, Princeton University Press, Princeton, New Jersey, 1967, pp 50-106.

2 Gérard, in 1793, claimed the arts should make 'one hate vice, love virtue, and they should charm the eye'. Quoted from Rosenblum, *op cit*, p 85.

3 *ibid*, pp 55-6.

4 Bravo has painted Danae in a bedroom being showered by gold coins, Bruno Civitico has painted her more convincingly in a New England living-room.

5 See catalogue devoted to his exhibition, *New Paintings and Drawings, James Valerio*, Allan Frumkin Gallery, New York, 1983, p 7.

6 For a good discussion of Ron Kitaj's work see Kitaj, *Paintings, Drawings, Pastels*, Thames and Hudson, London, 1983.

7 Anthropomorphism is discussed in Chaps X and XI of *PostModernism*.

8 Thomas Lawson, 'Last Exit: Painting', *Artforum*, Oct 1981 and reprinted in *Theories of Contemporary Art*, (ed) Richard Hertz, Prentice-Hall, Englewood, New Jersey, 1985, pp 143-57; quote page 150.

9 *ibid*, p 149.

10 Craig Owens, 'Honor, Power and the Love of Women', also reprinted in *Theories of Contemporary Art, op cit*, note 8, pp 131-41.

11 Eric Fischl, press release of Edward Thorp Gallery, New York, Feb 1982, quoted in *Eric Fischl Paintings*, Mendel Art Gallery, 1985, p 16.

12 R Hughes, 'Three from the Image Machine', *Time Magazine*, 14 Mar 1983.

13 Maurice Berger, 'The Dynamics of Power: An Interview with Robert Longo', *Arts Magazine*, Jan 1985, pp 88-9.

14 Ian Hamilton Finlay, 'Liberty, Terror and Virtue, The Little Spartan War and the Third Reich Revisited', *New Arcadians Journal*, No 15, p 20.

15 *ibid*, p 22.

16 See *Ian Hamilton Finlay, A Visual Primer* by Yves Abrioux, Reaktion Books, Edinburgh, 1985, pp15-21.

17 *Op cit*, note 14; quote also from *Studio International*, Apr 1984.

Post-Modernism: The New Classicism in Art and Architecture, by Charles Jencks, will be published by Academy Editions in October

THE POP ICON
Sheena Wagstaff

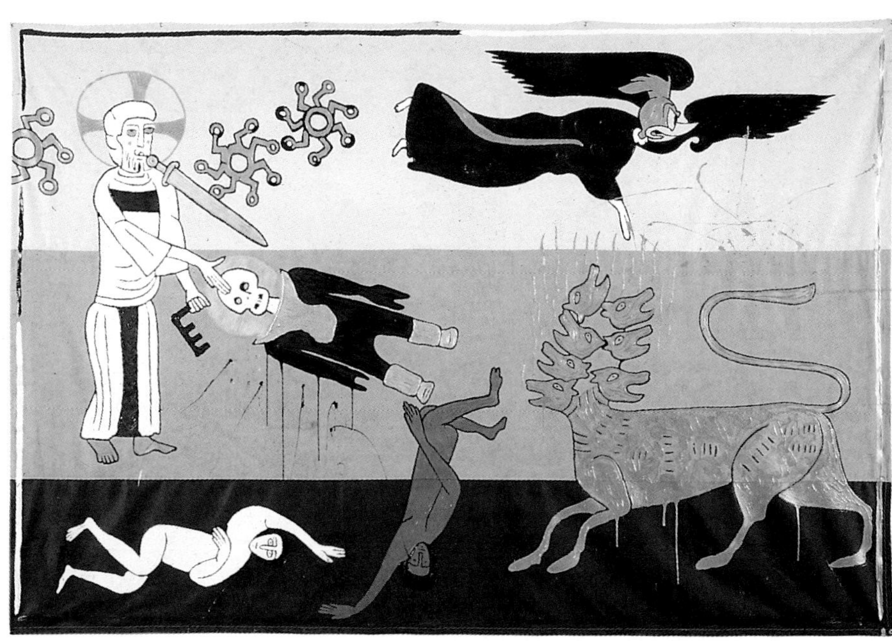

Ronnie Cutrone, *The Dead Christ in Space*, 1983, acrylic on banner

The 50s and 60s saw a simultaneous yet separate development of a Pop aesthetic on both sides of the Atlantic in the work of artists such as Warhol, Lichtenstein, Blake and Paolozzi. Sheena Wagstaff assesses a major modern movement that draws on iconography from the world of popular culture, and traces its impact on contemporary artists such as Kenny Scharf.

In 1962 Warhol chose a smouldering close-up photo of Elvis' face to repeat 36 times because he was a fan of the rock-and-roll star, and knew him like any other American kid – through the media. He might instead have tuned into another popular image whose well-oiled crooning filled the airwaves at the time, but Frank was simply out of the question. Elvis was Andy's generation. The cachet of this time, its lifestyle of swinging panache, its cool slick accoutrements, were vicariously esteemed by a newly emergent youth culture with a bit of money and ambition to burn. All this helped create a nouveau-riche art market – epitomised by socially ambitious men such as Robert C Scull (former cab-driver turned executive and Pop art collector) – which prefigured a corporate 'culture' that still today does not break faith with its youthful passions and generational allegiances: Britain's Charles Saatchi, for example, strictly rounds his collection at the year 1960.

Well before the 1960s, America possessed a vital popular culture which included the specific 20th-century developments of popular music (jazz), the Hollywood movie genre, animated cartoons, and the printed comic strip.

It is significant that during the immediate postwar period in the USA those artists earnestly striving towards establishing a peculiarly American artistic idiom did not consider the thriving (in their view 'philistine') indigenous culture on their walk-ups. And while

their scaled-up canvases and heroic dimensions successfully absorbed the exotic European mix of the previous influx of Modernist artists (such as Duchamp and Mondrian) with the resident-exiles (like Gorky and de Kooning) to result in what is recognised as an Americanised art, the Abstract Expressionist painters not only pursued a cerebral flirtation with European myth and Existentialism (Pollock, Rothko, Newman, Kline) but also unquestioningly subscribed to the model of a (European) avant-garde.

The American Pop artists clearly participated in the vanguard spirit of their predecessors in their continuing quest for a national vernacular. But they wielded a double-faced joker card: through their conscious plundering of the images and artefacts of their own popular culture, they continued to undermine both the pictorial conventions of European art and its attendant rigid hierarchy of highs and lows of taste.

So the 'borrowing' of comic images for inclusion in paintings, sculpture, and performance art was part of a deliberate strategy by some of the first artists to benefit from the huge explosion of university education in the US. Similarly in Britain the emergence of a new visual sensibility that found its expression in Pop was connected with a shift in the social composition of further education during the 1950s. 'It is often claimed that Pop embodied the aspirations of a new generation of art students – many

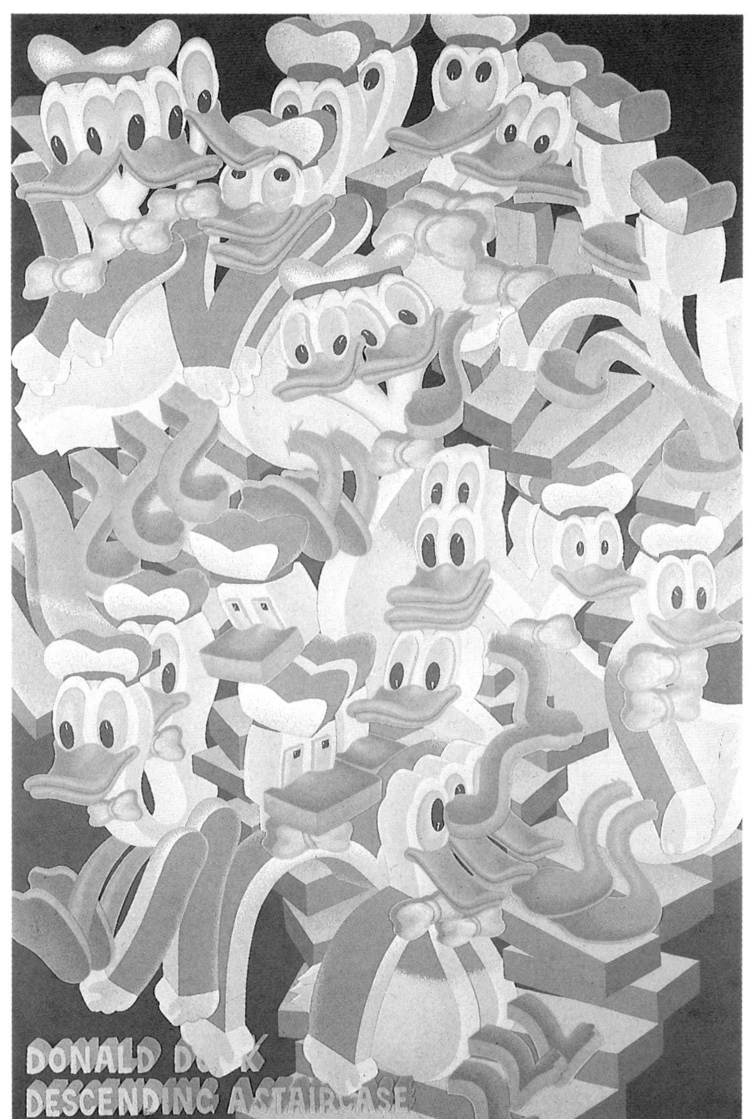

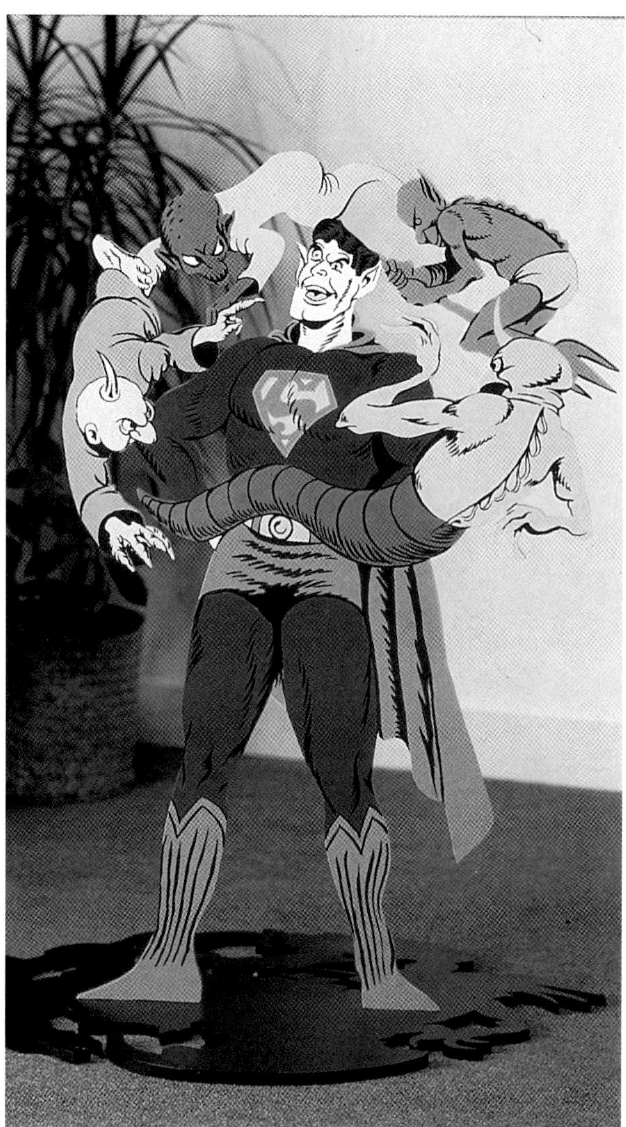

L to R: Peter Saul, *Donald Duck Descending a Staircase*, 1979, acrylic on canvas; Suzan Pitt, *Manic Superman with Devils*, 1983, acrylic on wood

from working-class or lower-middle-class backgrounds, the first beneficiaries in the immediate postwar period of servicemen's grants and the 1944 Butler Education Act'[1]. Pop, in Reyner Banham's words, represents 'the revenge of the elementary schoolboys'[2]. Banham was, along with Eduardo Paolozzi and Richard Hamilton, a member of the Independent Group founded in 1952 at the Institute of Contemporary Arts. 'The ICA became a home for ideas, a base for a congregation of minds which questioned given precepts with aggression and were alert to any new thought that could be hooked into their ambience . . . There was a noticeable change when Lawrence Alloway and John McHale convened the Independent Group. What had been cliquey, British, and laudably academic became, through their influence, cliquey, mid-Atlantic, adventurous, irreverent and relevant.'[3]

McHale was one of the earliest British artists to visit the US to study with Josef Albers at Yale University in 1955. Albers also taught Frank Stella at Yale and then, with fellow teachers Charles

Olsen and John Cage at Black Mountain College, he taught Robert Rauschenberg too. On both sides of the Atlantic a new breed of highly educated artists was shaping up an elastic comprehension which could swing from the shrewdly intellectual to the abjectly commercial – in the face of the full impact of a high-technology mass media which Europe would come to feel later. In addition to his educational experience (which included encounters with Duchamp and Buckminster Fuller) McHale returned to London with a large black wooden box crammed with magazines, catalogues and other American ephemera. This treasure chest of Americana, which spoke of a more affluent, attractive popular culture than was then to be found in Britain, heralded the burgeoning effects of the Marshall Plan and the personal passions of American European Tourers under the GI Bill. An avalanche of undifferentiated US popular culture washed through Europe. The sharp professional graphics of an expanding advertising industry, billboards, comics, widescreen movies, Detroit car styling, interior design, pop music and clothes design,

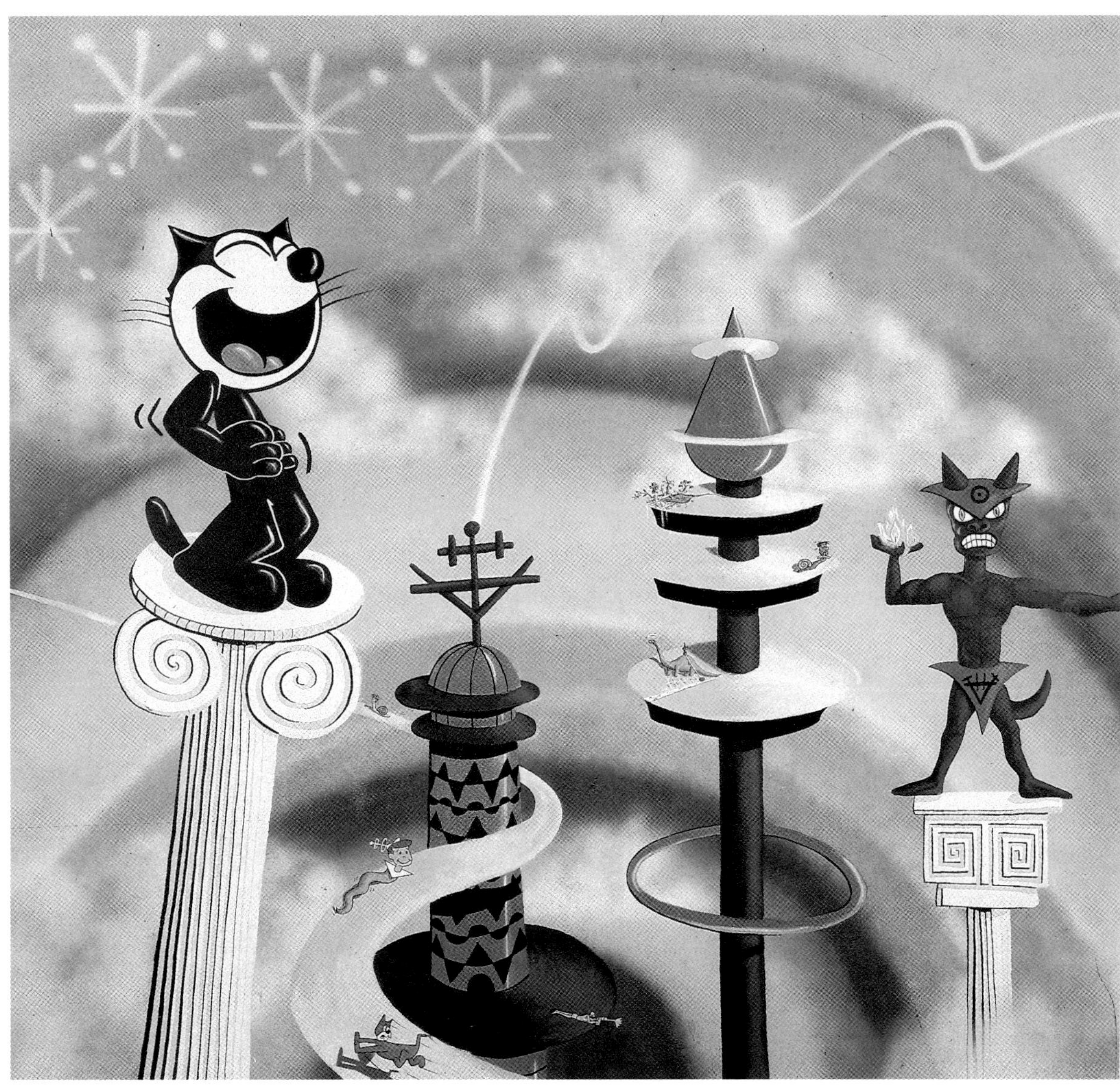

Kenny Scharf, *Felix on a Pedestal*, 1982, acrylic and spray paint on canvas, 96⅘ × 88⅘"

participated in the rapid growth of American corporate culture.

The word 'Pop' was originally coined by Lawrence Alloway who was referring to the raw material for Hamilton's and Paolozzi's work, rather than to their collages, prints and later paintings. For both camps of artists – British and American – 'Pop' promised a fun liberation from the strictures of an essentially European aesthetic tradition. However, through their 'discovery' and acknowledgement of a home-grown popular culture, American Pop artists were also defining themselves as 100 percent American, contributing towards the invention of their own cultural history.

Yet 25 years on, it is still considered plausible for artists to use popular comic images in their work: interest in and portrayal of the same comic characters has persisted, unabated, to the present day. Why? One of the main reasons is that comics continue to be a derided form of mass-produced popular culture, and as such they offer a complex formal and cultural status which can be seen to problematise many of the notions upon which the appreciation of art has traditionally rested. Yet the climactic impact of such a revelation to the 1960s artist has surely diminished by the 1980s. And while the descriptive handle to that practice has colourfully evolved over the years from 'copying', 'emulation/simulating', 're-producing', and 'quoting' to the current buzzwords, there has been no fundamental alteration to what is essentially an early Modernist passion for lifting images out of the common currency of urban dailiness. Nowadays, however, the 'appropriation' of an existing mode of visual communication is distinguished as characteristic of much 'Post-Modern' art, and the comic can perform endlessly in that exchange of visual and linguistic signs or images which contributes to a much-needed symbolic structure for our social, cultural, and economic existence.

Yet younger artists appreciate comics not simply because they fit neatly into that tirelessly recycled argument for Post-Modern art's cognisance of the omnipresent role of the sign in our society (though for many it may offer a dubious validation of what they

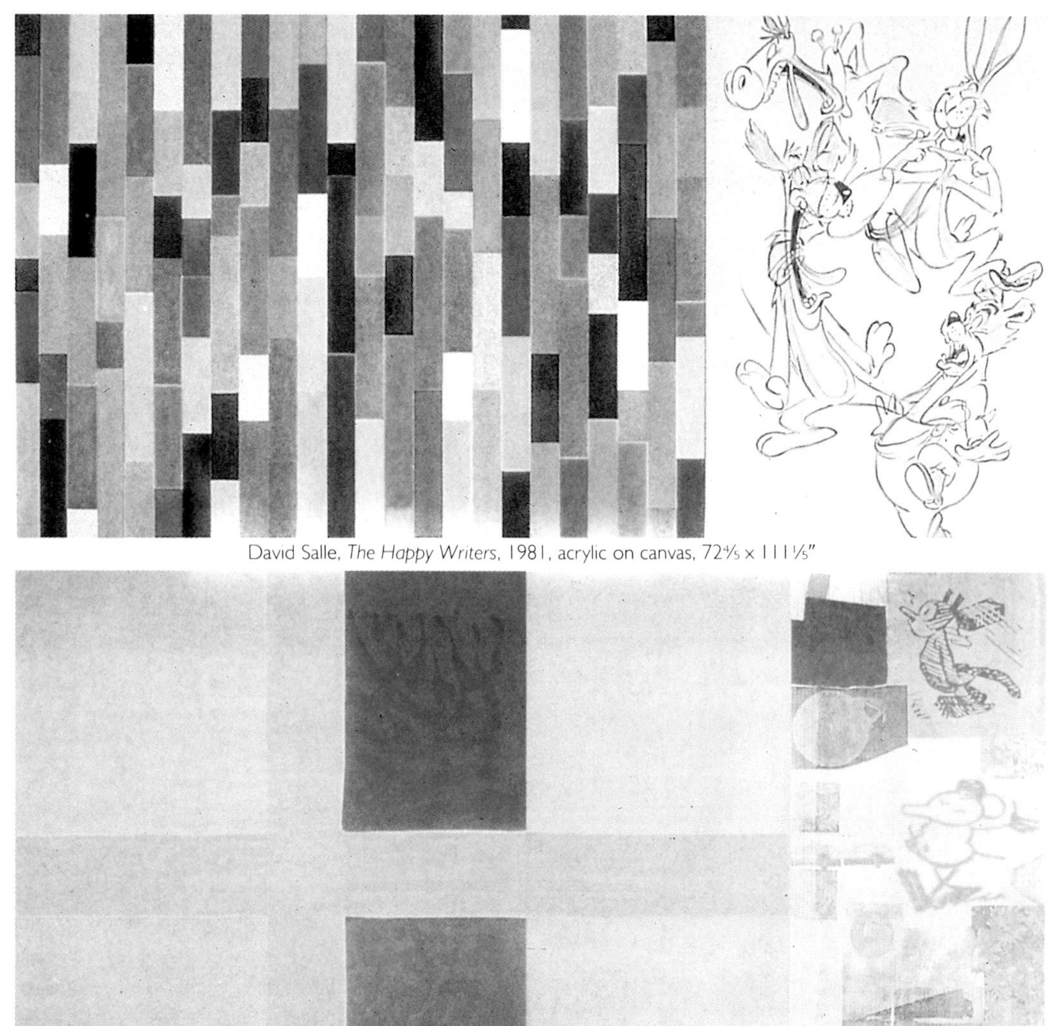

David Salle, *The Happy Writers*, 1981, acrylic on canvas, 72⅘ x 111⅓"

Robert Rauschenberg, *For a Friend and Krazy Kat*, 1976, silkscreen and solvent transfer and collage on wooden panels, 85⅕ x 146⅘"

do). The comics offer another significance – demonstrated by such consistent portrayal, decade after decade, of particular comic characters created mainly in the 30s and 40s in America. (For an astonishing 35 years, Superman has been artistically sanctified by 20th-century painting.) They offer the inheritors of a 1960s tradition an unchanging, ready-made, modern iconography.

An icon, as a representation of a hallowed being, is itself regarded as sacred. A perfect visual simile, the icon's devotional attraction does not require a conscious referral to the 'original' behind the image: it is one and the same. The ever-popular appeal of the comics, and their generation of 'heroic types' have recommended their iconic quotation by art in an age when religious archetypes have been replaced by consumer durables. And, like the icon, the comic may also be reproduced in different mediums, and in any size, an indefinite number of times, provided it retains certain identifiable characteristics. So the characters have become endlessly repeatable 'signs of the times'.

The nature of popular culture of any age is defined by its constant unvarying structures of expression. Not only does it miss an 'avant-garde' historical development as such, but it sustains itself through its very lack of fundamental change, and a strong sense of continuity. This is not to say that popular culture genres do not develop within themselves: high points of any cultural form are defined by those who are supremely skilful and inventive in their handling of its underlying formal skeleton. A discernable stylistic shift in a popular cultural form – for example the metamorphosis of rural acoustic blues to urban electric blues, due to outside economic geographic mobility and societal factors – nevertheless does not alter either the basic blues riff, or its continuation of a tradition passed down from one generation to another, through fathers/mothers to sons/daughters.

Likewise, the moral and iconic status of the comic strip Superman has not altered since his first muscular appearance in 1939; and his very creation as a comic character is only a modern extension of an age-old myth-making process, 'pouring a new substance into an essentially similar mould'.[4] The classic heroes of

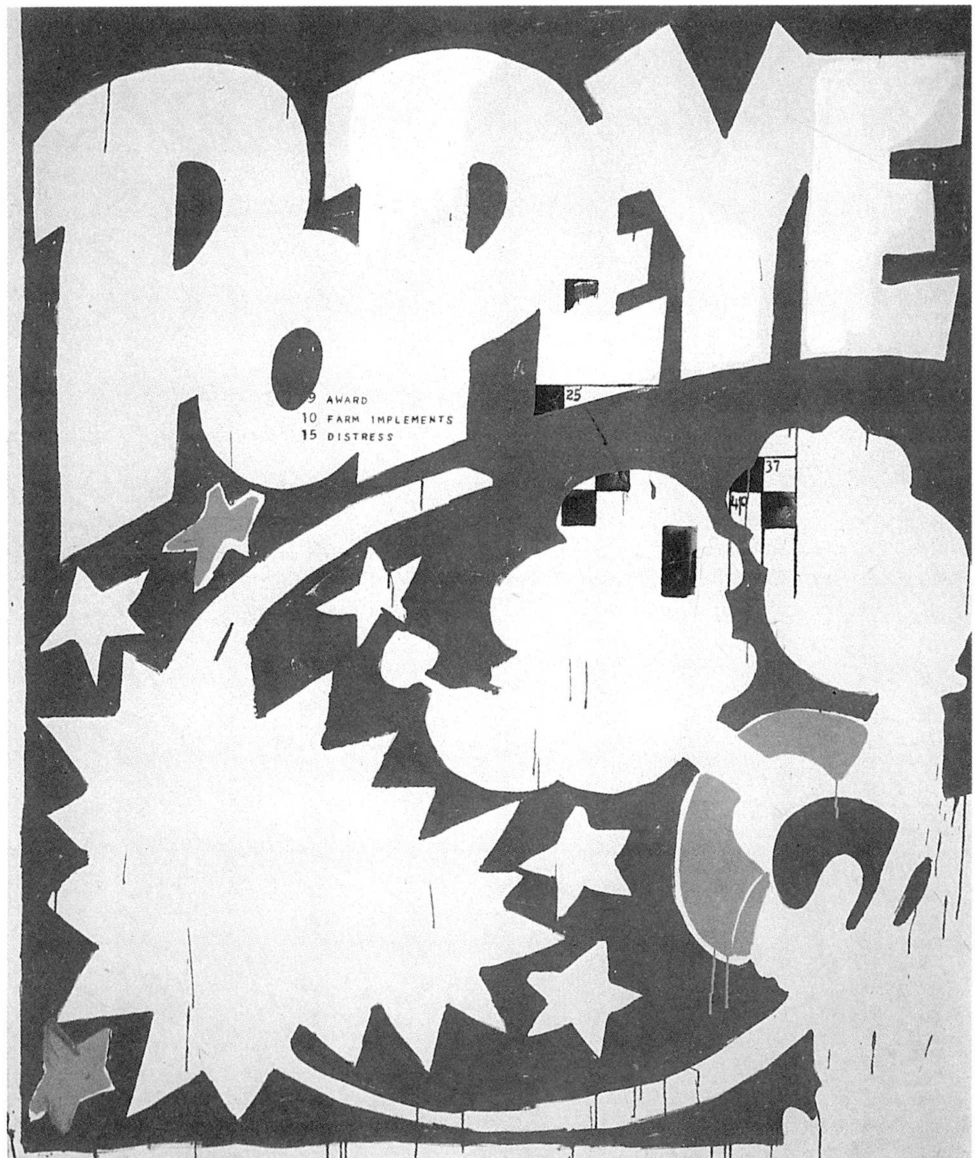

Andy Warhol, *Popeye*, 1961-62, pastels on canvas, 68⅕ x 59⅕"

Western civilisation such as Ulysses, Achilles, and Hercules were supplanted in America by Western heroes such as Daniel Boone, Davy Crockett and Buffalo Bill: tough frontiersmen who overcame a hostile environment. The preoccupation with the struggle against the vast awe-inspiring forces of nature had, by the 20th century, given way to one of fighting the urban problems of poverty, alienation, totalitarianism and crime: the province of comic heroes such as Superman and Dick Tracy. 'The central fantasy of the adventure story is that of the hero overcoming obstacles and dangers and accomplishing some important and moral mission. Often the hero's trails are the machinations of a villain. The true focus of interest in the adventure story is the character of the hero and the nature of the obstacles he has to overcome. This is perhaps the oldest and widest in appeal of any story type.'[5]

The creation of Dick Tracy in 1931 by Chester Gould was motivated by the crime wave of the Prohibition Era. Seven years later the first comic book superhero, Superman, joined the detective in crime fighting. Tracy's insistence on the primacy of law and order reflects Chester Gould's own virulent hatred of villains and his belief that he had a moral responsibility as a law-enforcer. 'Big gangsters were running wild but going to court and getting off scot free. I thought: why not have a guy who doesn't take the gangsters to court, but shoots 'em.'[6] The brutal stories of Dick Tracy, which included accurate details of the latest police procedural techniques, made J Edgar Hoover a fan of the strip, and a friend to Gould. Certainly the violence that 'progress' breeds is central to these comic genres, which are however generally seen less as carriers of an ideological standpoint than as tales of a lone vigilante upholding the forces of 'good' against immense odds (viz the Western).

While Clark Kent was a caricature of what individuals had become in an organised, depersonalised, technological world, it was his super-persona which represented a mitigation of his earth-bound feelings of impotence and frustration. In the dark days of the 1930s, the popularity of these adventure genres

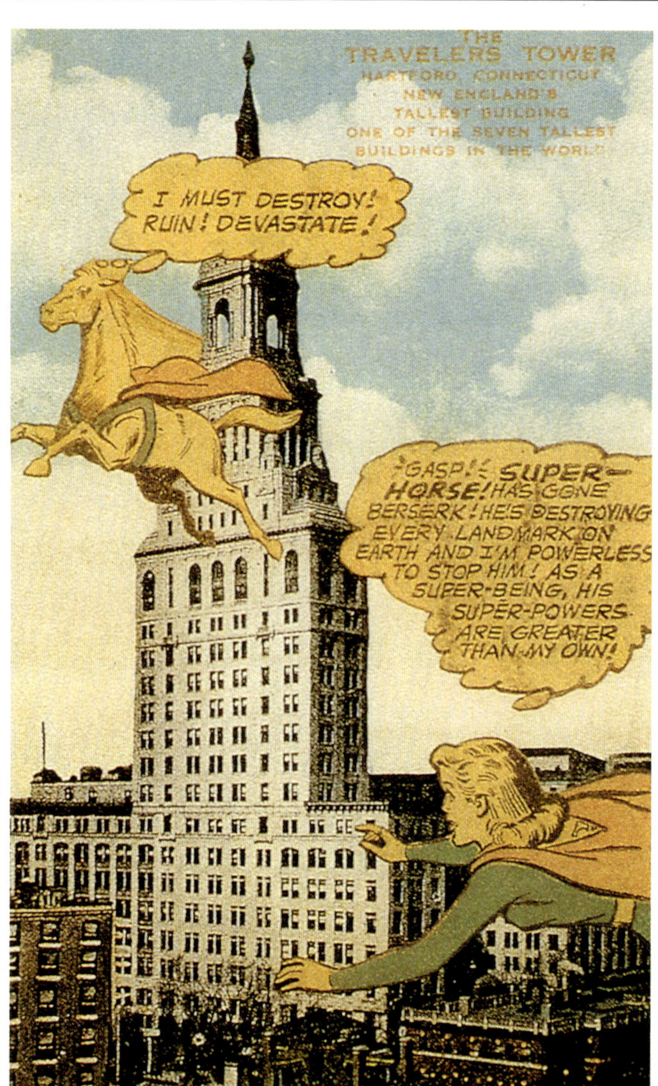
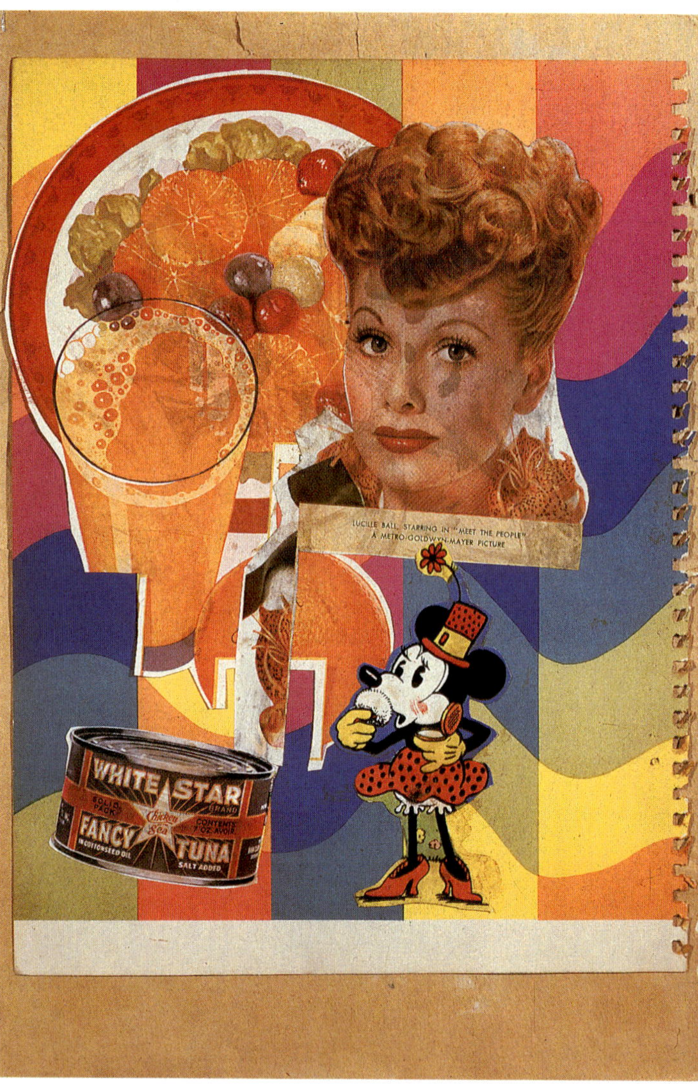

L to R: Peter Blake, *Souvenir for Judith*, 1973, collage, 10 × 7⅕″; Eduardo Paolozzi, *Meet the People*, 1948, collage, 143⅗ × 100⅖″

SHEENA WAGSTAFF

indicated the prevailing public unrest with the institutions and bureaucracies that shaped the contours of everyday life. Here were individuals who were free to bypass institutional constraints and emulate the procedures of the criminal in order to effectively institute morally sanctioned change. The comic strips thus offered projections for relieving tensions at the same time as expressing their feelings of despair concerning the future of both the individual and democracy. And just as the adventure genre developed its 20th-century idiom in response to the changing interests of its audience, so too the continued popularity of Superman and Dick Tracy may indicate something of today's moral climate. As Arthur Miller has expressed: 'A genuine social concern and a yearning for shared human values has been so thoroughly evacuated from American public policy and rhetoric in the 1980s that the past is invoked to restore a lost balance . . . that drab and painful decade [the 1930s] nonetheless generated a sense of genuine community.'[7]

Of course the quotation of Superman in art does not auto-matically reflect the historical context from which the character arose. And the audience for artists' complex paraphrases is not necessarily the same as that for the comics. Nevertheless, the heroic prototype has become a convenient, highly adaptable quotation.

And just as the popular cultural form redeems itself continually, often through stylistic variations, so too does much recent painting, assured of its emotive iconic status, achieve sub-genre formations while deviating only slightly from the Pop system. Comic iconology does however offer some younger artists symbolic objects for what has become an increasingly personal investigation.

Two young American painters, Kenny Scharf and Ronnie Cutrone, noted for their concentration on animated cartoon characters in their work, willingly admit to a common influence in the work of Warhol. 'It's Andy who inspired me. I remember growing up and learning about him and the whole scene.'[8] Scharf's multicoloured fun paintings are shaped by a desire to re-

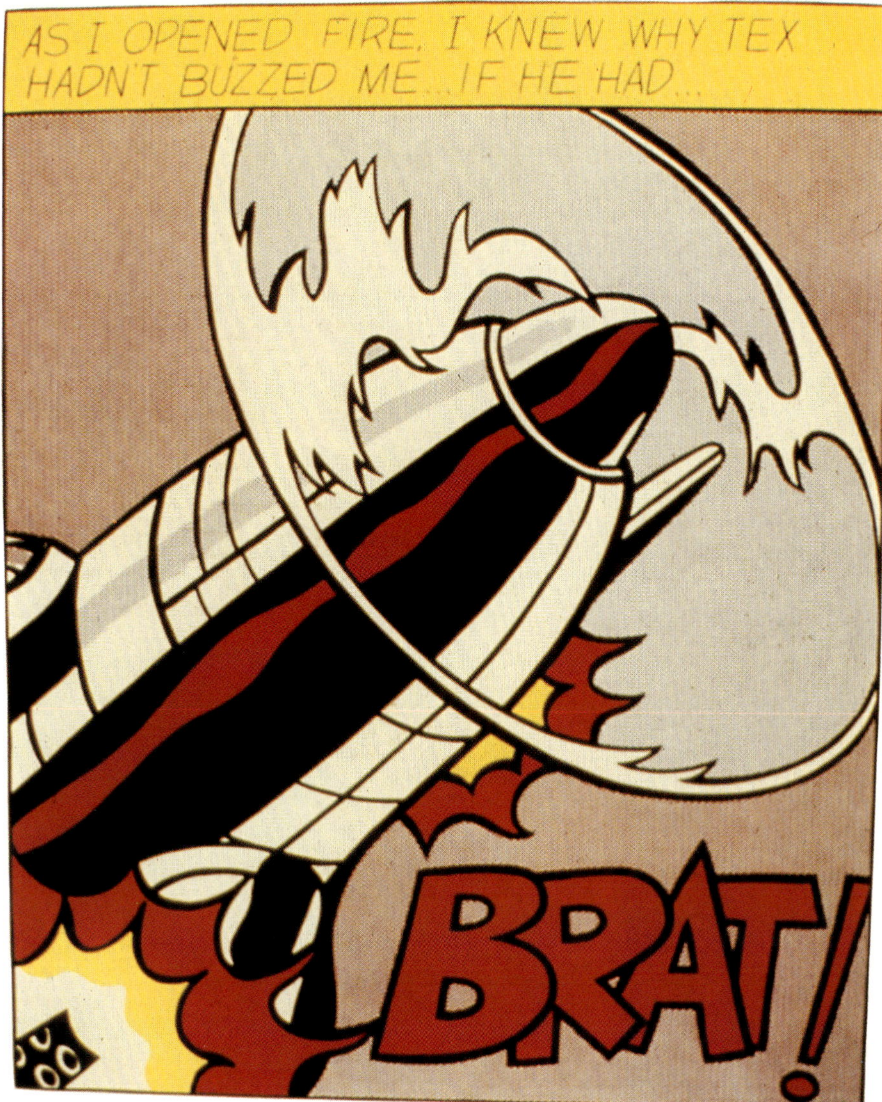

Roy Lichtenstein, *As I Opened Fire I . . .*, 1964, magna on canvas, 68 x 56"

create an experience of the 1960s 'scene' which he missed, being too young. His memories of that period are of watching a great deal of television, especially The Flintstones and The Jetsons cartoons by Hanna-Barbera, who is often cited as one of the chief figures in the so-called 'psychedelic revival' of the early 1980s. 'It is the creation – in the real world – of a television version of the 60s as remembered by those who saw the shows every night.'[9] Even today, the Flintstones and Jetsons continue to offer cartoon sit-coms, vignettes of an all-American family embroiled in domestic incidents, regardless of their respective settings of prehistoric or futuristic eras. In Scharf's work, Fred and Wilma and George and Elroy etc fraternise with dayglo amoebic mutants to add credence to the notion of the post-apocalyptic 'nuclear' family. 'There was this kind of metamorphosis – Flintjet, Jetstone. And then there was Felix the Cat . . . George and Wilma had a baby they called El Fredix. And then there were other offspring – millions and billions, sects and subsects . . . It's like the future is infinite and limitless.'[10] Scharf's unshakeable optimism recalls the

promise of new vistas with the 1950-60s 'space thing'. He aims to convey the 'space look' design of that period in his painting. 'That time was the best. We were all told we were going to buy tickets and get on board and go. It didn't happen.'[11] Maybe Scharf's faith in the 'future' is out of time with the present, but his unabashed belief in the technicoloured dreams of those summers of love is tempered by a darker mourning for their ultimate failure: a 1980s Peter Pan, Scharf keeps valiantly clapping his hands.

Although the cartoon characters Cutrone quotes – particularly Woody Woodpecker and the Pink Panther – share with Scharf's a national 'character', they have been assimilated not only for being recognisable TV personalities, but also for their potential to make unequivocal moral statements. His integration of these media characters with religious imagery, which 'are taken very seriously as icons but really they are just cartoons', is often for their (ahistorical) allegorical enactment of the battle betwen good and evil. This ritual conflict is often played on the face of a flag, a 'national symbol as environment', where the state is often

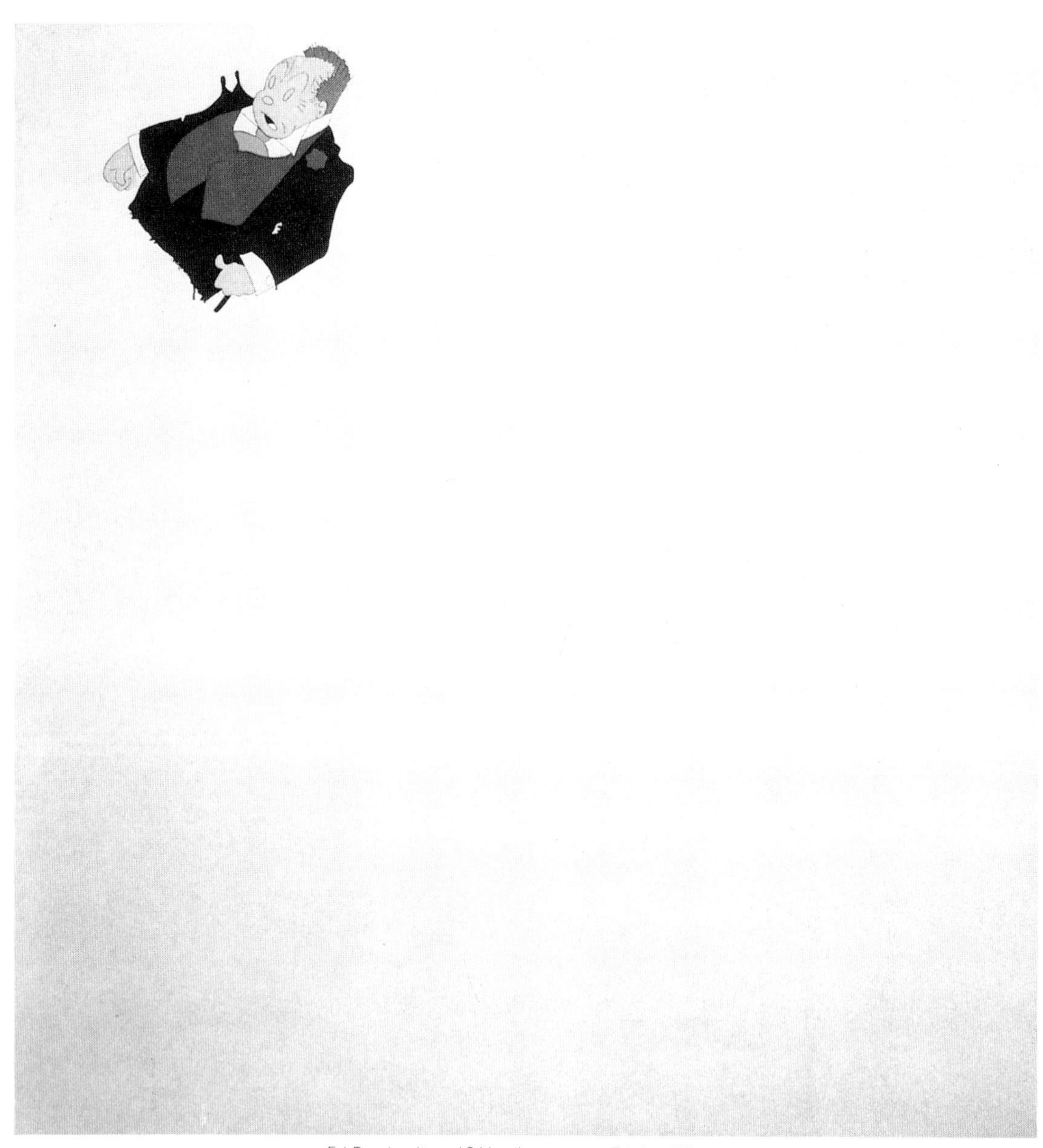

Ed Ruscha, *Jiggs*, 1961, oil on canvas, 71 ⅕ x 68"

proposed as the perpetrator of wrong, against which our hapless hero, Woody, struggles. The woodpecker's survival is never in question – 'Evil is already destroyed . . . The battle has been won. But I am a man and I have my problems; that is the struggle.'[12]

Unlike the work of his Pop mentor, Cutrone's confessional attitude reflects a 1980s prevalence of self-referential paintings which Christopher Lasch suggests 'testifies to the new narcissism that runs all through American culture. Americans have retreated from politics into "transcendental self-attention" because political failures and dehumanising social institutions have challenged their power to master reality. Thus detached, they perceive the external world as a fiction, themselves actors in it . . . Yet paintings do, in the end, communicate "a representative piece of reality". They show an America which is in the throes of a narcissistic identity crisis not unlike their own.'[13]

Cutrone's choice of specific cartoon characters relies on a wide understanding of the moral characters they portray in their television roles. As Walter Lantz has described his creation

Woody, 'He likes doing things that are just within the law – things we'd all like to do but don't have the nerve. Woody appeals to just about everybody; he's a universal character.'[14]

Cartoon characters with even more pervasive 'universality' are those of Walt Disney whose mythos has affected the perceptions of nearly everyone in the Western world. The most popular, Mickey Mouse and Donald Duck, have been presented in painting for over 35 years: 'Our work is a caricature of life.' Disney's popularity bears out his assumption that his larger-than-life animated parables offer particular aspirations and value systems which are similar to those of his audience, and which reconfirm their culturally privileged positions. David Kunzle has described Disney as 'the century's most important figure in bourgeois popular culture. He has done more than any person in disseminating around the world certain myths upon which that culture has thrived, notably that of an "innocence" supposedly universal . . . The Great American Dream still holds a global imagination in thrall.'[15] And like other comic characters such as

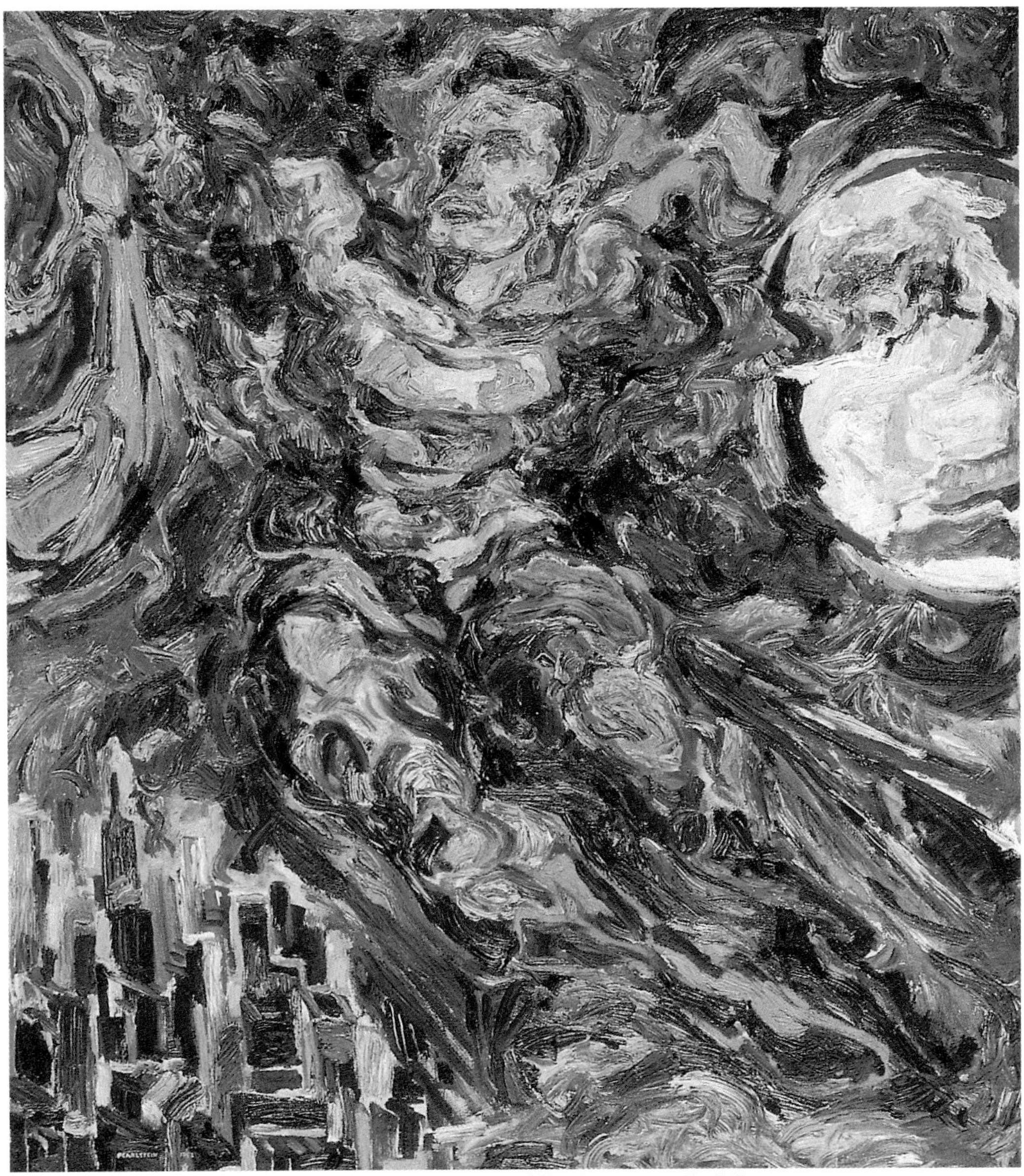

Philip Pearlstein, *Superman*, 1952, oil on canvas, 40 x 36"

Bugs, Woody, Dick or Superman, Mickey and Donald have become emblems of that dream.

It is astonishing that those European and American artists who continue to use comic icons to purposefully deconstruct existing systems of cultural security seldom, if ever, acknowledge or challenge the most obvious cultural constant since the 1960s: the continuous one-way global distribution of American corporate culture and marketing systems (which include those of the comics) which permits little, if any, exchange.

American comic icons have come to stand for a self-perpetuating popular dream, rejuvenated over the years by a phalanx of both American and European artists whose deliberate emulation of popular cultural systems suggests an accordance with Thomas Hart Benton's remark: 'Throughout American time, epic fantasy has been the popular culture's solution to dealing with historical change.'[16]

Sheena Wagstaff is curator of the Comic Iconoclasm *exhibition at the ICA, London. We would like to thank the ICA for providing the illustrations used in this article.*

Notes

1 Dick Hebdige, 'In Poor Taste', *Block 8*, 1983.
2 Quoted by Hebdige, *ibid*.
3 Richard Hamilton, *The Expendable Ikon: Works by John McHale*, Albright-Knox Art Gallery, Buffalo, New York, 1984.
4 Max Lerner, *America as a Civilisation*.
5 John Cawelti, 'Notes Towards a Typology of Literary Formulas', in *Adventure, Mystery and Romance*, University of Chicago Press, 1976, p 40.
6 Quoted by Art Spiegelman in 'Chester Gould', *New York Times*, 1983.
7 Quoted by Christopher Bigsby in 'Arthur Miller', *The Guardian*, 4 Aug 1986.
8 Kenny Scharf, quoted in Gerald Marzorati, 'Kenny Scharf's Fun House Big Bang', *ArtNews*, September 1985.
9 Gerald Marzorati, *op cit*.
10 Kenny Scharf, *op cit*.
11 *ibid*.
12 Ronnie Cutrone, quoted in T Trini, 'Ronnie Cutrone', *Flash Art*, No 117, April 1984
13 Christopher Lasch, *The Culture of Narcissism*, Abacus, London, 1980.
14 Danny Peary, 'Reminiscing with Walter Lantz', in *The American Animated Cartoon*, Dutton, New York, 1980, p 195.
15 David Kunzle, 'Introduction' to Ariel Dorfman and Armand Mattelart, *How to Read Donald Duck: Imperialist Ideology in the Disney Comic*, International General, New York, 1984, p 11.
16 Quoted in Prof K A Marling, 'Thomas Hart Benton's Boomtown', *Prospects VI*, 1981.

Mark Rothko, *Orange, Red and Red*, 1962, oil on canvas, 93×80″

INTERCHANGES
British and American Painting 1945-87

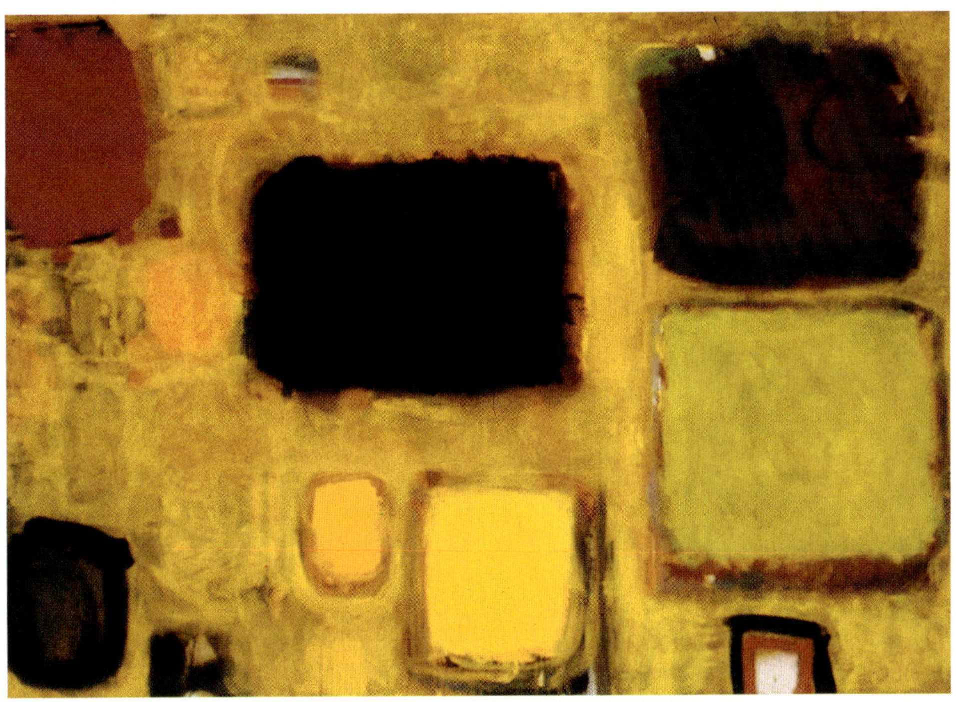

Patrick Heron, *Yellow Painting: October 1958-June 1959*, oil on canvas

The present day provides a unique opportunity to look back and assess the nature and development of British and American art since 1945. The post-war period saw in America the ascendancy of a coherent unified group of artists, the Abstract Expressionists, who succeeded not only in establishing America as the centre of aesthetic innovation, but in

creating a peculiarly American aesthetic. That said, Britain in the 50s saw the emergence of a group of abstract artists who became consciously aware of the work of American artists such as Pollock and Rothko. Abstraction went on to become one of the dominant modes in both countries. Aside from abstraction, both Britain and America developed, independently, Pop art movements that at their height can be seen to have benefited from a shared influence that comes not only from imagery drawn from American rock, comic and film culture, but from the work of the respective artists.

At a significant symposium at the Tate Gallery this year the relationship of British and American art since 1945 was the subject of a major discussion by a selection of important and influential artists and critics. The British American Arts Association* successfully brought together artists such as Grace Hartigan, Patrick Heron, John Baldessari and Steven Campbell with critics such as Irving Sandler and Robert Rosenblum, as well as influential figures such as Bryan Robertson, the former director of the Whitechapel Gallery. The Association was able to provoke a vivid analysis and questioning of the nature and relationship of British

and American art since 1945. Organising the symposium into groups of three panellists, the aim was to cover three significant eras, starting with the Abstract Expressionist generation.

Grace Hartigan, Patrick Heron and Bryan Robertson provided unique perspectives on the influential decades following the war. Grace Hartigan who knew and worked with many of the significant Abstract Expressionists conveyed the lasting effect of the atmosphere of that era. Patrick Heron highlighted the British contribution to the development of abstraction, emphasising his early fascination with the work of Rothko and Pollock. Bryan Robertson provided a complementary viewpoint, that of an influential gallery director who was responsible not only for showing many Neo-Romantic artists, but also introducing many American artists to Britain.

The second panel benefited from a strong and succinct series of questioning comparisons by Robert Rosenblum of British and American abstract and Pop art. What he sought to stress was the difference in tone and scale between British and American Pop, as well as the shared formal and thematic concerns, which are often surprisingly similar, if not identical.

Speakers such as John Baldessari and

Michael Baldwin provided personal viewpoints of their own development as artists, as did Michael Craig Martin and Tom Lawson. Steven Campbell emphasised the importance of going to America in order to achieve his present reputation.

The symposium produced a series of enlightening and unexpected opinions on the relationship of British and American art. It is clear that Britain and America shared a synonymous and deep-rooted fascination with aesthetic innovation since 1945. Artists at the heart of abstraction and Pop especially have admired each others' work and shared many similar formal concerns. Moreover audiences in both countries have benefited from a powerful exposure to the work of the significant artists of the age.

Here we include significant extracts by Grace Hartigan, Patrick Heron, Bryan Robertson and Robert Rosenblum which testify to a powerfully imaginative cultural interchange between Britain and America since 1945.

For further information contact the British American Arts Association, 49 Wellington St, London WC2 who are planning to publish the proceedings in full.

GRACE HARTIGAN

I lived in New York from 1946 to 1960. I think the best thing I can do is to try to briefly describe that time to you. I wasn't trained as an artist. When I was young, I trained as a mechanical draughtsman and machine designer and I did work on small parts of planes. My first husband was in World War Two. I studied painting privately in New Jersey. Around 1946 my teacher Ike moved to New York, and very soon we met Milton Avery there. I remember Milton Avery and his friends sitting around – this was '46 – discussing with great derision the work of a man named Jackson Pollock. I had been taught the School of Paris: I was painting still-lifes like Matisse. I was extremely curious about why they would be mocking this man. So I saw the first show of Pollock, of drips, and I was confused, but quite fascinated.

Harry Jackson and I had been talking about Kooning. At that time he had just finished painting *Attic* and was about to begin *Excavation* which I think of as his greatest work. Bill – who was sharing a studio with Jack Tworkov – then introduced me to Franz Kline, and then we all started to hang out. There was also Rothko who had been a friend of Milton Avery and who liked his work very much. There was something about the subtle transitions of the colour that I think interested him.

It's hard to describe to you the kind of world that was. First of all I think I might mention the extreme poverty. A chilling example is the story that Elaine de Kooning tells of Franz Kline when he was living on nothing but coffee with a lot of sugar in it. A friend made the mistake of leaving a police dog with him to take care of, and he came back home one day and found the dog dead with a half-chewed bar of soap next to him. And Franz said, 'Look, an artist can live where a dog dies.' And that was the kind of

going to make something that never existed before. And I hadn't gone through the life they'd gone through and the painting experiences they'd gone through. I'd never had any art history, I'd never had anything but the natural way to draw. So in 1952 I painted my way through my own art history and then, in the next few years, came smack up against what was known as Abstract Expressionism.

I was looking at a canvas, over and over again, a blank canvas, for the very first time with no memory, with people who were extremely developed and had wonderful memories. I realised they were involved with stripping bare the self to face the canvas with conscience, and with the mysteries of the unknown in their hand, and making the unknown known on the surface. What I was involved with was trying to send the painting, through the paint, into a state of trembling chaos and oblivion, and then at that point of

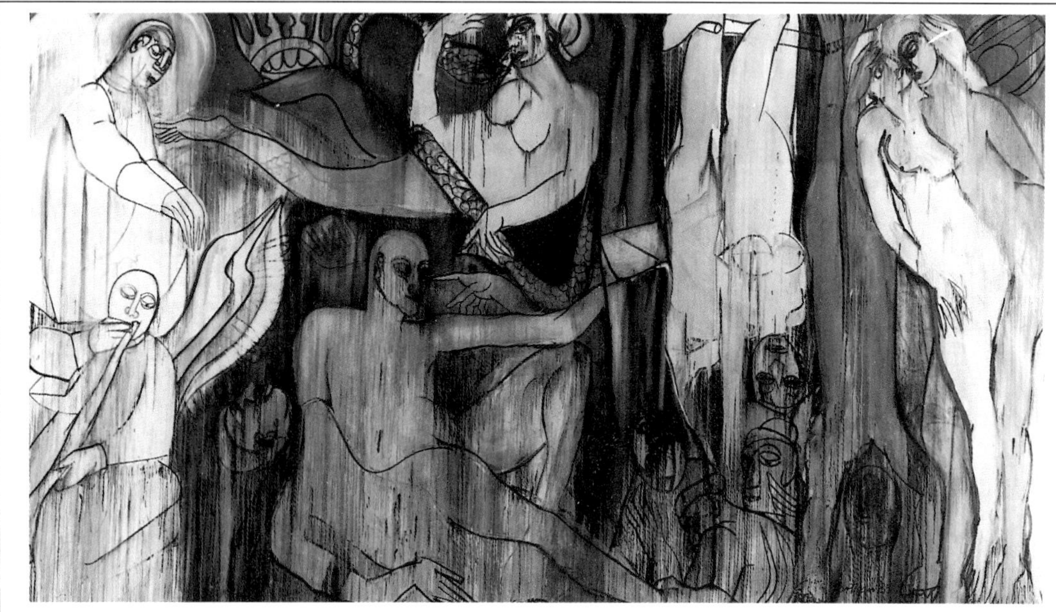
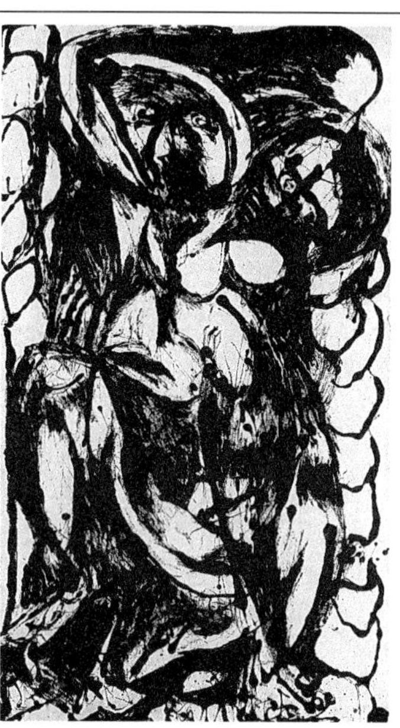

L to R: Grace Hartigan, *Vision of Heaven and Hell*, 1985; Jackson Pollock, *Number 5*, 1952

Jackson Pollock. A friend of ours said that he'd just moved to the country and was very lonely and didn't know that any young people liked his work, so why didn't we call him. We called him and he said 'Come on out and see me'. I don't know if I can convey to you the feeling of walking into a barn in Long Island and seeing wet Pollocks on the floor and on the walls, all drips. I had this incredible feeling that I was seeing something that I'd never seen before in my life, and that was true. And sitting that evening with Pollock and Lee I asked Pollock who he liked and he said, 'They're all shit, but de Kooning and me.' And I said, 'Who's de Kooning?' He said, 'He and Gorky, I thought they'd never get out of European painting. But at last de Kooning has and he's just had his first show. Now it might still be on but if it isn't, why don't you drop by and see him. Say I sent you, he likes young artists.'

The show was down so I went to see Bill de

life we lived: we all borrowed the same dollar bill back and forth.

Franz hadn't started really doing the black and whites when I first met him. And no-one was called anything, incidentally. As Bill said, 'It's death to name yourself.' How Abstract Expressionism came into being surely the art historians know, but I don't. I'm not sure about it. I saw a new way to make a painting, an overall painting, one where the painting was the image and there were no images within the painting – a painting that projected into your eyes all at the same rate of speed.

By 1950 I had assimilated the work that I'd seen of de Kooning and Pollock and started to do a series of paintings that probably had something of my own in it. But in a sense they were using the aesthetic that had been given to me by these older artists. I had a bout of conscience about this. I know that you don't start with the way a painting looks if you're

destruction, summon up something of the world that I could believe in. That's what I felt in this unique aesthetic that was given to me by my friends. The thing they were involved with was killing off Picasso and I joined that attitude. A 1951 painting of mine was called *The King is Dead* and the king was Picasso who had a way of living for a long, long time.

I will briefly give you a little anecdote about Franz Kline which expresses a certain attitude towards English painting. I was a friend of Larry Rivers and I said to Franz one day, 'Larry Rivers and I go to the Metropolitan Museum and we trade. I'll agree to spend 15 minutes in the room with English landscape painting if he'll spend 15 minutes with me looking at Spanish painting.' Franz said, 'Hum, English landscape painting. You know how it is when you're in the country and you're taking a walk, and you're looking at your feet, and it starts to rain and you bump into someone, and you say

"Excuse me!" and he says "No, excuse me!" That's English landscape painting.'

PATRICK HERON

I'm in a slightly difficult position as some of you may imagine because any painter who's ever written anything other than an anecdotal account of events really does put himself in rather a hot spot, and in the case of my relationship with New York the situation is very, very complex. The other difficulty for me is that my very admiration for American painting when I first encountered it was expressed in criticism published in New York in *Arts Magazine*. This has never been republished in spite of the fact that when I resigned from *Arts* in 1958 its editor Hilton Kramer did in fact press me to allow him to bring out the American articles I'd written for them over three years in book form. I actually refused

in the following way: my friend Alan Davie had got to know Peggy Guggenheim in Venice while he was a student on a scholarship there and been very impressed by three or four early Pollocks which she owned. Alan raved about this totally unknown painter, so I heard that there were Jackson Pollocks from 1948 on but it meant nothing to me. You can't imagine this but there were no reproductions, no exhibitions, no magazine articles. This again is difficult for people to understand but there was absolutely no trace of this painter or of any of his colleagues until another great friend of mine, William Scott, whose work was seen in an exhibition, *Space in Colour*, I'd organised in July/August'53, was visited by two very influential New Yorkers. One was James Johnson Sweeny whom I knew quite well at the time. He came to see this show and was more impressed with William Scott's paintings than anybody else's, and he asked, 'How can I get

can call it.

So the moment William got home in September 1953, he rang me up in a state of high excitement and said: 'Do you realise that there's a great deal of extremely interesting modern painting going on in New York?', and I said 'You're kidding, who the hell, what on earth are you talking about?' He said, 'Well there's Rothko'. So I said 'And who is he, and how do you write that?' So he wrote it down. I said 'What does he do?', so he then did a William Scott of a Rothko and we went right through all the Abstract Expressionists. The only painter I'd heard about myself was Motherwell. But I didn't really know what Motherwell was up to. Anyway that was a good enough introduction for me because I immensely respected William Scott's judgment. So that's how I became aware of the fact that something important was possibly happening in New York.

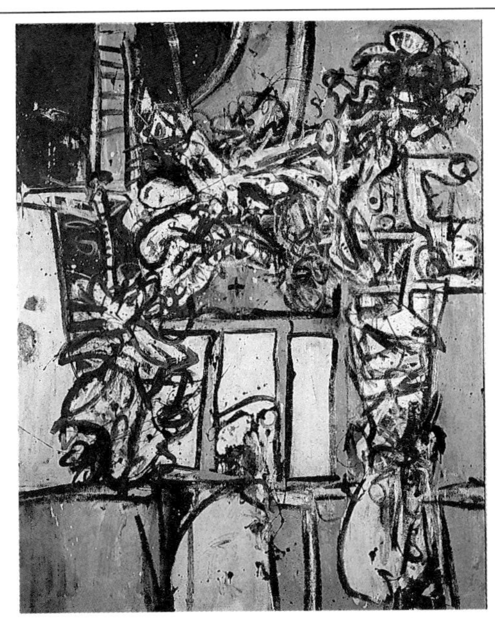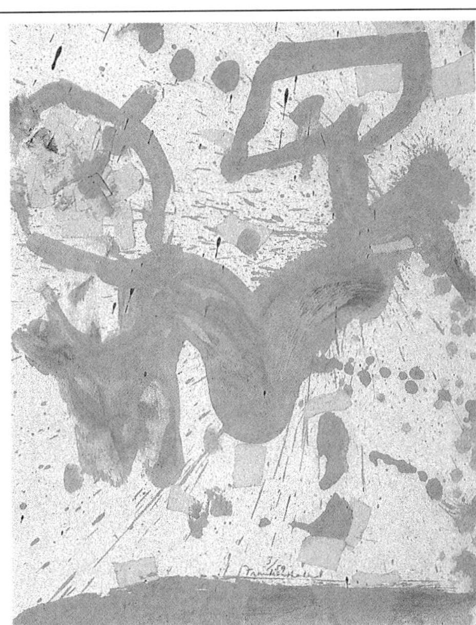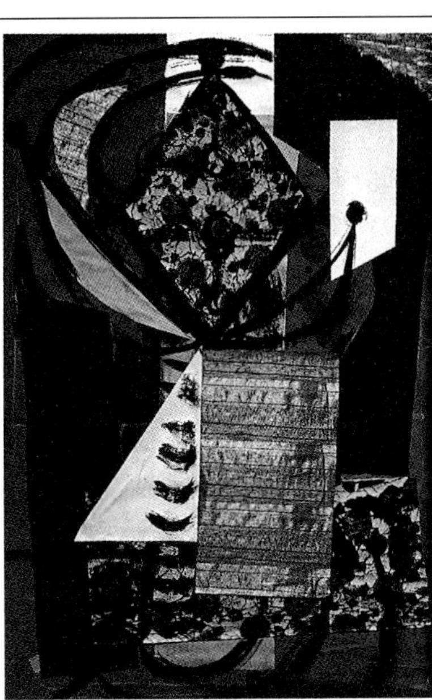

L to R: Alan Davie, Farmer's Wife No 2, 1957; Helen Frankenthaler, Untitled, 1959; Robert Motherwell, Collage No 2, 1945

because my reason for resigning was that to write seriously about the painting of contemporaries had become far too complicated a thing for me as a painter. I was introducing American painting to the British, in so far as they ever read *Arts Magazine*. I was also introducing contemporaries to the New York scene; painters like Alan Davie, William Scott, and Peter Lanyon. So I resigned and took a vow of silence which I maintained with absolute rigidity for nearly nine years. That is all detail however.

It's obvious that the most difficult thing in the world for anybody at any time is to project back into a given situation and to become aware of the total reality of that situation'. Nobody in the world today can imagine a state of total ignorance of, for instance, the Abstract Expressionists. But that was in fact the situation in London right up to 1956. I had premonitions, as you might say, of something going on,

William Scott to New York? He should be showing there. Where is he?' and I said, 'He's actually just gone off to teach summer school in the Rockies.' The other American, who was then curator of sculpture at MOMA, also turned up at this show and he, curiously enough, had exactly the same response to William Scott. I gather therefore that they got back to New York, the next week and sent a message to William asking him to come home via New York which he did, in order to be introduced to a dealer, and not – as he said to us when he came back - to visit the Mecca of modern art, since none of us knew that anything except Pollock was happening there. Don't forget that Pollock's name was known internationally at least five years in advance of everybody else; and I think that possibly his arrival at his maturity was also about five years in advance of the other painters of the Abstract Expressionist group, if that's what you

It wasn't until 1953 that the first Pollock to be shown in this country was exhibited at the ICA. It nearly filled the end wall of the small room which was number 17 Dover Street. There were also three or four works on paper – just black paint on which the oil spread in oily circles, which again greatly appealed to Alan Davie. Incidentally, the exhibition in January was called *Opposing Forces* because the other five or six painters in it all came from Paris. They included an American Parisian called Sam Francis, whose works I liked better than anything else there, even more so than the Pollock at the time. I had a certain resistance to that very first Pollock, while I had no resistance to those two Sam Francis paintings and I've always proclaimed that they influenced work which I made about two years later. But of course Sam Francis was really regarded by the establishment in New York as being tainted by the School of Paris, and you'll notice that he wasn't included in the major American shows of the very, very early years.

I wanted to talk for a minute about the first appearance of any modern American painting, other than that single Pollock, which was of course at that show at the Tate which was sent over by MOMA. I think the title of the show was *Modern American Painting* or *Modern Art in the United States*. I had been invited by Hilton Kramer – who I think was put up to it by Clement Greenberg, whom I'd met the year before in London – to become London correspondent for *Arts Magazine*, New York... But what I was going to say was that although that was the title of the show, and although the show came from MOMA, only one room out of six or seven was devoted to the Abstract Expressionists, and they had only one small – by modern standards – painting each, except for Pollock and de Kooning who somehow managed to have two each. The sole Rothko

review "Yankee Doodles"' – I'm now quoting from my article – 'but one feels that his comments on Pollock, no less facetious than his title, only convey in reverse, as it were, an unwilling preoccupation with this painter.' (Nearly all the British critics had of course devoted the mass of their space to the older artist, to Andrew Wyeth and to major figuration.) 'Having, he says, been told "on authority" that Pollock "slapped the canvas with his paint-covered hands" the Sunday Times critic ends up "but I don't think in this case that it was the canvas that deserved the slap".' There was also John Berger, of course, who was a Marxist critic, and you can imagine that he wasn't very keen on the Americans. Rather curiously, the Manchester Guardian said this extraordinary thing: 'As this is the first notably representative exhibition of modern American art to be seen in this country, one looks for signs of a movement independent of European influence, the

first sight of them as they hung in consort in the big Tate room at the private view a month ago.' (This was January 1956.) 'A month ago, I was instantly elated by the size, energy, originality, economy and inventive daring of many of the paintings. Their creative emptiness represented their radical discovery, I felt, as did their flatness or rather their spatial shallowness. I was fascinated by their consistent denial of illusionistic depth which goes against all my own instincts as a painter. Also there was an absence of relish in the *matière* as an end in itself, an absence of worked-up paint quality, such as one never misses in the French – sometimes a superbly manipulated surface texture is all one can find in Paris. These American painters were so direct in the execution of the idea that their paintings, their gestures, their statement on the canvas had an almost over-dry immaculateness, and I mean this even in connection with such wet paint

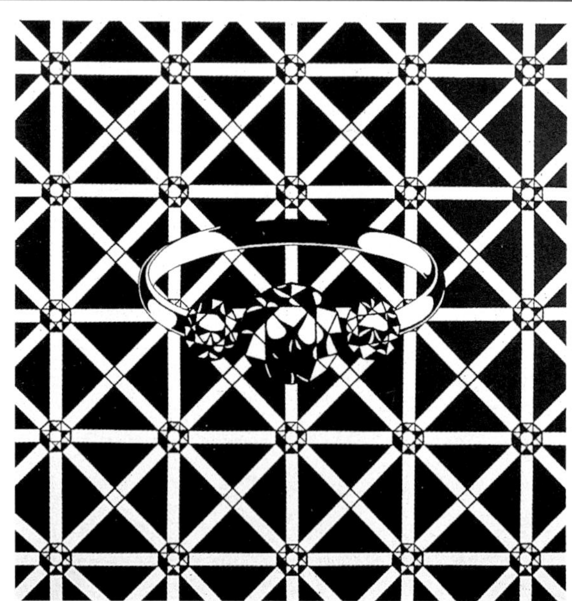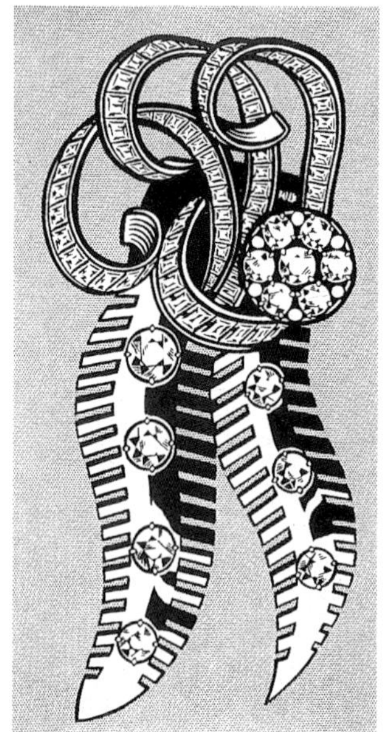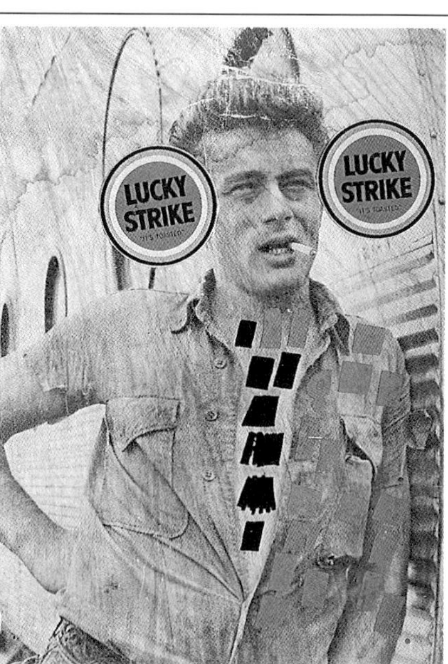

L to R: Patrick Caulfield, *Engagement Ring*, 1963; Roy Lichtenstein, *Large Jewels*, 1963; Ray Johnson, *James Dean*, 1957

was hanging on a screen as you came into the room. It was the first Rothko I ever saw, or anybody in England ever saw. But just to complete the point about the show: looking back, one feels now that it was a sort of try-out by MOMA – is there anything in all this or isn't there? And in fact half the major figures still didn't qualify. There was no Newman, no Gottlieb, there was no Ad Reinhardt and so on. So it was a very incomplete show, a very partial show, of small works, and it was all I had to react to.

If I may just bore you, I'll tell you one or two things that I said about it. First of all Hilton Kramer was, curiously enough, anxious to know what other London critics thought about the show, so I did a précis of a few of the articles. I won't relate the lot here but I do think that it's rather amusing for you to know for instance that 'the Sunday Times art critic' – I spared mentioning him by name 'heads his

characteristics of a specifically American creative activity. At first sight, to European eyes, the show is interesting without being deeply impressive. There is much individual exciting work, but no overwhelming masterpiece, no seducing master or theorist likely to lead the young artist ahead or astray.' We won't say who that was ... he's dead anyway so it's all right. 'Now', I went on, 'whatever one may ultimately feel to be the value or direction of the American Abstract Expressionist painters, three facts are already obvious: firstly they *do* constitute a movement; secondly this movement *is* specifically American, *is* notably free of European influence; and thirdly Pollock, in particular, *is* just such a seductive artist, as anyone acquainted with the youngest non-figurative painters of Europe of America can testify.' Well I then went on to say what I felt: 'My own feelings about these painters have shifted one way and then the other since my

canvases as Pollock's. Those always have a lack of resonance in colour. I finished with: 'Whatever I have said, I would like to end by insisting that to me and to those English painters with whom I associate, your new school comes as the most vigorous movement we have seen since the war. If we feel that far more is suggested than is achieved that is in itself a remarkable achievement. We shall now watch New York as eagerly as Paris for new developments, not forgetting our own, let me add, and may it come as a consolidation rather than a further exploration.'

BRYAN ROBERTSON

The Anglo-American dialogue as I remember it did not take place in a vacuum and was not an isolated phenomenon; there was a context, in which it happened, began to happen, and gathered in strength.

In 1952 I went to the Whitechapel Gallery, and my eternal principle in directing that institution was to give British artists a new kind of level of estimation and visibility with a series of one-man shows on a scale which had not been tackled before in this country. These were artists in mid-career: artists never used to be given a retrospective until they died. This, although it seems a very ordinary thing now, was innovatory at that time. Artists in their thirties and forties were given a huge show with, what is more, a very copiously detailed and documented catalogue. I wanted to present British artists in Britain at the same level as good foreign artists, and show good artists from history, some old masters. These included Turner in 1953, which I think had a great impact in this country among artists. It was the first Turner show since his death in 1851. Turner had been put down by Roger Fry who described him as an artist who had no original

really set much store by groups and movements and the ones that were going on at that time in England seemed to be rather vapid and bad, like, for example, the so-called Kitchen Sink thing, which seemed to be completely journalist-contrived, nothing at all to do with reality and which quickly fizzled out.

So the people that I presented included Cecil Collins, Merlyn Evans, Ceri Richards, Prunella Clough, Keith Vaughan and Stanley William Hayter, a forgotten artist, but a very important one indeed. In 1927 Hayter was the creator of the Atelier 17 for the propagation of print-making along original lines as opposed to a mere means of reproduction, and in the 1940s he conducted quite radical experiments with Mark Rothko. Others were Armitage, Philip King, Hepworth, twice, Robert Colquhoun, Craxton, Ayrton, Nolan and Boyd (the Australian painters were very important in the English context of that time, giving a refreshing

Catlin, the 19th-century American artist, who with great braveness and courage, worked with and painted the American Indians. And with this at the same time were American primitive arts from the Rockefeller Collection which at least showed English visitors a sense of the American Arcadia.

The first contemporary American shows that I put on were Pollock in 1958, followed by Kline, Rothko, Guston, Johns, Rauschenberg, Tobey, Motherwell, Louis, and Frankenthaler. Earlier in the 1950s there was a very important show on an American artist called Charles Howard who is completely forgotten in his native country. He was a pre-war Surrealist painter who worked on Mendlesohn's Bexhill Pavilion with Edward Wadsworth, and one of the most serious and remarkable American painters of this century. He was a West-coaster and of course he got nowhere, because of the extraordinary snobbism and pro-

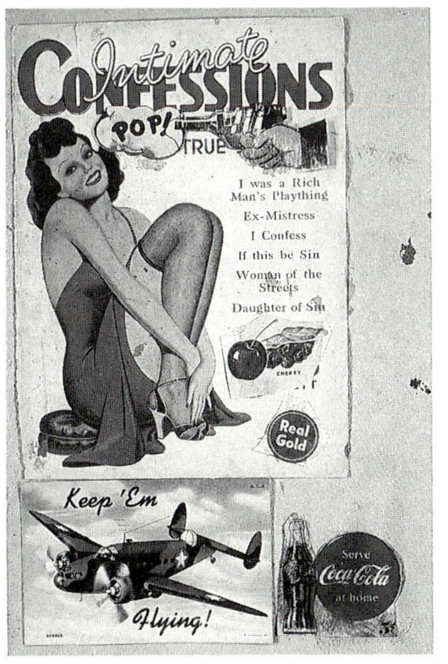

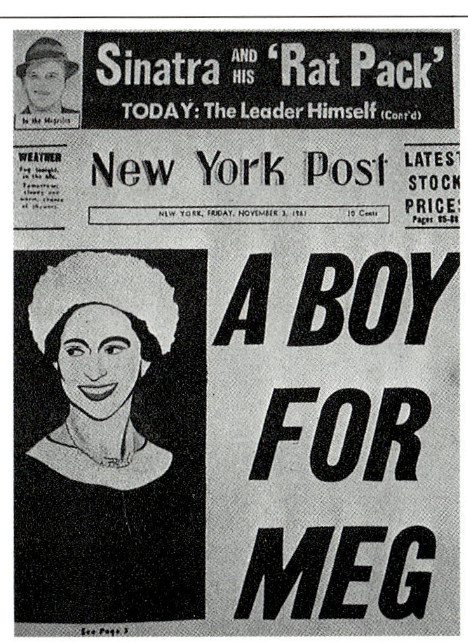

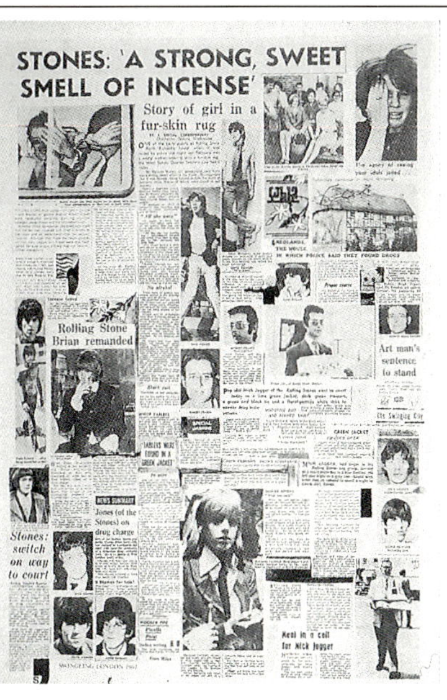

L to R: Eduardo Paolozzi, *I Was a Rich Man's Plaything*, 1947; Andy Warhol, *A Boy for Meg*, 1961; Richard Hamilton, *Swinging London*, 1967

visual experience in the face of nature. And Turner was a revelation, I assure you, in 1953; Stubbs also, because in my estimation he was one of the very few English artists whose work we could look at without embarrassment in the same context as great European art.

In 1945, '46 and '47, I had become aware of American art in a very lop-sided way through articles and things in magazines. The most serious artist I became aware of, very early on, in about 1947-48, was Robert Motherwell, through his writings and notably through his collaboration with Wolfgang van Thalen and Gordon Onslow-Ford. I also became aware of some middle-of-the-road, rather conservative American painting through magazine articles, but still I realised that something was going on.

From 1952 onwards the English artists that were presented in Whitechapel were all individuals. None of them had any real role in any kind of group or movement, because I don't

window on something new to us), Hoyland, Alan Davie, Jack Smith, and later on Richard Smith.

I resisted theme shows, with the exception of an exhibition called *This is Tomorrow*. This was none of my doing, being made by other people, but I gave up the premises willingly. It included collaborations between artists, like Pasmore and Paolozzi, and architects, sculptors and designers, and saw the first definition of English Pop art. There've been many claims made about English Pop art – 'we did it first', and all the rest of it – but these have always seemed to me to be perfectly frightful, that is to say, full of nostalgia and a kind of infantilism. English Pop appears rather dinky as opposed to the American variety, which seems to me to have great guts and to be totally differently conceived and at its best absolutely creative.

Now the very first American show that I ever put on in England was a show of George

vincialism of New York towards all artists coming from the West Coast. They extended the same snobbism and ignorance towards Mark Tobey, an absolutely sublime artist who was working along Abstract Expressionist lines with his 'white painting' paintings at Dartington Hall in 1936-37. But talk about Mark Tobey in New York and the conversation freezes and everybody looks out of the window. He doesn't exist! He was a West-coaster and then he had the effrontery to go and live in Switzerland.

Other artists included Krasner. I think there were 12 shows in all. I rejected an exhibition of Hans Hofmann though he seemed to me to be a very good artist. I knew him quite well, and greatly admired the last phase of his work which I'd seen up at Provincetown the same summer it was made. But I thought he was essentially a teacher-artist and not in the first rank of those other people like Pollock and

Rothko.

I should say that the Pollock show created a furore in 1958, an absolute furore. We had to have police to control the crowds queuing to get in, and the same thing happened a few years later with the Rauschenberg show. I mention this only to try to convey the excitement of that period. I gave a lecture for the Arts Council on Pollock, and more than 300 people were turned away. It was an extraordinary time of great excitement. There was a real dialogue going on, with many visits to England from American artists and lots of English people going to New York.

ROBERT ROSENBLUM

I wanted to take off on a point of Bryan Robertson's which fits right into place as a transition, and that is the extraordinary parochialism of New York art people, which especially includes the Museum of Modern Art.

One of the few things that I recall making me a little bit nervous about assuming the imperial centre of the world was New York was the fact that British Pop art seemed to turn up in the late 40s and 50s – God forbid it should have been a kind of prototype for the likes of what we had in New York in the 60s! There was Paolozzi from 1947 and, unbelievably precocious there in 1956, the famous Richard Hamilton that appears in all the traditional histories of Pop art as a kind of incunabula item. There is also the fact – which I think needs exploration – that Kurt Schwitters was here in England in the late 40s, around 1947, the same date as Paolozzi's *I was a Rich Man's Plaything*. Schwitters was said to be a progenitor of Pop art, which tends to internationalise things . . . Also, the recent catalogue by Henry Geldzahler, *Pop Art*, has all kinds of Continental entries.

However, we're talking about Anglo-American dialogues here. Very recently in two Pop exhibitions – and this includes the marvellous *Comic Iconoclasm* which I just saw at the ICA – some American artists of the 50s have turned up, thereby offering, in terms of historical timetables, a kind of synchrony with what the British were doing. There's a Ray Johnson from 1957 of James Dean, and another of Elvis Presley. There's Jess' comic strip from the mid 1950s. These of course offer a kind of prelude, as do Paolozzi and Richard Hamilton, to American events of the 60s. These events of the 60s also seem to offer a perfect example of Anglo-American dialogue sometimes right on target even in terms of date. There are two pictures of 1963 – a Roy Lichtenstein of costume jewellery and a Patrick Caulfield engagement ring, which are fascinating examples of the way these two artists and other British and American Pop artists tended to – well, 'join forces' isn't quite the word – at least coincide across the Atlantic. Nevertheless, one of the

things that certainly catches the attention of at least the American eye, and possibly the British one, is the discrepancy between the look of things American and the look of things British. Comparing a Caulfield and a Lichtenstein from 1964, you can see that sense which Americans, at least, feel in England; that things are sort of smaller, more complicated, diminutive in feel, scale, and so on, vis-à-vis America. I recently read something by Martin Amis in which he said how shocked he was when he got back to England after America: everything, Frigidaires included, looked so itsy-bitsy. There is certainly a general experience of change of scale that we feel not only in Pop art, but in the abstract art of the period.

This is a point that can be made by multiple comparisons, sometimes with the same sort of subject. Look at Richard Hamilton doing Marilyn Monroe in 1966 vis-à-vis Rosenquist doing her in 1962, and that sense of things being more diminutive, more compartmentalised in the British work is very clear. Compare especially the front pages of newspapers, as in the case of Richard Hamilton's *Swinging London* of 66 and a *Strong Blast* by Andy Warhol, the late great Andy Warhol, of 1964.

It's interesting to see that exactly this kind of visual discrepancy which seems to be so conspicuous in any discussion of Anglo-American relations holds up as well for abstract painting. Put a Patrick Heron of 1959 next to a Rothko and I would say, looking at things from the top of an Olympian mountain in the middle of the Atlantic, that the relationship between these two pictures is rather like that between the Richard Hamilton and the Warhol I've just mentioned. The same kind of point can be demonstrated by other transatlantic comparisons. For example, the kind of blazing emblems of Robert Indiana's *The American Dream* of 1962 have any number of parallels in England, such as a work by Peter Phillips in 1961 that again becomes more intricate, more convoluted by the addition of photographs, girly photos and the like.

In a peculiar way the British relationship to New York Pop parallels that of the other non-New York American artists. For instance the 60s work of Peter Blake and the Chicago painter Ed Paschke show the same kind of peripheral relationship to the grand-scale, skyscraper conventions of New York Pop or abstract art in the late 50s and 60s. The same is true, it would seem to me, of the reverberations of Johns, Rauschenberg and company in London. Look at their work in relation to an Allen Jones and a Richard Smith, both of which seem to offer peripheral – some might say provincial – variations on the 'Drop dead on target' images of the Americans of the late 50s.

Other interesting comparisons, or dialogues, to use a fancier word, between American and British artists of the time have occurred to me. For example the work of Larry

Rivers very often, at least in the late 50s and 60s, seems to correspond to the kind of thing that David Hockney was doing. That's true not only of the common gay subject, evident for example in Rivers' picture of Napoleon called *The Greatest Homosexual* (in reference to the fact that Napoleon looks pretty campy in those clothes) and Hockney's *The Most Beautiful Boy in the World*. Apart from such matters, there's a funny kind of shuffling here between a kind of illustrational style – some literary point, something specific and personal – and a kind of adaptation of the rough-and-tumble look of de Kooning as it survived into the 1960s. There's another curious parallel which is so unexpected it sort of blows my mind: I always wondered who it was Kitaj reminded me of on our side of the Atlantic, and it turned out to be Romare Bearden, a black American artist of considerable repute in the 60s and 70s.

One of the more fascinating things in terms of the dialogue we're involved with today is the impact of the big picture and the manner in which this seems to have been translated – less generously, one would say diluted – by any number of British artists in the early 60s, and above all by the tyrannical critic Clement Greenberg, who was recently called the Reverend Moon of the 1960s. Compare a Stella with a Robyn Denny and the latter seems to disintegrate before our eyes. Here is the kind of picture that obviously wanted to be big and grand and bold like a suit of armour, rather like the Stella, which at least to my eyes always looked as though it had an ancestral figure, whose name might be Ben Nicholson. That kind of atmospheric, one might say moist, quality in the colour and in the finer subtlety of British art is something that always seemed to surface even when the pictures tended to look at first glance like clones of what was going on in New York in the early 60s.

Lastly, I wanted to point out a couple of dialogues between the 60s and the 80s. We have first a comparison which has to do with the interesting break in a very young group of artists from the 80s. New York artists who've become famous in the last few years frequently tend to pick up on visual ideas from anywhere in the 60s but quite often, say, from Bridget Riley. Compare her with the hot young artist Philip Taaffe who is, in the phrase of our time, appropriating her in various guises. Then we have Cohen and Scharf. As an American I am always wondering what happened to Bernard Cohen. His work seems to have disappeared, but I remember looking at it with great astonishment in the 60s – those spaghetti tangles of dayglo paint – and this kind of art from Britain in the 60s still looks very fresh to me. You can see its influence on new artists like Kenny Scharf.